# Crisis in the "Great Republic"

# CRISIS in the "GREAT REPUBLIC"

Essays presented to
Ross J. S. Hoffman

Edited by *Gaetano L. Vincitorio*,
with the assistance of James E. Bunce,
Elisa A. Carrillo, and Joseph F. X. McCarthy

*NEW YORK:*
FORDHAM UNIVERSITY PRESS
MCMLXIX

© Copyright 1969 by FORDHAM UNIVERSITY PRESS

Library of Congress Catalog Card Number: 70–79567

SBN 8232–0820–6

**LIBRARY
FLORIDA STATE UNIVERSITY
TALLAHASSEE, FLORIDA**

Printed in the United States of America
by The Colonial Press Inc., Clinton, Mass.

# Contents

Preface ix

Foreword xi
    ROBERT I. GANNON, S.J. *President Emeritus, Fordham University*

An Appreciation xiii
    LAWRENCE HENRY GIPSON *Lehigh University, Pennsylvania*

1. William Dowdeswell's *Thoughts on the Present State of Public Affairs*     1
    M. FRANCIS DE SALES BORAN, R.S.H.M. *Marymount College, Arlington, Virginia*

2. Edmund Burke and the First Partition of Poland: Britain and the Crisis of 1772 in the "Great Republic"     14
    GAETANO L. VINCITORIO *St. John's University, New York*

3. The King's Purse and the Absentee's Pocket in Eighteenth-century Ireland     47
    SAMUEL J. FANNING *St. John's University, New York*

4. The Role of Prudence in Burke's Politics     85
    PETER J. STANLIS *Rockford College, Illinois*

5　The British Career of a New York Federalist　107
　　Joseph F. X. McCarthy　*Fordham University*

6　The Whigs and the Invasion Crisis of 1779　131
　　James E. Bunce　*St. John's University, New York*

7　The Forces of the Crown in Ireland, 1798　155
　　William D. Griffin　*St. John's University, New York*

8　"Young England" and Its Political Debut: 1843　181
　　Nicholas Varga　*Loyola College, Baltimore, Maryland*

9　Napoleon III, Venetia, and the War of 1866　200
　　John W. Bush, S.J.　*Le Moyne College, Syracuse, New York*

10　Crisis in East-central Europe: The Teschen Dispute　220
　　Eugene Kusielewicz　*St. John's University, New York*

11　Alcide De Gasperi: The View from the Vatican, 1929–1943　256
　　Elisa A. Carrillo　*Marymount College, Tarrytown, New York*

12　The New Nationalism and the Old: America and Europe　276
　　C. Richard Cleary　*La Salle College, Philadelphia, Pennsylvania*

13  Crisis and Progress in Postwar France  291
   JOSEPH N. MOODY  *The Catholic University of America, Washington, D.C.*

A Select Bibliography of the Works of Ross J. S. Hoffman  309
   PAUL R. ZIEGLER  *Assumption College, Worcester, Massachusetts*

Index nominum  317

# Preface

PROFESSOR ROSS HOFFMAN'S scholarship, wisdom, dedication, and sterling qualities of character have been a source of inspiration to those who had the singular good fortune of studying with him during his distinguished career of over forty years—the greater part of it spent at Fordham University. The authors of the following articles and essays wish to present their work to him as a token of their esteem and affection. Eleven of the authors attended Fordham; two, Samuel J. Fanning and Peter J. Stanlis, though pursuing doctoral studies at the Universities of California and Michigan respectively, also consider themselves students of Professor Hoffman.

The title of this collection comes from one of Professor Hoffman's most perceptive works, *The Great Republic*. The essays deal therefore with some British and European crises which vexed the "great republic," or the common political and international community of Europe and the mother of all Western nations during the past two hundred years.

It is fitting that the Foreword comes from the pen of the Reverend Robert I. Gannon, S.J., himself a noted biographer and historian of Fordham, who was President during the university's golden years. The Appreciation is the work of the dean of British imperial studies in the United States and Pulitzer-Prize recipient, Professor Lawrence Henry Gipson of Lehigh University, whose crowning achievement is his magisterial *The British Empire Before the American Revolution*.

A special word of thanks must go to Dr. J. Jean Hecht,

Kew Gardens, N.Y., for his generous and expert assistance to the editors, and to Professor Hoffman's long-time colleague and friend, Dr. A. Paul Levack, for his wise counsel and encouragement. The editors also wish to thank Professor Helen F. Mulvey of Connecticut College for reviewing an article, and Dr. Geoffrey Bruun, Ithaca, N.Y., Dr. Blaise Opulente, St. John's University, Reverend Edwin A. Quain, S.J., Director, Mr. John E. Connolly, Associate Director, and Mr. H. George Fletcher, Editor of Fordham University Press for advice and assistance. They are also indebted to the Earl Fitzwilliam and the Trustees of the Fitzwilliam Settled Estates for their kind permission to quote from the Rockingham Papers in the Wentworth–Fitzwilliam MSS, and to Professor Howard H. Peckham, Director of the Clements Library, University of Michigan, for his courtesy in permitting the citing of the Dowdeswell Papers. Finally, the editors are grateful to Mr. Daniel J. McCarthy of Brooklyn, N.Y., and Mr. Ralph H. Schust of Locust Valley, N.Y., for making possible the publication of this volume.

GAETANO L. VINCITORIO

# Foreword

A REAL EDUCATOR is not a single-minded man. He wears a dozen hats, even if his field is in graduate work. Some who have never studied in the academic stratosphere may think that the professors there have just one aim—discovery by research; may even sneer a little at their discoveries. You know the old refrain: "more and more about less and less." Such superficial observers may conclude that a scholar who can lose himself in the Letters of Edmund Burke or World War Statesmanship or even down-to-earth American Politics could never devote himself wholeheartedly to his home, his church, or his students. But that is because they never met Ross J. S. Hoffman.

When this particular researcher came to Fordham some thirty years ago he was not looking for a better library or more congenial associates. He had been very happy where he was. His reasons had nothing to do with prestige or finance. It is true that he was joining a distinguished group made up of men like Hess, Halecki, Timasheff, Pegis, and von Hildebrand—not to mention the greats still in the ranks or Jesuits gone to their reward—but he was leaving a school of established reputation with bright lights of its own. It is true that the new policy of salary, rank, and tenure introduced about that time give him a feeling of security in his new surroundings; but this he had already with a brilliant future at New York University. The fact was that he wanted to do something special for the Church he had recently entered.

Once here, Dr. Hoffman was not satisfied to publish dozens of books and scores of articles. He was to be, first of all, a teacher: a rare blend of Socrates and Mr. Chips on the other end of a log. To one with a few English memories, his manner brought a youthful echo of A. C. Benson, Arthur Quiller–Couch, and Gilbert Murray. He soon became known in the school for his model lectures. They always had a beginning, a middle, and a calculated end. The voice, the tone, the presentation, and, above all, the substance always satisfied.

Is it any wonder, then, that his disciples, now professors in a dozen colleges and universities, are taking the occasion of his retirement to present this testimony of their admiration and affection? Is it any wonder that an old office-worker, regarded all his life as fit for nothing higher than administration, considers it an honor to join them?

ROBERT I. GANNON, S.J.

Ross J. S. Hoffman

# An Appreciation

IT HAS BEEN IN MY EXPERIENCE the privilege of coming to know few men who have brought to their scholarly activities a greater zeal, a more persistent dedication, than has my friend, Ross J. S. Hoffman. His historical labors have been to a high degree purposeful, not only in the sense that he has had as an objective accuracy in details in dealing with the past, but also in the sense that he has had as an even more important objective: the illumination of each aspect of history that has concerned him in a manner that will harmonize with the comprehensive interpretation of the past that has been fundamental to his approach to it. This becomes evident as one surveys a list of his many writings which gives an impressive unity to them as a group.

The writing of history is to a remarkable extent a subjective thing. In other words, if the writer of history is true to himself—that is, to his convictions—he will, in the light of these convictions, inevitably record what he is persuaded is true after the weighing of available evidence—in itself only too frequently a highly subjective process.

Among American historians of standing there is probably no person more highly regarded as a spokesman for the faith of the Roman Catholic Church than Ross Hoffman. Nor do I know of an historian with a deeper commitment to that faith. It is indeed refreshing in this turbulent, iconoclastic age, when so much that had been held up to deep respect and even reverence during ages past is now challenged, to find a writer who holds so firmly to traditional moorings and defends his position so cogently.

It may seem strange to many that the writer of this appreciation was the one selected to present it as a part of the *Festschrift* honoring Professor Hoffman. On its face nothing could seem less appropriate. For I am descended from Elder William Brewster of the Pilgrim Fathers, who viewed Rome as a mortal enemy to much that they held sacred; I was reared in a home where the tenets of Protestant puritanism were rigidly upheld, and am a member of the Congregational Church which rejects much of Roman Catholic faith and tradition. The invitation to me by Professor Hoffman's former students was surely nothing less than a manifestation of the growing spirit of ecumenicity, so heartening a sign today of the drawing-together of all those who are persuaded that a basic Christian outlook on life has such transcendent values to the individual—values which must be preserved and defended in this period of testing—that it rises above lesser differences, great as they may be, with respect to the Christian religion and the resulting difference in the historical interpretation of the past. Beyond this heartening spirit of ecumenicity is the fact (doubtless taken into account by the planners of this *Festschrift*) of the deep friendship that exists between Professor Hoffman and myself. I shall not soon forget his generosity in placing at my disposal in 1951 source material of great importance to my British Empire series that he had secured in Ireland; nor can I forget the gracious hospitality extended to me as a guest in the Hoffman home in Rye, New York during the days when I was working with this material. The bond that has continued to hold us together beyond that of friendship is our common interest in eighteenth-century British history.

Professor Hoffman was born in Harrisburg, Pennsylvania, in 1902. As was true of the writer of this appreciation he became as a young man involved in newspaper work which developed his facility in reporting events. He received his undergraduate training at Lafayette College, an excellent institution. Thinking in terms of a career as a foreign correspondent he went to Germany in 1923. But this plan did not work out and as a result he wisely entered the graduate school of the University of Pennsylvania where he worked under such shining lights as Professors William E. Lingelbach and Edward Potts Cheyney and secured his doctorate in 1932.

Hoffman's doctoral dissertation under title of *Great Britain and the German Trade Rivalry, 1875–1914* was published in 1933 by the University of Pennsylvania Press. It was accorded the coveted George Louis Beer prize by the American Historical Association and was reprinted in 1964. An important economic study, it helps to throw much light on the field of international tensions before the outbreak of the First World War.

Likewise, Professor Hoffman's historical writings during the next fifteen years relate chiefly to international politics. In 1939 appeared his *The Organic State: An Historical View of Contemporary Politics,* and in 1942 his *The Great Republic; An Historical View of the International Community and the Organization of the Peace*—both very timely and scholarly works. In collaboration with Professor Charles Groves Haines of Syracuse University he wrote *The Origins and Background of the Second World War.* Published by the Oxford University Press in 1943, it was issued in revised form in 1947. In reviewing the book in the January 1944 number of the *American Historical Review* Dr. Raymond C. Miller of Wayne University wrote:

The publishers will do the world a disservice if they publicize this volume only as a textbook. Here is a vivid and dramatic story of our age. It is an enlightening, indeed a shocking, experience for any reader to re-examine at one time the cumulated record of our generation, to feel again the impact of portentous events and the agony of fateful decisions. . . . For the good of the nation one may wish this book great success.

This was followed in 1944 by Hoffman's *Durable Peace; A Study in American National Policy,* also published by the Oxford University Press. In 1951 appeared the last of his studies on international politics, *The Spirit of Politics and the Future of Freedom*. In this he contrasts the outcome of the American Revolution with that of the French Revolution and also stresses the problem of government and the moral law.

Professor Hoffman's academic advancement meanwhile was steady. He was assistant in history at the University of Pennsylvania between 1924 and 1926; an instructor of history at New York University between 1926 and 1935; an assistant professor at the same institution between 1935 and 1938; an associate professor at Fordham University between 1938 and 1944, and then from 1944 onward a full professor in the same institution.

With his growth in prestige as an historian the emphasis of his teaching gradually shifted to the graduate school and to the careful preparation of his students who would later occupy posts in the academic world. The standards that he set were high, as is indicated by this *Festschrift*.

While Professor Hoffman by no means lost his interest in contemporary international affairs, his attention was increasingly drawn to the eighteenth century. In 1948 there appeared *Burke's Politics; Selected Writings and Speeches on Reform, Revolution and War,* which he and Dr. A. Paul Levack, also of Fordham University, compiled and carefully edited. The writings are preceded by a very thoughtful and penetrating essay on "Burke's Philosophy of Politics," which shows both the limitations and the vast reaches of Burke's thinking. One great merit of the work is that closely interrelated topics are brought together from various parts of the writings of Burke so that the reader is able to get the unity of his thought whether it relates to the American Revolution, the oppression of the Catholics, the government of India or of Ireland, or the French Revolution. In fact, this volume is the most convenient vehicle that

I know of for the student of today to approach Burke's views on public issues.

In one respect there is a serious omission in the volume. For it may be regretted that while, in dealing with India, there are presented abundant Burke reflections on the misgovernment of that great subcontinent by the United East India Company and its servants in India, there is lacking any of the thunderous charges levied by the great orator directly against Governor-General Warren Hastings. The explanation for this omission doubtless lies in the feeling of the editors—a very proper feeling—that Burke was not at his best in the violent polemics uttered against Hastings. They observe that impartial historians are agreed that Burke's "powerful imagination and hot passions clouded his judgment, and that partisan prejudice crept into and corrupted his sense of justice in the Hastings case" (p. 276).

But Professor Hoffman was not through with Burke. In 1956 there was published by the American Philosophical Society in its *Memoirs* series his important *Edmund Burke, New York Agent, With his Letters to the New York Assembly and Intimate Correspondence with Charles O'Hara, 1761–1776*. The letters to the New York Assembly are introduced by an illuminating essay of 178 pages. The larger part of the volume is given over to the O'Hara correspondence between Burke in England and O'Hara in Ireland; it sheds much light on Anglo-Irish relations. These original source materials were uncovered by Hoffman among the Fitzwilliam manuscripts in the Sheffield Public Libraries and in the O'Hara family archives at Annaghmore in County Sligo, Ireland. The work places all students who are interested in the eighteenth-century British Empire in debt to the editor of it. One final item relating to Burke may be mentioned—as contributing to an understanding of the great man; this is Hoffman's interesting article entitled "Edmund Burke as a Practical Politician" that was printed in *The Burke Newsletter* of 1963–64.

From this time on, Professor Hoffman's specialized interest has shifted from Burke to his close friend the Marquess of Rockingham. I myself feel that the latter has not received the credit by historians for the quality of statesmanship that he brought to bear on the problems facing Great Britain in the latter half of the eighteenth century. This is now destined to be rectified by Hoffman with a forthcoming political biography of Rockingham.

Two years after the appearance of the Burke Correspondence there was published a cooperative work by Doubleday under the title *Man and his History; World History and Western Civilization*. Professor Hoffman not only acted as its editor-in-chief but contributed the first unit as well as the last two units to it—the book is divided into units. The volume is one in the *Christian Democracy Series* and is designed as a textbook for Catholic high schools. I have never seen its equal in textbook form with respect to the beauty of its illustrations (a number of them in color) and the attractiveness of its many maps. Moreover, the book is carefully written. After going through four printings, the original edition was revised in 1963. It deserves to have a long life.

Professor Hoffman is also the author of numerous other briefer works that are largely concerned with the position of the Roman Catholic Church in world affairs. The importance of his contribution to this field is manifest in these other works, especially in the volume *Restoration* published in 1934 that is concerned with Hoffman's conversion to the Roman Catholic faith.

Although a Protestant and therefore outside the Catholic fold, may I say that I know of no other living American historian of high reputation who is more justly entitled to the accolade "Defender of the Catholic Faith" than is Ross Hoffman. That this is also the attitude of Roman Catholic scholars seems evident by the fact that an honorary doctorate was conferred upon him by Villanova University in

1936, followed by Marquette University in 1937, Fordham University in 1946, the University of Detroit in 1950, and the National University of Ireland in 1957. Hoffman has also been honored by the Catholic Historical Association. His presidential address "Catholicism and Historismus," published in the January 1939 number of *The Catholic Historical Review,* seeks to make clear the nature of the insights into the reality of human events that can come only by the rejection of positivism and the purely materialistic approach to the study of history in favor of an approach based upon spiritual insights. I could not more heartily agree with such a position when stated in the above terms.

In concluding this appreciation I, as one who has long been interested as a student in the eighteenth-century British Empire, salute Ross Hoffman as a distinguished contributor to the history of this empire. Fordham University may indeed take pride in having had the services of such a man for a period of some thirty years.

LAWRENCE HENRY GIPSON

# Crisis in the "Great Republic"

# I

# William Dowdeswell's *Thoughts on the Present State of Public Affairs and the Propriety of Accepting or Declining Administration*, July 23–24, 1767

## M. FRANCIS DE SALES BORAN, R.S.H.M.

OSCAR WILDE once postulated (in *Lady Windermere's Fan*, Act II) that *discontent* is the first step in the progress of a man or nation. Professor Butterfield may well be correct in his charge that much of the history of the Age of George III suffers from the taint of a Whig interpretation, that is, from the prejudgment that anything which conduced to the present situation is "progress," while anything which has had some other result is not progress; that only Whigs were capable of effecting progress. But if the definition of progress—even historically—is disputable, there can be no dispute about the fact that in the early part of George III's reign the Rockingham Whigs suffered *discontent*. In fact, they believed themselves to be in the *crisis* of their political lives. Was this crisis productive of progress in the reassessment and development of political party?

Edmund Burke's *Thoughts on the Cause of the Present Discontents,* which first appeared in 1770, gave the well-known classic exposition of the Rockingham Whig analysis of the prevailing distempers in the nation. William Dowdeswell's hastily composed and more modest pamphlet is not as well known. Indeed, it has never been published in toto. Yet, on its own merits, it is of no small historic interest. I know of no occasion more timely than this commemorative one to bring Dowdeswell's *Thoughts* into print. It was Professor Ross J. S. Hoffman who first aroused my interest in the document as a history student.

William Dowdeswell (1721–75) first stepped on to the English political stage in 1747 as a Tory member for the family borough of Tewkesbury. He retained his seat until 1754, and was then out until 1761, in which year he was returned, again as a Tory, for Worcester. A number of factors combined to prompt him to cross the shadow-line separating his *old toryism* from the whiggism of virtuous aristocracy professed by the second Marquess of Rockingham and his followers. When, in July of 1765, Rockingham had completed the membership of his first short-lived administration, Dowdeswell was Chancellor of the Exchequer. Upon the fall of the ministry in the following July, he refused to remain in the new government of Chatham, and turned down "the first seat of the board of trade, or a joint pay-master's place" offered him by the king.[1] Instead, he elected to go into opposition with his new political friends; he remained in opposition to the end of his life. In the meantime, the Chatham administration went into rapid deterioration; Chatham himself was rendered increasingly incapacitated and withdrew absolutely from all public business from May 1767 to October 1768. The ministry was

[1] Dowdeswell to Chatham, July 31, 1766, Dowdeswell MSS in William L. Clements Library, University of Michigan, Ann Arbor, Michigan.

then known by the Duke of Grafton's name. The Rockinghams, who had been wont to flirt with the idea of winning Chatham to a government of their own, now became disenchanted with his politics. As early as November 27, 1766, Edmund Burke denounced it as that "tesselated pavement government," "beat about like footballs." [2] And Dowdeswell castigated it as a ministry "of fine discordant atoms." [3] As traditional proponents of the existing party system, the Rockinghams were disgusted with Chatham's proscription of all parties as mere factions tending to place their petty interests above the interests of the state. They rejected his thesis that ability alone was the touchstone of selection for public office. They were strongly convinced that his "men-not-measures" policy was ranging him irrevocably on the side of the monarch and opening him to undue pressures from the court and the *king's friends* part of the court. The Rockinghams realistically foresaw that the weakness of the administration would eventually compel the king to approach them as the dominant Whig group with a request to strengthen government. They had learned in the crucible of bitter experience that it was futile to attempt to form a ministry with but their own scant following. Hence, beginning in the summer of 1766 they had undertaken negotiations with the leaders of the other prominent Whig groups, preeminently the Bedfords and the Temple–Grenvillians, in an effort to effect some measure of Whig union. These negotiations, though they bore no positive fruit, lasted on one basis or another until July 1767. In the meantime, by March 5, 1767, the king was sounding Lord North for the exchequer. Upon North's refusal, the Duke of Grafton, in July (6–7) requested assistance from Lord Rockingham. Reluctantly, George III agreed to informing Rockingham in Grafton's name that when he had a plan of administration

[2] Burke to Charles O'Hara, O'Hara MSS, in possession of Mr. Donal F. O'Hara, Annaghmore, Collooney, Co. Sligo, Ireland, printed in Ross Hoffman, *Edmund Burke, New York Agent* (Philadelphia, 1956), 374.
[3] Dowdeswell to his wife, July 30, 1766, Dowdeswell MSS.

he would admit him to the closet. A consummate realist, George III rightly expected that, given time, the disparate Whig leaders would bicker irreconcilably over the disposition of employments. Therefore, he elected to leave Lord Rockingham ignorant of the precise extent of authority he might exercise in the formulation of his plan. On his part, Rockingham, believing "the present administration at an end," proceeded on the basis of constructing *a totally new* government.[4] The Rockinghams became increasingly enfuriated with the king's actions, particularly with his tactics, which, rightly or wrongly, they imputed to the influence of the *king's friends* principle of government, of refusing to do business directly with Rockingham but rather through a third party. This, they felt, robbed their leader of that confidence and prestige in the eyes of his Whig peers which was rightfully his as the royally selected formulator of the projected ministry. On Wednesday, July 22, 1767, Rockingham had to inform the king that his attempts to form a comprehensive government had failed. The following day, however, he found himself once again summoned to meet the Duke of Grafton, who informed him that both the king and the duke himself desired that Rockingham attempt anew to see "if some new plan could not be hit off" which would bring the Rockingham friends into administration.[5] Newcastle's *Narrative* clarifies that Rockingham adhered to his principle of a comprehensive plan of government based on a Whig union, or no government at that time under his aegis.[6]

Such was the political situation which prompted William

[4] G. F. R. Barker, ed., *Memoirs of the Reign of George III* (4 vols., London, 1894), III, 51.
[5] M. Bateson (ed.), *A Narrative of the Changes in the Ministry 1765–1767 as told by the Duke of Newcastle* (London, 1898), 154. The treasury was not actually offered on this occasion, as apparently it was in the former negotiation, to Rockingham. It was mentioned as "open."
[6] *Ibid.*

Dowdeswell to compose his *Thoughts*. He sent his paper to his political chief on July 24 (1767) with the proviso:

You will be so good as to remember that it is for your information only and for Lady Rockingham's if she will take the trouble of reading it. You will take a copy in your own hand or in Lady Rockingham's and when you send it safely let me have the original.[7]

[7] The copy is in the hand of the marchioness who frequently copied *special* papers for her husband, in the Fitzwilliam MSS, in the Central Library, Sheffield, England.

## Dowdeswell's Thoughts[8]

*In the present distempered state of public affairs it is hardly possible for a well-meaning man to look forwards and see what can be done to put himself and his friends in a situation the most likely to serve the public.*

*So many changes of administration[9] in so short a time have rendered sensible and well-meaning men indifferent to office. The short duration of each administration not only curtails the reward of merit but check'd every good disposition as it rose and aspired to do something for the service of the State. Opinion of want of continuance, shortness of the duration and limitation of power have disabled you in foreign negotiation and domestic enterprize. Officers have not time to learn the duties of their offices before they are discharged. They continue just long enough to learn how to perplex their successors and no longer. The civil list runs in debt year after year and no minister has had time to look into the cause. The many divisions which have been the consequences of so many changes have so disunited men that though no opposition can be successful, no administration can stand.*

*All mankind calls aloud to have union and permanency but men however discordant in their former opinions wish that there be permanency in administration, whatever hands it may happen to be placed in.*

*With this view it was that administration was lately offered to Lord Rockingham.[10] He endeavoured to form a plan as comprehensive as possible.[11] He failed. It behoves him to take care in his future conduct not to lose that merit which the sincerity of his attempt entitles him to. Why it failed and how pure he stands in his behaviour on that occasion is considered in another paper.*

[8] Only the abbreviated names and offices in this transcription are altered: they are completed.
[9] In the seven years following 1760 there were six changes of ministry.
[10] July 1767. See *supra*.
[11] That is, on the basis of a Whig union, particularly with the Bedfords.

*What can he now do but stand still and leave it to chance to bring about those events which may possibly enable him to be useful to his King and Country.*

*Suppose administration were offered to him: In these circumstances and upon these conditions only I think he could undertake it.*

*First the King would send for him to give him powers from his own mouth without the interposition of any of his ministers. This will give him weight and is absolutely necessary at this time, there having been in the former negotiation a point not rightly understood tho' no less essential than whether he was to be at the head of the Treasury.*[12]

*Secondly at his audience he must give the King to understand as tenderly as he can, but at the same time as truly, the real cause of all the public misfortunes. They must be imputed not to the influence of particular persons but to the prevalence of a political principle which says that the power of the Crown arises out of the weakness of the administration.*[13]

*The Public misfortunes necessarily resulting from that weakness should be set forth as the distress of the Crown in its income and its honour. At the same time that these representations are made, with all possible deference and submission, there should appear a manly resolution not to maintain the pageantry of administration an hour after it is divested of its necessary weight in the Closet and its necessary power in other places.*[14]

---

[12] Rockingham learned in the closet interview of July 22, 1767, that in the king's opinion the treasury had not been offered him. However, both he and Dowdeswell believed that it had, and interpreted this as a conscious tactic to confuse: Newcastle's *Narrative,* 150; Albemarle, *Memoirs of the Marquis of Rockingham* (2 vols., London, 1852), II, 54.

[13] Dowdeswell here castigates the court party of the *king's friends.*

[14] Edmund Burke is ordinarily credited with being the first to enunciate the *modern* principles of "responsibility" and solidarity for a satisfactory system of political party: *Discontents* (2d ed., London, 1770), 110. Dowdeswell here implies the same principles, and the date was July, 1766.

*If after this he is directed to proceed, he should not fall into a common error that the removal of a particular set, supposed connected with the prevailing influence either gives or marks the power of an administration. At the same time, for example sake, he should invariably remove such of them as have been most insidious in their conduct to any of the former administration. He should not confine his discipline to that particular set. There are others who belong to other Corps. Example should be the object in the first list of removals. The rest may be taken as it shall be thought best in that political management which tho' no part of our constitution, is become, I am afraid, inseparable from our Government.*

*In filling up the offices, he should attend determinedly to forming a comprehensive plan, if possible; he should apply to the Duke of Bedford and in the first place remove those stumbling blocks which were in his way in the former negotiation. If I mistake not, they were these: First, Lord Rockingham not being able to produce the necessary power by going into the closet before he undertook the work, the Duke of Bedford treated on a par.*[15] *Secondly, the Grenvilles' interposition could not be with any good design and must necessarily excite suspicion in Lord Rockingham.*[16] *The Duke of Bedford should therefore be told that as soon as he had the King's orders to proceed, he returned to his former idea of a comprehensive plan and resolved to carry it into execution if he could; that he would be fair enough to tell his Grace that if he could not compleat what he most*

---

[15] George III in one *coup* had helped to put Bedford forward and to harass the whig attempts at coalescence (1) by undertaking his own negotiations apart from the overture to Rockingham, and (2) by electing to proscribe the inclusion of George Grenville in Rockingham's government. The Bedfords would not join the Rockinghams without the Temple–Grenvillians.

[16] Grenville had made it known at the meeting of July 20, 1767, that he and Temple would back the comprehensive plan for a ministry on the condition that it would adopt "the capital measure of asserting and establishing the sovereignty of Great Britain over its colonies." This was interpreted by the Rockinghams as an insinuation that their repeal of Grenville's stamp act had sacrificed English interests: Newcastle's *Narrative*, 143.

wished, he would still proceed and that though he might foresee that possibly in this case his administration might be short-lived, it should be an honest one and such an one as however it might be opposed by his Grace while it existed, should have his approbation after its death.

That in order to show his fairness, he would ease his Grace's mind and not appoint Mr. Conway secretary of state; Mr. Conway's late declaration that he would not act with the Bedfords will justify this conduct in Lord Rockingham.[17] There might be other grounds of justification if they were wanted; that whether Mr. Townshend [18] or Mr. Dowdeswell were to be the leader he would reserve to himself at present;[19] that he must desire his Grace not to recommend Mr. Townshend to them because he intended himself to offer what he hoped might be acceptable; that after this fairness he hoped he should not appear presuming if he told his Grace that he could not treat on par; that he must consider himself as the Former of the Administration and answerable for its success, and would therefore preserve in all offices of business a manifest superiority for his own friends; but that if his Grace would make a list of his friends with the nature of his wishes for them, he would find Lord Rockingham as earnest as he could wish in giving all possible proof of his desire of what might be perfectly satisfactory.[20]

[17] Rockingham desired that General Henry Seymour Conway (1719–95) be his trusted lieutenant in the sensitive posts of secretary for the southern department (which still included the American colonies) and leader of the House of Commons. The Duke of Bedford stoutly opposed Conway's candidacy: Newcastle's *Narrative,* 145; *Rockingham Memoirs,* II, 61; *Grenville Papers,* IV, 78.

[18] Charles Townshend (1725–67), chancellor of the exchequer in the Chatham-Grafton administration, brilliant but unreliable. See L. B. Namier, *Charles Townshend* (Cambridge, Eng., 1959).

[19] The Duke of Bedford had counterproposed Dowdeswell for the secretaryship and leadership of the Commons at the meeting of July 21, 1767: Newcastle's *Narrative,* 149.

[20] Dowdeswell was as interested in securing union with the Bedfords as was Rockingham himself, but he saw clearly that Rockingham would have to retain "leadership."

*That as to the friends of Lord Temple and Mr. Grenville he certainly would himself most earnestly wish to provide for some of them, but after what had passed he must object to the interposition of Lord Temple and Mr. Grenville. However, if he could receive a list of them from the hands of the Duke of Bedford he would certainly do all he could to comprehend them. That as to Mr. Grenville himself he should pay all possible civility and attention to him; that at present it would be impossible to go further towards, but that he would live in hopes that upon his experience of Mr. Grenville's fairness and Mr. Grenville's experience of Lord Rockingham's behaviour towards him, they should in time get nearer to each other.*

*This being opened by degrees to the Duke of Bedford, I do not see why he might not become as tractable to Lord Rockingham as he has been to Lord Chatham. The advantage given to him by making him the person from whose hands Lord Rockingham was to receive the list of Mr. Grenville's friends would of course bring on a negotiation between the Duke of Bedford and Mr. Grenville, which could not turn out to the prejudice of Lord Rockingham. The rule laid down from the beginning of treating Lord Temple and Mr. Grenville as the friends of the Duke of Bedford would make this proceeding very correct and the perseverance in it might give the Duke of Bedford an opportunity of struggling with Mr. Grenville for some of their common friends, in case Mr. Grenville should not agree and the event of such a struggle must do some good.*

*In the arrangement Lord Rockingham should take care to be so liberal to the Duke of Bedford for his friends, Lord Temple and Mr. Grenville, that the sincerity of his intention for a union may be manifest beyond contradiction and that the Duke of Bedford may be most clearly in the wrong if they do not agree. In that case Lord Rockingham will stand justified for taking upon narrower ground. Mankind does not wish to see this Country without an adminis-*

*tration though it expects with reason that every possible attempt be made to form one that shall be powerful and to that end it would be broad and comprehensive. This will secure it against the intrigues of the Closet and nothing else can.*

*It will be much to be wished that Mr. Townshend may be confidential and take the Secretary of State. Making the Plantations Department separate from the Southern is a very right measure especially with the view of putting Lord Dartmouth*[21] *into it, but will have its difficulties if Lord Gower*[22] *and Mr. Townshend are to be the other secretaries. It should be understood early to be a determined matter before the Duke of Bedford chooses a secretaryship for Lord Gower.*

*If Mr. Townshend will not be confidential he may have the pay office with or without the Cabinet and he must be given to understand that he must give an active support. In this case Mr. Dowdeswell must necessarily have the lead. Mr. Townshend is much to be wished as a friend and therefore all possible means should be used to make him one.*

*A new parliament should certainly be called by which not only the number of Lord Rockingham's particular friends might be increased but our line of speakers also enlarged. Wedderburn*[23] *should undoubtedly be gained and Dunning*[24] *too. The only fear will be that not being able to trust in the man the most fit for the lead,*[25] *you should be overpowered in debate. If all this is thought too great and impracticable, the question then is whether it is better to undertake a weak administration than not to undertake it at all.*

*To do it would be so contrary to all our former assertions that unless some great good is to be got by it, or some*

---

[21] William Legge, 2d Earl of Dartmouth (1731–1801).
[22] Granville Leveson–Gower, 2d Earl Gower (1721–1803), later (1786) 1st Marquess of Stafford, brother-in-law to the fourth Duke of Bedford.
[23] Alexander Wedderburn (1733–1805).
[24] John Dunning (1731–1783), later (1782) 1st Baron Ashburton.
[25] Charles Townshend.

*great evil prevented, it is surely a thing not to be thought of. A weak administration is of course to expect to be a short one. It can do no good; it cannot enterprize; it would not probably be allowed to hold to the general election; it would not dare to shorten the continuance of this parliament; it would be insulted at home and despised abroad. As to the evil to be prevented it is this; a worse administration may be formed; if so, it must still be a weak one. It must be so bad an administration that mankind would wish it to be a short one. It would be short for it must consist of men who will have no opinion of each other.*[26] *The secret promoter of it and the first open actor in it would probably be two men the least conciliating in their manner and the most unpopular in the Kingdom. It must consist of men who have joined us in avowing the necessity of a strong administration. Why should we by taking, contradict ourselves through fear that if we do not they will contradict themselves.*

*By taking, we should prevent them from being put to the trial. We have said, and I fear it is true, no good can be done till the administration is offered in every quarter and refused by all. Till then it is to be feared that the same political principle will prevail and no administration will be formed that is not weak.*

*We must therefore permit the offer to go round, or the refusal will not be general. Possibly those to whom the next offer is to be made may be as cautious as ourselves. This is certain, that by taking we leave it in their power to make us as black as they please, and themselves as white as the unsullied snow. They may say that we were not desirous of a union. Nothing has done us so much honour as that attempt to form a comprehensive plan. Nothing can justify our putting an end to that negotiation so much as our self-denial on this occasion. If we take they may say against us*

---

[26] Here in July 1767 Dowdeswell at least *implies* what Burke later raised to the status of party platform—mutual confidence and party responsibility.

*that we were not sincere, that we broke off for the sake of being in office a place taking administration; that if we had not taken, they also would have refused and the King would have been under the necessity of forming what the nation most wishes—a strong comprehensive administration not to be shaken by the intrigues of the Closet. Whatever they may be pleased to say of the purity of their intentions, they may safely for they cannot be contradicted. We shall have prevented the trial.*

*Perhaps also the thing is not practicable. The treasury has indeed been offered to Lord Rockingham and his friends might be provided for. Have we reason to believe that Mr. Yorke*[27] *might be made Lord Chancellor and the Duke of Portland* [28] *Lord Chamberlain? If these things are not to be done at the same time could we with honour accept? What then can be done? Nothing but to finish with honour. We have hitherto acted with the strictest honour. If our friends will not join us it is impossible for us to join them. Their adherence to office may possibly prevent an offer to Mr. Grenville. It is as likely to prevent one to Lord Rockingham conveying to him what the former offer did not: all the necessary power, the continuance and assistance of the Crown.*

*I confess that I see no fair prospect before us—standing still is the only thing we can do. It depends upon the virtue of our friends whether it will or not, but I am sure it will do us honour as individuals. In these unhappy times when we find ourselves well in the opinion of mankind the best thing we can do is to stand still and enjoy the reputation which we have, not resign it for something new, the chances of which are so much against us.*

[27] Charles Yorke (1722–70).
[28] William Henry Cavendish Bentinck, 3rd Duke of Portland (1738–1809).

2

# Edmund Burke and the First Partition of Poland: Britain and the Crisis of 1772 in the "Great Republic"

## GAETANO L. VINCITORIO

THE POLES PRIZED LIBERTY so much in the eighteenth century that they overlooked the order, stability, and the purpose that would render it viable. Like the Greeks of antiquity their obsession with freedom and free government provoked endless internal quarrels which led their neighbors to exploit their lack of unity and intervene on behalf of one Polish party or another. Their leaders squandered their energies on factious disputes that sapped national strength —no longer nourished by a deep religious faith[1]—and that weakened the determination to continue the unique experiment of the Royal Republic.

Contemporaries easily identified a root cause of Polish misfortune in their anarchic constitution. Edmund Burke observed that Poland carried liberty to the extreme. Real power was vested in the gentry, any one of whom could end discussion in the Diet by exercising the *liberum veto*. "Each

[1] O. Halecki, *A History of Poland* (New York, 1961), 212–13.

Pole," he said, "seems rather an independent sovereign than a citizen."[2] The nobles were enamored of the anarchic constitution. "The idea of personal dignity they entertain, from seeing so many people in a servile condition below them," he added, "flatter in the highest degree their pride and self-importance." The result of the anarchy is that the Poles "sacrifice all the security and all the dignity of the state; and they are, in effect, governed in their most important concerns rather by their powerful and ambitious neighbours, than their own national council."[3]

The elective monarchy was a source of weakness. It injured not only the Poles but Europe which it frequently involved in blood and confusion.[4] The laws and institutions of the Poles, according to a history written by Burke, resembled those of the Saxons in early England. The Saxon and Polish love of freedom closed their minds to a constitution in which one person or a few could exercise the powers of government, and to the idea of deputed authority or representation. The result was that when any important matter had to be considered, it was first necessary to assemble the whole body of the nation so that "every individual might consent to the law, and each reciprocally bind the other to the observation of it."[5] The elective monarchy

[2] *Annual Register,* VI (1763), 44. This publication reflected the views of Burke, who was its first editor. Professor Copeland maintained that Burke was always in a position to dominate the periodical that he had founded and that virtually everyone associated with it was either a close friend or professed disciple. It can be proved that Burke worked on it from 1758 to 1763; that he probably worked on the 1764 and 1765 numbers; and that he probably made occasional contributions and suggestions from 1766 to 1792. (Thomas W. Copeland, "Edmund Burke's Friends and the *Annual Register,*" *The Library,* 5th Ser., XVIII [Mar. 1963], 29–39.) My own researches support the position that Burke wrote parts of the Historical Article which opened each number, perhaps as late as the 1780s. At the very least, the Historical Article faithfully mirrors Burke's mind. See also Carl B. Cone, *Burke and the Nature of Politics* (2 vols., Lexington, Ky., 1957–64), I, 122.
[3] *Annual Register,* VI (1763), 46.
[4] *Ibid.,* VI (1763), 44.
[5] "An Essay Towards an Abridgment of the English History [1757]," *The Works of the Right Honorable Edmund Burke* (12 vols., Boston, 1877), VII, 291. The Abridgment is a posthumous work (see Cone, I, 31). In his cele-

meant that the several candidates from Europe's competing dynasties who vied for the Polish throne that became vacant in 1763 sought support not only from leading Polish families like the Czartoriskis but also from rival foreign courts, which were ever ready to extend their influence in Warsaw. As a British diplomat commented to his superiors in 1768, "the Polish constitution is so near to anarchy, that violence must be expected on every vacancy of the Throne" and that left to themselves the Poles "cut one another's throats." [6]

Another source of debility was the religious quarrels between the dominant Roman Catholics and the Protestant and Orthodox Dissidents. The persecution of the Dissidents touched off protests by foreign governments and offended European opinion. Burke wrote in 1756, for example, that though Poland was a republic, its little finger of government was heavier than the loins of arbitrary power in most countries.[7] Despite the fact that the religious rights of the Dissidents had been guaranteed since the formation of the Republic, as the widely read *Annual Register* commented, these rights had been periodically violated because of the perverse disposition of almost every denomination of mankind to despoil and oppress all others, which, when accompanied by power, always discovered words to ignore explicit guarantees.[8]

---

brated Speech on Conciliation of 1775, Burke referred to the spirit of liberty that existed in the Southern American colonies in the midst of slavery— "those who are free are by far the most proud and jealous of their freedom." Freedom is a kind of rank and privilege. "Such were all the ancient commonwealths; such were our Gothic ancestors; such in our days were the Poles; and such will be all masters of slaves, who are not slaves themselves. In such a people, the haughtiness of domination combines with the spirit of freedom, fortifies it, and renders it invincible" (*Works,* II, 124).

[6] Lord Cathcart to Lord Weymouth, St. Petersburg, Nov. 1 (12), 1768, *Sbornik imperatorskago russkago istoricheskago obschestva* [The Collection of the Imperial Russian Historical Society, hereafter cited as *Sbornik*]; (148 vols., St. Petersburg, 1867–1916), II, 397.

[7] "Vindication of Natural Society [1756]," *Works,* I, 36.

[8] X (1767), 16. The author commented in the Preface: "While our humanity is deeply engaged in the cause of the Dissidents, we cannot but lament the

The Poles were unmindful of the dangers to their independence posed by the treatment of the Dissidents. Czarina Catherine the Great extended Russian influence over Poland by placing on the vacant Polish throne in 1764 her former paramour, Stanislaus Poniatowski, and by continuing to intervene in Polish affairs on the pretext of assisting her Orthodox coreligionists.[9] A British diplomat observed that the Russian demands on the Poles were imperious and dictatorial and that nothing but absolute impotence could prevent a free nation from resisting. Out of despair they would throw themselves into the arms of any other power.[10] Their fanaticism, he added later, seemed to "make them forget every sense of danger, and rather hazard the loss of all than admit the Dissidents to a chance of the smallest share." Because the Czarina wanted full concessions accorded to the Dissidents and refused compromise, she bore the refusal of the Poles with great impatience.[11] Catherine's minister, Count Panin, told his son-in-law and Russian representative in Poland:

It is necessary to resolve the Dissident affair not for the sake of propagating our faith and the Protestant in Poland, but for the sake

fatality by which a great nation is surrounded in its capital by a foreign army; and the senators of a republic that was once free and independent, carried off by a military force for a discussion of their own affairs.

[9] *The Annual Register* (VII [1764] 11) said that Poniatowski "was a man, by his personal qualifications, by his striking virtues, and his various acquirements by study and travel, fitted to fill and dignify any station. If the constitution of Poland would ever suffer it to emerge, it could not have better chances for becoming considerable under any prince."

[10] Sir George Macartney to the Rt. Hon. Mr. Secretary Conway, Nov. 1 (12), 1766, *Shornik*, XII, 281. The British government considered the international danger in the Dissident question. Shelburne wrote to the British Ambassador in Paris, Rochford, on Nov. 13, 1767, that "there reigns . . . amongst the Polish nobility such a spirit of discontent and resentment that the least prospect of foreign assistance might kindle a great flame in that country." He asked Rochford to learn if the courts of Versailles or Vienna would continue to look with an indifferent eye on the affairs of Poland (Royal Historical Society, *British Diplomatic Instructions, 1689–1789*, Vol. VII: France, pt. iv: 1745–1789, ed. L. G. Wickham Legg [Camden Third Series, Vol. XLIX; London, 1934], 101).

[11] Macartney to Conway, Nov. 28 (Dec. 7), 1766, *Shornik*, XII, 288–89.

of acquiring for ourselves, through our coreligionists and the Protestants, a firm and reliable party with the legal right to participate in all the affairs of Poland.[12]

The Polish Diet was compelled to accept a Perpetual Treaty (March 1768) that in effect reduced Poland to a province of the Czarina who now "guaranteed" its independence. The *Annual Register* remarked that Poland was humiliated and became a vast field of carnage, and that Stanislaus was an impotent witness who was under obligation to his enemy for his defense.[13] In light of the fact that Poland fell victim to all the calamities that followed weak government and proximity to mighty neighbors, the publication observed that it might be better for that unhappy country to become a province of one of them.[14]

In February 1768 the smaller Polish nobility not unexpectedly rose up in rebellion in Podolia and announced a confederation at the small fortress town of Bar. The effort to regain freedom, of course, brought the Poles to blows with the Russians in June. The *Annual Register* reported that the unfortunate country was the scene of the most malignant and complex of wars—one that was in part civil, religious, and foreign.[15]

The defeat of the Confederation of Bar did not end Polish resistance, which became enmeshed in the age-old Russo–Turkish enmity. When some Poles fled from their pursuers to sanctuary on Turkish soil, they were followed by Russians. Incited by the French, the Turks turned on the Russians in October 1768 and began another Russo–Turkish War (1768–74). The paradox was that Poland

---

[12] Aug. 25, 1767, as quoted in Herbert H. Kaplan, *The First Partition of Poland* (New York, 1962), 67.

[13] XI (1768), 4–6. Henry Shirley wrote to Henry Conway, Jan. 24 (Feb. 4), 1768, that "the King of Poland is very uneasy, and has reason to be so; for I must confess, that I think, she [Catherine] looks upon him as a tool; as long as he is useful to her. She will protect him, but no farther." *Sbornik*, XII, 325–26.

[14] XII (1769), 5–6.

[15] XI (1768), 4.

looked to Turkey for protection and the Sultan became the guardian of Polish freedom. As the *Annual Register* exclaimed, "the Catholic religion fled for protection to the standard of Mohammed!"[16] It had earlier noted that the Turks had played a "truly neighbourly part" in the Polish affair and it regretted that no sovereign in Europe—where rulers were educated in principles infinitely better calculated to form it—had helped the Poles.[17] Russia would have kept the peace if she could have dominated Poland without war. But she chose war on the grounds of observing existing treaties on the protection of Dissidents, a claim that the periodical labelled superficial and always available as a pretext to maintain an army in any country on ostensibly benevolent principles. Similar grounds might justify dispatching a Russian force to Constantinople to maintain regularity and to restore the ancient and transgressed rights of Christians.[18]

The Russo–Turkish War helped bring on the partition of Poland. The striking successes of Russian arms in the campaign of 1769 wrenched Moldavia and Wallachia from the Turks. The courts at Vienna and Berlin were understandably uneasy about the increase in Russian influence and they therefore took measures to mediate the conflict and prevent further Russian victories. France, however, encouraged the Turks to continue hostilities. As diplomats clearly perceived, the continued success of the Czarina's forces near the Danube would provoke Austria to enter the war. To balance the power that Russia had gained, Austria and Prussia would have to seek acquisitions at the expense of Poland, who would be made to pay for the defeat of the Turks.

After Austrian troops occupied territory in the County of Zips south of Cracow in the fall of 1770, Frederick

[16] *Ibid.*, XI, 2.
[17] VIII (1765), 6.
[18] XI (1768), 7.

the Great determined to restore the balance that had existed between Prussia and Austria prior to the acquisition. He accordingly decided to assert his "ancient rights" which his archives would furnish him and to take "some small province of Poland." [19] For many months projects involving the dismemberment of Poland became the subjects of discussion in the courts of Berlin, St. Petersburg, and Vienna. In October 1770 Prince Henry, the brother of Frederick, had tentatively proposed a tripartite deal to end the Russo–Turkish War and let Poland pay the price of peace. Frederick began action on partition in the following February, and a year later, a Russo–Prussian treaty had been signed. Prussia and Russia then negotiated with the wily minister of the Austrian empress, Kaunitz, who maneuvered successfully to get the lion's share.[20] A tripartite convention was signed at St. Petersburg in August 1772 that cost the Polish Commonwealth almost thirty percent of its territory and about thirty-five percent of its population. The Czarina, who had enjoyed exclusive sway over Warsaw, now had to share her dominance with two suspicious partners.[21]

The Poles had no choice but accept the enormity. The king could not prevent it. "Whatever future revolutions may take place," the *Annual Register* sneered, "the Poniatowski family will always be certain of a secure refuge in Siberia." [22] The partitioning powers were eager to have the Polish Diet ratify their acquisitions and had assembled it in

---

[19] Frederick to Count Solms, Prussian Ambassador to Russia, Feb. 20, 1771, as quoted in Kaplan, 141.

[20] See Chap. XIII, Kaplan. Robert Howard Lord maintained that the partition of 1772 "was brought about in the first place by the common and equal cupidity of Russia and Prussia; and, in the second place, it was singularly facilitated by the extraordinary situation of Europe at that time, which made a partition a plausible means for averting a general war, forced Austria to become a partner in this nefarious business, and prevented the Western Powers from intervening" (*The Second Partition of Poland: A Study in Diplomatic History* [Cambridge, Mass., 1915], 53).

[21] *Ibid.*, 188–89.

[22] XV (1772), 7.

April 1773. Faced with the choice of yielding or of witnessing further threatened losses in the event they demurred, the great senators gave in. They "already experienced, in the frozen wilds of Siberia, or in the gloom of a dungeon, the danger of holding an opinion, or of giving a vote, when surrounded by Russian troops."[23] In September the Diet finally regularized what was already a fact.

The two countries able to pressure the partitioners were ill prepared, singly or jointly to help the Poles. The failure of France, the traditional protectress of Poland, to prevent the amputation or even to be consulted was a body-blow to the monarchy and brought the government into deep disrespect.[24] Britain similarly stood aside. The British regretted but did not resent the partition to the point of demanding its reversal. Poland was too remote from the British Isles: news from Warsaw took many weeks to reach London.[25] The Poles, besides, adhered to the detested Roman Catholic religion which was a symbol in the eyes of many Englishmen of intolerance, discrimination, and supernaturalism. Were not Poles persecutors of Protestants? Other considerations that contributed to the remoteness of Poland included her traditional friendship for France, the inveterate enemy of Britain, and the relatively few points of contact in culture and trade between the two countries.[26] British leaders could not identify themselves with the plight

[23] *Ibid.*, XV (1772), 43.

[24] Leopold von Ranke, "The Great Powers," in Theodore von Laue, *Leopold Ranke: the Formative Years* (Princeton, N.J., 1950), 207–8.

[25] The comment of a friend of Charles James Fox reflected the attitude of many Britons: he would "rather be a commissioner of the customs in London than King of Poland," if he were obliged to pass his life at Warsaw (James Hare, quoted in D. B. Horn, *The British Diplomatic Service 1689–1789* [Oxford, 1961], 86).

[26] See William Fiddian Reddaway, "Britain and Poland 1762–1772," VII[e] Congrès International des Sciences Historiques, *Résumés des communications présentées au Congrès Varsovie 1933* (2 vols., Warsaw, 1933), I, 183–87; and David Bayne Horn, *Great Britain and Europe in the Eighteenth Century* (Oxford, 1967), Chap. VIII.

of the Poles. The Republic was not part of the Grand Tour of the Continent made by Milords anglais who regarded it as some sort of terra incognita.

However much some Englishmen resented the partition, their government did not act.[27] Constitutional crises at home, discontent in the colonies, together with the old insularity, turned the gaze of most Britons and the government away from Europe. After her striking victories in the Seven Years' War, Britain seemed to withdraw from European affairs. In analyzing Britain's shying away from continental politics, Albert Sorel said that "statesmen on the Continent paid very little attention to her, and even pretended that she no longer entered into their calculations," and that "Old Europe witnessed this spectacle with astonishment mingled with disdain." [28]

A reason for Britain's isolation was the breakup of the

[27] See David Bayne Horn, *British Public Opinion and the First Partition of Poland* (Edinburgh, 1945), and Wladyslav Konopczynski, "England and the First Partition of Poland," *Journal of Central European Affairs,* VIII (Apr. 1948), 1–23. The *Annual Register* (XI [1768], 65) summarized the British attitude toward Russo-Polish hostilities: "The war in Poland, from distance of situation and remoteness of interest, can have little immediate effect upon this country. Our minds are more strongly attracted by domestic concerns. The great and growing state of our Colonies in North America, the unhappy contention which has arisen between the mother country and the colonies; the vast extent of the empire acquired in India, and the various discussions which have arisen upon that subject between the Oriental Powers and the East–India Company, and between that Company and the English Government, afford sufficient matter to engage all our care and prudence, without looking for further employment in foreign politicks than evident necessity shall exact."

[28] *The Eastern Question in the Eighteenth Century* (London, 1898), 78, 83. Another student of international events commented that from 1763 to 1786 British foreign policy was largely blank: "few things in our history are more startling than the sudden obliteration of British influence in Europe after the Seven Years' War" (Sir Richard Lodge, *Great Britain and Prussia in the Eighteenth Century* [Oxford, 1923], 139). Recently, Herbert Butterfield has remarked that a comparison of British and French or Prussian diplomatic documents "might raise the question whether the British at this time sufficiently gave their minds to diplomacy or realized its creative possibilities." The British were single-minded on the importance of the Russian connection as the chief anti-French force in Europe ("Review Article: British Foreign Policy, 1762–5," *The Historical Journal,* VI, I [1963], 137).

Anglo–Prussian alliance, which fell apart during the negotiations that ended the Seven Years' War. In casting about for another ally that possessed a mighty army on the Continent, Britain could not find it in Austria or in her old enemy, France. The formula applied by British statesmen was "economize, promote trade, watch the Bourbons." Francophobia deprived Britain of the opportunity of concerting with other powers to curb Austria, Prussia, and Russia in their Polish enterprise; and even led some Englishmen to rationalize that the dismemberment had some benefit for them because it humbled the Bourbons.

The ally that British diplomats sought was Russia.[29] This explains to a large extent why they did not wish to alienate Catherine in the matter of Poland. A close look at the abortive efforts in the 1760s and 1770s to conclude an Anglo–Russian alliance renders intelligible the British failure to prevent the partition. British isolation, the military potential revealed by Russian armies during the Seven Years' War, the hostility toward France expressed by the Czarina, and vital Anglo–Russian commercial ties formed the bases for an eventual accord, in the eyes of the British.[30] Britain was Russia's biggest customer and imported on the average over half of Russia's exports.[31] Of paramount importance to His Majesty's maritime security were the naval stores from the Baltic.

In 1763 the British ambassador in St. Petersburg was reminded that his government looked to no alliance with so great desire as that with Russia, and that it shared the

[29] The *Annual Register* (VII [1764], 2) reported that Russian friendship was an eagerly sought object: "The emulation which, for this century past, has subsisted amongst all the maritime countries in augmenting their marine, has, without the exertion of any deep policy on her side, operated peacefully in her favor; as nature has made her the great magazine of naval stores to Europe."

[30] See M. S. Anderson, "Great Britain and the Russo-Turkish War of 1768–74," *English Historical Review*, LXIX (Jan. 1954), 39, and *id., Britain's Discovery of Russia 1553–1815* (London, 1958), 134–35.

[31] John Ehrman, *The British Government and Commercial Negotiations With Europe 1783–1793* (Cambridge, 1962), 97–98.

greatest attention to the desires of the Czarina in the matter of her candidate to the Polish throne "as upon every occasion that has offered." In this natural alliance between Britain and Russia both countries could speak with dignity and weight and could be heard with attention. As things stood, however, they were both mere capita mortua in European politics.[32] The Czarina instead concluded a treaty in April 1764 with Frederick, according to which he agreed to support her candidate to the Polish throne. The Prusso–Russian agreement was renewed in 1769 and was in force until 1780.

English efforts persisted. The English envoy was reminded that King George III was anxious to see formed a Northern League of Britain, Prussia, and Russia as a counterbalance to the dangerous combination of the Great Powers of the South of Europe, namely the Bourbons and Austria.[33] The highpoint in the negotiations toward alliance was the commercial treaty concluded in 1766 by George Macartney who plainly said: "We wanted Russia more than Russia could ever want us." [34] The longed-for political accord never came. The instructions given to Lord Cathcart, the new ambassador, alluded to the "invariable disposition to cement the good understanding so happily subsisting between the two courts." [35] After Count Panin had communicated to him his ideas on a possible alliance,[36] Cathcart informed London that Russia was *decidedly* English and that the moment was favorable for negotiation.[37] To his colleague in Constantinople, he wrote that Russian troops

[32] Earl of Halifax to Buckingham, June 24, 1763, *Sbornik*, XII, 102–3.
[33] Conway to Macartney, Dec. 19, 1766, *ibid.*, XII, 285–87.
[34] Macartney to Conway, July 4, 1766, *ibid.*; on Macartney see W. F. Reddaway, "Macartney in Russia, 1765–67," *The Cambridge Historical Journal*, III (1931), 284. Macartney's description of Russia in 1767 is printed in extract in John Barrow, *Some Account of the Public Life, and a Selection from the Unpublished Writings of the Earl of Macartney* (2 vols., London, 1807), II, 1–93.
[35] July 21, 1768, *Sbornik*, XII, 334.
[36] Sept. 29 (Oct. 10), 1768, *ibid.*, XII, 371–79.
[37] Cathcart to Weymouth, Oct. 7 (18), 1768, *ibid.*, XII, 382.

should not evacuate Poland "for were Poland to be left to itself without a principle of force either foreign or domestic to support government of some sort, anarchy must be the consequence." The Czarina, he added, would try to reunite the Poles among themselves! [38]

Britain tried to mediate the Russo–Turkish War by offering her good offices, a proposal opposed by France and Prussia, as well as by the principals. She further revealed her good will toward Russia by assisting her to transfer her Baltic fleet to the Eastern Mediterranean in 1769–70. Among other reasons impelling the English to aid the Russians was the misguided idea that the Czarina's maritime expansion would result in her greater dependence on Britain, who would be in a position then to exploit the commercial advantages that Catherine would secure from the Sultan.[39]

Prior to the partition, the British government left no doubt that Poland lay within the Russian orbit. The Earl of Rochford, Secretary of State for the Northern Department, reminded Cathcart

> not to engage his Majesty, to guaranty anything that should be settled, both on account of the little connection of interests, which this Kingdom has in general with that of Poland, and of the disturbances so frequently arising from the monstrous constitution of that country, which might some time or other make it a very burthensome obligation.[40]

He later said that he had told the Russian ambassador, Count Burzyinski, that "it was thought civil to pass over in silence the request desired to be made of us to the Empress of Russia to withdraw her troops from Poland" and that "we could not advise the Empress to such a step in the present situation of that country." [41]

[38] Cathcart to John Murray, Nov. 1 (12), 1768, *ibid.*, XII, 401.
[39] M. S. Anderson, "Great Britain and the Russian Fleet, 1769–70," *The Slavonic and East European Review,* XXXI (Dec. 1952), 150.
[40] Feb. 3, 1769, *Sbornik,* XII, 420–21.
[41] Jan. 26, 1770, *ibid.,* XIX, 1–2.

Early in 1771 the British government even instructed its envoy in St. Petersburg to warn Count Panin that Prussia had designs on parts of Poland.[42] Cathcart commented on the possibility that Austria and Prussia would support Russia in regard to peace terms with Turkey in exchange for dismembering Poland.[43] His subsequent allusion to the mutual suspicions of the powers, which were concerned in the Polish and Turkish questions, and to Russian desires to preserve Poland entire, is interesting. Although the courts at Berlin, St. Petersburg, and Vienna were mutually in open and direct correspondence, they really did not understand each other. And Cathcart added: "Russia is threatened by Austria; and Austria by Prussia, if Russia is attacked; and great warlike preparations are going on in all quarters." [44]

When London requested its envoy in St. Petersburg to look into the widespread belief that the three great powers intended a Polish partition,[45] Cathcart replied that as yet there was "nothing fit to be relied upon" concerning Frederick's intentions.[46] A week later he reported that Panin denied knowledge of a treaty that was ratified between Austria and Prussia on the subject of Poland.[47] Cathcart just could not bring himself to believe that the dismemberment had occurred or that Panin had duped him. Finally, on June 1, 1772, he admitted that reasons were sufficient to persuade him of a tripartite partition.[48]

[42] Halifax to Cathcart, Feb. 22, 1771, *ibid.*, XIX, 175–76.
[43] Cathcart to the Earl of Suffolk, July 12 (23), 1771, *ibid.*, XIX, 224–25.
[44] Same to same, Jan. 31 (Feb. 11), 1772, *ibid.*, XIX, 259.
[45] Suffolk to Cathcart, Mar. 20, 1772, *ibid.*, XIX, 259.
[46] Apr. 17 (28), 1772, *ibid.*, XIX, 264–65.
[47] Apr. 24 (May 5), 1772, *ibid.*, XIX, 268–69.
[48] Cathcart to Suffolk, June 1 (12), 1772, *ibid.*, XIX, 271–72. A week later he provided an interesting explanation of the partition: "Austria was jealous of Prussia's intention of encroaching upon Poland; Prussia was suspicious of the intention of Austria to make war, and was resolved to strike first. Upon information of the cause of the jealousy in Austria, and of her real dispositions, Prussia unknown to Russia, brought Austria over to the opinion of taking each a part, and invited Russia to do the same, under the pretence that the conduct of the Czartoriski's, and the situation of affairs rendered the measure, and a concert for that purpose indispensably

The British government knew what was afoot, however. Rochford informed the English ambassador in France that Britain would not favor the seizure of Danzig and Polish Prussia by Frederick—a measure that would affect the free commerce of Englishmen—and that she certainly would not concert measures to prevent the annexations. "Your Excellency is well aware," Rochford continued, "of the use that might be made at other Courts of any communications of our sentiments to that of Versailles on points of such delicacy." [49] Furthermore, the British minister in Berlin had informed London on March 1, 1772, that a treaty of partition had been signed at St. Petersburg on February 15th.[50] He received word in August that "his Majesty does not consider the affair of such importance as to justify acting to prevent it, yet nothing has been expressed which can be construed into the remotest *approbation* of it, or indeed convey an idea that the King regards it with indifference." [51] The Polish representative in London presented a note to the British Government requesting its intervention against the dismemberment.[52] On October 27, 1772, King Stanislaus—

necessary, in order to prevent a war, of which Poland would be the source. It is plain this proposal could not be relished by Russia, but in the shape in which it came, and at the moment when those two powers have so much to say upon the question of peace, it was impossible for her absolutely to reject it, and if she submits to their taking parts of Poland, it is likely that, in order to preserve the balance, she may also think herself obliged to take a part of that kingdom. I am persuaded that, as yet, there is nothing more concerted than general propositions; and that the issue of the question relative to dismemberment and partition, is as yet, uncertain. Events ever determine, in a great measure, the free agency of Russia or the weight she will have in this determination, but those events seem in a great degree to depend upon the other powers, which seems much in favour of the success of their wishes" (June 8 [19], 1772, *ibid.,* XIX, 274-75).

[49] Rochford to Lord Harcourt, Feb. 21, 1772, *British Diplomatic Instructions, 1689-1789,* France, pt. iv: 1745-1789, 124.

[50] Sir James Harris to Suffolk, Mar. 1, 1772, *Diaries and Correspondence of James Harris, First Earl of Malmesbury,* ed. by his grandson, the Third Earl (4 vols., London, 1844), I, 79.

[51] Suffolk to Harris, Aug. 7, 1772, *ibid.,* I, 85.

[52] Count Renaud Przezdziecki, *Diplomatic Ventures and Adventurers: Some Experiences of British Envoys at the Court of Poland* (London, 1953), 204.

Augustus wrote to King George III asking that Britain—the safeguard of the European equilibrium—be the protector of Poland's cause. The British king replied on November 17 that "these misfortunes have reached such a point that they can only be redressed by the Almighty" and he could see no other intervention which could be of any remedy. Although sovereigns should be guided by justice, at times they were motivated by material interests. George III hoped that justice would come into her own again in better times.[53] The King of Poland in commenting on English ministers at his court said that although they showed great personal attachment to him, they were not effective in Polish affairs. They were very careful, he added, not to displease the Russian Ambassador or injure the interests of their court with the Russian.[54] According to a Cabinet minute of November 12, 1772, although the British ministers regarded the action of Austria, Prussia, and Russia toward Poland as "arbitrary and tyrannical," they were in a quandary about what to do. They wished to avoid being drawn into war or "yielding too far to the tone of the times on the mere principle of preserving peace." And, of course, they sought to avoid giving France, their "natural great rival," an opportunity of augmenting her power in Northern Europe. If the French were to send a fleet to the Baltic in support of the Swedish Revolution, the British could not be idle spectators, and a general war would thereby follow. If the Russians received support for their interests in Sweden, on the other hand, they would act forcefully and a war would ensue. The possibility existed, the ministers concluded, that if the Russians were discouraged too strongly, they might even reach an accommodation with the French.[55]

In a secret and confidential letter to Mr. St. Paul in

[53] *Ibid.*, 206.
[54] *Ibid.*, 211.
[55] *The Private Papers of John, Earl of Sandwich, First Lord of the Admiralty 1771–1782,* ed. G. R. Barnes and J. H. Owen [Publications of the Navy Records Society, London], I (1932), 30–32.

Paris, Rochford commented on the overtures of the French Minister, the Duke d'Aiguillon, to prevent the partition. Britain could not, for many reasons, Rochford said, enter into a formal engagement with France to operate jointly for any purpose whatever. "The Fact is true but the consequence does not follow that we are equally interested in the late dismemberment of Poland, however we may be concerned to see the misfortunes that have fallen upon that Kingdom and the Ballance of Power." France was nearer to the immediate consequence than Britain, he continued, and was of too restless and intriguing a disposition to wait for rebuking mishaps. The French proposal of an alliance among Britain, France, Spain, Russia, and Sweden was romantic.[56]

Rochford repeated his views in a cipher message to the British Ambassador in Spain, Lord Grantham. "It is too romantic to suppose we could seriously enter into a formal Concert with them upon any political Transaction whatever." Prudence dictated that Britain should wait to see the turn of events and not take a decisive part.[57]

George III prepared a memorandum on the partition which judged that the very extraordinary coalition of Austria, Prussia, and Russia was so subversive of the idea of their mutual jealousies and the European balance that it would lead the other countries to consider alliances. The commercial interests of Britain, France, and Holland, the king said, would be adversely affected by Polish events. Those three injured powers would eventually be induced to unite and to ally themselves and thereby extricate Poland from the tyranny that now seemed impending. The monarch realized that such an Anglo–Dutch–French plan would appear chimerical. But if Britain and France "would with temper examine their respective situations," he argued, "the

[56] Dec. 11, 1772, Coxe Papers, CLXV (1766–73), Brit. Mus., Add. MSS, 9242, fo. 90.
[57] Dec. 15, 1772, Grantham Papers, Official Correspondence, Brit. Mus., Add. MSS, 24,158, fo. 196.

antient animosity would appear absurd" and responsible for aggrandizing other powers while weakening themselves. As if he were partitioning world influence, George III speculated that England would be left to flourish with commerce, while France would have a natural preeminence on the European continent by virtue of her great army.[58] Yet nothing came of his musings.

The French Minister of Foreign Affairs, the Duke d'Aiguillon, had proposed to Britain a joint Anglo–French declaration at Vienna. Rochford told the secretary of the British embassy in Paris that the French ambassador "is continually throwing out to me how alarmed his Court is, and how much ours ought to be at the Dismemberment of Poland," and maintained that it was not too late to do something about it. Rochford added, however, that partition was viewed with the utmost displeasure and that if France had been as zealous in the beginning as she appeared now, the evil might have been avoided.[59] Indeed, in April 1773 when France and Spain prepared armaments against Russian power in the Mediterranean, the British king employed firm language to prevent the French government from taking the steps that would provoke British measures in support of Catherine.[60]

Meanwhile, Robert Gunning, who had come to St. Petersburg from Copenhagen to replace Cathcart, told Suffolk of his conversation with Count Panin. The latter's ambiguity and manner, he said, confirmed what he had already surmised about the dismemberment of Poland.[61] Gunning forwarded Cathcart's assessment of the impact of the partition on the old project of an Anglo–Russian alliance. In Cathcart's judgment, Catherine could never march her ar-

---

[58] No. 1180 (1772), John Fortescue, ed., *The Correspondence of King George the Third from 1760 to December 1783* (6 vols., London, 1927–28), II, 428–29.
[59] Rochford to Mr. St. Paul, Mar. 16, 1773, Coxe Papers, CLXV (1766–73), Brit. Mus., Add. MSS, 9242, fo. 146.
[60] *Correspondence of King George the Third*, II, 339, 470, 474.
[61] July 6 (17), 1772, *Sbornik*, XIX, 284–85.

mies into Germany without first securing the permission of Frederick—who might, in these circumstances, turn to France against Austria and to Sweden against Russia. If the British were to be allied to the Russians, Cathcart continued, they would then be obliged to assist their allies in an action that would impel Frederick to possess himself of George III's Hanoverian possessions.[62]

Gunning related to the government the information that Count Panin told him that the Czarina believed that Britain would certainly approve a good consequence of the partition: namely, that the court of Vienna was detached from that of Versailles. Panin explained too that his silence about the negotiations leading to dismemberment was due to the necessity of keeping any knowledge of it from France "whose intriguing spirit" Russia dreaded.[63] The English envoy observed that Panin was not as friendly to England as had been previously reported and that his reluctance to reach an agreement with Britain did not stem from any inclination to come to terms with France.[64]

The British were deeply concerned about the threat to their Baltic trade that was created by Frederick's seizure of the port duties and custom house in Danzig.[65] Gunning complained to Panin of English commercial losses and reminded the Russian that though the "delicacy and great friendship" which George III had for Catherine caused him to say

[62] Cathcart to Mr. Robert Gunning, 1772, endorsed in Mr. Gunning's to Suffolk, July 13 (24), 1772, *ibid.*, XIX, 289–90.
[63] Gunning to Suffolk, Sept. 7 (18), 1772, *ibid.*, XIX, 317.
[64] Same to same, Sept. 27 (Oct. 8), 1772, *ibid.*, XIX, 326.
[65] Ehrman, 112. "You in England are apt to say, 'We are an island, and what have we to do with affairs of the continent?' True, sir, if you have enough of primitive simplicity, and self-denial to give up your wealth, the convenience and luxuries of life, and live contented on the produce of your own farms, then you have nothing to do with them; but if you cannot do this, then you must owe the value of your lands, your wealth and your importance in Europe; and therefore wherever the transactions on the continent affect your commerce so materially, as the present designs do, you are as much concerned in them, as the powers on the continent themselves." Letter IV, Feb. 27, 1773, [John Lind] *Letters Concerning the Present State of Poland* (London, 1773), 304.

nothing about the partition, the king could not be insensitive to the interests of his subjects. What was required now, according to the diplomat, was the interposition of Russia on behalf of English interests. Without the concurrence of Catherine, Frederick could not have acted as he did in the Danzig affair.[66] For his part Panin justified the dismemberment on the grounds that it avoided a general war by preventing Austria from drawing the sword; that it estranged Austria from France; and that in any case Britain did not have to worry about the free navigation of the Vistula.[67] The British government underlined the fact that it had every reason to expect the Czarina to support the English complaint if she wanted to prove her friendship. It did not intend to negotiate with Frederick because such a step would acknowledge the right and the validity of his Polish acquisitions. Even if British commercial interests were large enough to justify actively pursuing them, it deemed that the moment was not right.[68] Notwithstanding its acquiescence in the deeds of 1772, London refused to acknowledge their legality. The British minister in Russia was reminded that in his discussions about possible alliance "a guaranty of the usurpations in Poland can never compose a part of it." [69]

Although the dismemberment is now regarded as a gross violation of the law of nations, it was not so viewed by many major figures in the eighteenth century who smugly said that the Poles got what they deserved. Frederick—admittedly not a disinterested party—voiced "enlightened" thinking in telling d'Alembert about the rustic, fanatical, ignorant, impudent, cowardly Poles. "I pity the philosophers who interest themselves in this people, so contemptible in

---

[66] Gunning to Suffolk, Dec. 3 (14), 1772, *Sbornik,* XIX, 336.
[67] Same to same, Dec. 3 (14), 1772, *ibid.,* XIX, 337.
[68] Suffolk to Gunning, July 30, 1775, *ibid.,* XIX, 374–75.
[69] Same to same, Aug. 27, 1773, *ibid.,* XIX, 366. In the judgment of D. B. Horn, "that Britain played such a sorry part in the partition of Poland, was the fault of the government at home, not of its representatives on the spot" (*The British Diplomatic Service 1688–1789* [Oxford, 1961], 118).

every way." Theirs was the worst government in Europe except that of the Turks.[70] Philosophers like Voltaire and Diderot, prisoners of the good opinion they professed of Frederick and Catherine, praised their Polish deeds. Voltaire was happy that the partition ended anarchy; while Diderot was cheered by the blow that it struck at Poland, the asylum of fanaticism and superstition.[71]

Burke, however, perceived it as destructive not only to the interests of his country, but to the great republic, the society of European states. Although he was in no position to direct British foreign policy or even to affect it profoundly, he was not without influence. As a leading member of the Whigs who looked up to the Marquess of Rockingham for leadership and a member of the House of Commons since 1765, he had a powerful voice. As a Rockinghamite, he intended to oppose the domestic and foreign policies of the ministry headed by Lord North, and to return the Marquess to office from which he had been turned out in 1766.

Accordingly, Burke and other Rockinghams sought to make parliamentary motions to embarrass North's government, defeat it in the Commons, and supplant it in the king's confidence. The Rockinghams had clear notions of Britain's role in the European system and what they could contribute to it. *They* were the descendants of the Whigs used by King William to thwart the aggressions of King Louis XIV of France, and therefore *they* knew best how to protect England's vital interests against the power of the

---

[70] Quoted in G. P. Gooch, *Frederick the Great: The Ruler, The Writer, The Man* (Hamden, Conn., 1962), 83–84.

[71] Pierre Renouvin, *Histoire des Relations Internationales,* vol. III by Gaston Zeller, *Les Temps Modernes, II, De Louis XIV à 1789* (Paris, 1955), 261. See also Philippe Sagnac, *La Fin de l'Ancien Régime et la Révolution américaine (1763–1789),* Peuples et Civilisation series, Vol. XII, ed. Louis Halphen and Philippe Sagnac (Paris, 1952), 274. Raynal's opinion was that "it is in the security of peace, without rights, without pretexts, without grievances, without a shadow of justice, that this revolution has been effected by the terrible principle of force, which is, unhappily, the best argument of kings" (quoted in Lord, *The Second Partition of Poland,* 55).

Bourbons.⁷² Long before the Polish crisis, Burke reflected the Rockinghamite concern that the "appearance of good understanding which Britain had with her neighbours indicated stagnation rather than tranquility." Foreign governments, he maintained, did not choose to interrupt the tranquility of the British government which had neither the spirit to assert a right nor to resent an injury. "The Bourbons may not have been an object of terror," he said, "but they were no object of contempt." ⁷³ Burke's comments on international affairs, nevertheless, possess an importance not only in the political struggles in the reign of George III, but also in the consideration of the strivings of the great powers whose actions he interpreted with keen insight.

Late in June 1772, Burke wrote to a friend about Frederick's seizure of parts of Poland and of Danzig, which affected Britain navally and commercially. Despite the fact that any increase in the power of Prussia would be harmful to Britain, Burke said that he knew of nothing that the government was doing to prevent it.⁷⁴ Four months later he remarked that "to make a partition of Poland formerly put all Europe in a ferment; now it has four kings, and all Europe is quiet." ⁷⁵

When Parliament was convened before Christmas in 1772, Burke believed that things at home and abroad were in a critical situation; but he did not know if foreign affairs were an additional reason for summoning it.⁷⁶ In a speech

---

⁷² Suspicion of France is reflected in Rockingham's letter to Burke which reports some speculation on Austria's receiving Alsace and Lorraine from France. The Marquess argued that if France would be thereby weakened, on balance Britain would suffer less harm than France would, and the scale would preponderate in Britain's favor (Nov. 20, 1772, *The Correspondence of Edmund Burke,* ed. Thomas W. Copeland, II [ed. Lucy S. Sutherland; Cambridge, 1960], 380).

⁷³ Speech, Nov. 24, 1767, clipping from the *Political Register,* Collection of letters and papers concerning Edmund Burke, Osborn Collection, Yale University, Box 74, No. 24A.

⁷⁴ To John Cruger, June 30, 1772, *Correspondence,* II, 310.

⁷⁵ To John Stewart, Oct. 30, 1772, *ibid.,* II, 359.

⁷⁶ Burke to William Dowdeswell, Oct. 27, 1772, *ibid.,* II, 349; same to

he gave in the Commons on December 7, 1772, Burke spoke satirically of the precedent lately given by three great and glorious monarchs who entered Poland to make it a glorious kingdom, just as the English did when they cut off the head of Charles I to make him a great and glorious king.[77]

Several months later he attributed Britain's passivity to this act of violence—that was mischievous in the short run and in the future to the balance of power—to the supine neglect of the court to European affairs. The result was that Britain had either to stand aside or "join in an alliance with those [the French] whom we have most reason to fear, without much probability of success even by that measure, considering the situation of the Theatre of war." On possible Anglo–French cooperation to confront the partitioning powers, Burke said that while he doubted that the ministry could act decisively, he judged the political merits of such an alliance as problematical and, at any rate, as contrary to the general inclination of the English people. What might bring the British court to join with France would be a threat by Frederick to Hanover, whose Elector was George III. It was not likely, however, Burke argued, that Frederick would wantonly provoke to war those powers that were otherwise disposed or necessitated to allow him to enjoy his usurpation in peace.[78]

It is probable that during his visit to France early in 1773, Burke discussed the Polish problem with French

---

same, Nov. 6, 7, 1772, *ibid.*, II, 364; Burke to Rockingham, Nov. 11, 1772 and Nov. 23, 1772, *ibid.*, II, 369, 385.

[77] Brit. Mus., Egerton MS 243, f. 91–92, Debates of the House of Commons on the East India Company (1772–73).

[78] Burke to John Cruger, Apr. 16, 1773, *Correspondence*, II, 429. The *Annual Register* said that the partition raised the question whether Britain should depart from the system of considering her nearest neighbors as her first object of jealousy and therefore "induced her not to obstruct the growth of other great powers on the continent, though this growth might be at the expense of weaker powers, with regard to whom the protection of the European system of ballance would be lost." XV (1772), 6.

leaders whom he met.[79] Years later, he said in retrospect that to his certain knowledge, although the interposition of other nations to prevent the partition was not easy, France (then weary and under a lethargic king) would have wished intervention on behalf of the Poles if the British went along. In this matter Britain and France had a common interest. "But a languor with regard to so remote an interest, and the principles and passions which were then strongly at work at home, were the causes why Great Britain would not give France any encouragement in such an enterprise." [80]

Burke told an old confidant that in foreign affairs Britain was absolutely asleep though Frederick did everything in his power to awaken her.[81] In the same vein he wrote to the Committee of Correspondence of New York, which he represented as colonial agent, that, if there were not a total disregard of foreign affairs, there was a deep silence.[82] Britain just could not be aroused.[83] He complained that the present temper of the nation operated as little as the division of Poland. The government was not to be moved and would not be embarrassed by foreign affairs: "the northern powers are too remote; and France is certainly disposed to be pacific." [84]

Long after the time for action had passed, Burke continued to refer to the sorry events of 1772. Standing armies threatened peace. The parsimony of Frederick the Great, he commented, was intended to support immense armies which he poured into neighboring countries with as little conscience as notice. Burke denounced Lord North for say-

---

[79] Thomas Macknight, *History of the Life and Times of Edmund Burke* (3 vols., London, 1885), II, 9.
[80] Thoughts on French Affairs [Dec. 1791], *Works*, IV, 329–30.
[81] To Charles O'Hara, Nov. 19, 1773, Ross J. S. Hoffman, *Edmund Burke, New York Agent, With His Letters to the New York Assembly, and Intimate Correspondence with Charles O'Hara 1761–1776* (Philadelphia, 1956), 551.
[82] Jan. 5, 1774, *ibid.*, 237–38.
[83] Burke to Rockingham, Sept. 18, 25, 1774, *Correspondence*, III (ed. George H. Guttridge; Cambridge, 1961), 30.
[84] Same to same, Sept. 25, 1774, *ibid.*, III, 31.

ing that the national honor did not consist in being busy meddlers in every European quarrel and for holding forth a system of blindness and infatuation

as an excuse for that conduct which saw Corsica seized in one part of Europe, and Poland dismembered in another, with the most torpid indifference; when, by having little of that busy spirit of intermeddling, both might have been prevented by mere force of negotiation, had the powers of Europe any respectable idea of this country, once the refuge and protectoress of distressed nations. But the time will come when the new system will be seen in all its impotence and folly; and when the balance of power is destroyed, it will be found of what infinite consequence its preservation would have been.[85]

He scoffed at the despoilers of Poland who were fortunate to find a fourth power unable to resist any of them, let alone the three together. If Poland had not been their victim, they "might have been obliged to find a discharge for the superfluous strength of their plethorick habits in the destruction of the finest Countries in Europe." The past was disheartening; the future was foreboding because these powers continued armed: "Their arms must have employment. Poland was but a breakfast; and there are not many Polands to be found—Where will they dine. After all our love of Tranquility and all our expedients to preserve it—alas poor Peace." [86]

Frederick's remark that the partition was the first example in history of a division settled and terminated peacefully among the powers[87] was callous to the injury suffered by Poland and the European state-system. A markedly different view was taken in the *Annual Register* for 1772. Its perceptive comments on the long-range effects of the

[85] Speech on the Budget for 1774, May 18, 1774, *The Speeches of the Right Honourable Edmund Burke, in the House of Commons and in Westminster-Hall* (4 vols., London, 1816), I, 244.
[86] Burke to Adrian Heinrich von Borcke, *post* Jan., 1774, *Correspondence*, II, 514.
[87] As quoted in Albert Sorel, *L'Europe et la Révolution française* (8 vols., 19th ed., Paris, 1926), I, 40.

dismemberment appear to have been written by Burke[88] or at the very least to mirror his sentiments. The anarchical events of the early 1770s distressed Europe and tore asunder its system:

> The breach that has been now made, in those compacts that unite states for their mutual benefit, establishes a most dangerous precedent; it deprives, in a great measure, every separate power in Europe, of that security which was founded in treaties, alliances, common interest, and public faith. It seems to throw nations collectively into that state of nature, in which it has been supposed, that mankind separately at one time subsisted, when the security of the individual depended singly upon his own strength, and no resource was left when it failed.[89]

The *Annual Register* asserted that the partition destroyed one of the most ancient nations in the world by cutting away half its population and a third of its land. Without the pretence of war, or even the color of right, the partition constituted the "first very great breach in the modern political system of Europe" and laid the axe immediately to the root of the constitution of "our great western republic" in a way that threatened the complete ruin of Europe.[90]

[88] Some writers (e.g. Macknight, II, 2) maintained that Burke was responsible for the account of the partition that appeared in the History of Europe in Vol. XV (1772) of the *Annual Register*. Sir James Mackintosh's "An Account of the Partition of Poland" asserted that "the sentiments of wise men on the first partition are admirably stated in the Annual Register of 1772, in the Introduction to the History of Europe, which could scarcely have been written by any man but Mr. Burke" (*The Miscellaneous Works of the Right Honourable Sir James Mackintosh* [3 vols. in 1, New York, 1860], 216n. See also William Massey, *A History of England During the Reign of George the Third* (4 vols., London, 1858), II, 169; and Alfred Cobban, "The Partition of Poland: A Commentary by Edmund Burke," VII<sup>e</sup> Congrès International des Sciences Historiques, *Résumé*, I, 188–90.

[89] XV (1772), Preface.

[90] *Ibid.*, XV (1772), 43–44. In assessing responsibility for the dark deed, it asserted that Russia did not originate the scheme but joined in it only from the necessity of the existing conjuncture. Catherine's purpose was to maintain Poland whole, to uphold the name and form of the ancient form of government in the republic, but simultaneously to preserve it as a virtual Russian province. She was led into the dismemberment by various ways and degrees. It also commented that Austria's hesitation revealed that she

Europe was a great republic:

> The idea of considering Europe as a vast commonwealth, of the several parts being distinct and separate, though politically and commercially united, of keeping them independent though unequal in power and of preventing any one, by any means, from becoming too powerful for the rest, was great and liberal.[91]

Although this system was the result of barbarism, the periodical continued, it was founded upon the most enlarged principles of prudent policy. From it was derived European superiority over the rest of the world. Asiatic nations, though potent and civilized, perished for lack of any union or system of this sort. Beholding the annihilation of their neighbors with malignant pleasure and supineness, they failed to realize that the weapons and power derived from this destruction would soon be turned to their defeat.[92]

The idea that Poland and her sister European states formed a distinct civilization and an international system, a *respublica Christiana,* was commonplace. In 1751 Voltaire, for example, spoke of Christian Europe, without Russia, as a sort of great republic in which several states possessed the same principles of public and private law that was unknown in other parts of the world. And he added that they wisely maintained among themselves, as far as possible, an equal balance of power.[93] Similarly, the Swiss jurist, Emer

---

was either abashed at the robbery or shocked at the outrage (*ibid.,* XV [1772], 24-25). The *Annual Register*'s treatment of Frederick was unsympathetic. It reported that he was not satisfied with his share and seized the port duties and customs house of the free city of Danzig, thereby depriving English merchants of their treaty-rights of 1707. Although British grievances should be redressed, it said, the real damage was irremediable. The seizure showed the "dangers to which commerce will be exposed, by the transfering of so considerable a share of the maritime power and property, into such grasping, oppressive, and arbitrary hands." The fate of the free city revealed the "futility, if not the absurdity of treaties of guarantees of security" (*Ibid.,* XV [1772], 40).

[91] *Ibid.,* XV (1772), 2.
[92] *Ibid.,* XV (1772), 2-3.
[93] Le Siècle de Louis XIV, *Oeuvres historiques* (Paris, 1957), 620.

de Vattel, whose treatise on the law of nations was consulted as the authoritative guide, observed that Europe formed a political system and was not a "confused heap of detached pieces, each of which thought itself very little concerned in the fate of others and seldom regarded things which did not immediately relate to it." Europe was a kind of republic, and, Vattel added, the independent states united, through ties of common interest, for the maintenance of order and liberty by means of the balance of power.[94] Edward Gibbon too considered Europe as one great republic whose various inhabitants have attained almost the same level of politeness and cultivation. Its system of arts, and laws, and manners have placed the Europeans and their colonists above the rest of mankind.[95]

In the same spirit, the *Annual Register* maintained that in conformity with nature, states like individuals needed society. It was the "language of a frivolous and voluptuous age" that though a country prospered and endured no immediate abuse from other states, it had therefore no grounds for concern in the disasters of its neighbors.

A single man, cast out from the laws, the protection, and the commerce of his whole species might in that solitary situation, with as rational and well-grounded a probability, propose to himself conveniences and security, as any single state, in the present political and

[94] *Law of Nations or the Principles of Natural Law Applied to Conduct and to the Affairs of Nations and Sovereigns [1758]* (3 vols., Washington, D.C., 1916), III (tr. Charles G. Fenwick), Book III, Chap. III. Albert Sorel rejected the belief that the great republic was a regularly constituted international society in which established law governed relations and dictated treaties; and he averred instead that in modern times it was only an august abstraction. He agreed nevertheless that there was a public law, by quoting Montesquieu that "even the Iroquois have one" (*L'Europe et la Révolution française,* I, 9, 11). In the same vein, Georges Lefebvre more recently contended that European unity was only an illusion. "Cosmopolitanism was in reality nothing more than an aristocratic and bourgeois veneer, a modish idea in intellectual circles. Mobility was still too restricted to dislodge the particularism of different European groups" (*The French Revolution from Its Origins to 1793* [London, 1962], 71).

[95] *The History of the Decline and Fall of the Roman Empire,* ed. J. B. Bury (7 vols., London, 1925), IV, 163.

physical state of Europe, could expect independence and safety, unconnected with all the others.

International society did not eliminate strife. Wars, evil as they might be, were inevitable in every state of human nature. Conflict could be postponed; but it could not be avoided. To purchase present quiet at the price of future security, the writer concluded, was humiliating pusillanimity.[96]

The balance of power sought the preservation of peace and the maintenance of the *status quo*. Herein lay its fundamental weakness. The continual striving of the powers for advantage, the reshufflings that aimed at the restoration of a lost equilibrium or the establishment of a new one, and the endemic wars that resulted weakened the great republic. Yet judged by the standards of total war in the twentieth century, the conflicts of the eighteenth century are tame in comparison and local in character. The limited objectives of princes, coupled with the limited weapons of the generals, lessened ferocity and minimized defeat. Edward Gibbon echoed the sentiments of his "enlightened" age when he asserted that a civilized nation could not think of total victory, a concept he found alien to civilization itself:

> The abuses of tyranny are restrained by the mutual influence of fear and shame; republics have acquired order and stability; monarchies have imbibed the principles of freedom, or at least, of moderation; and some sense of honour and justice is introduced into the most defective constitution by the general manners of the times.[97]

The *Annual Register* alluded to the ambitions of the great powers which were cloaked in transparent pretensions to certain territories and rights. Their claims were based on ancient titles, and thereby violated prescription, the foundation of international order. These pretensions disturbed the

[96] XV (1772), 2–3.
[97] *The Decline and Fall of the Roman Empire,* IV, 165.

"long and unimpeded possession acknowledged by universal consent of mankind," it said, "as the most certain and equitable title, by which a right can be claimed in any thing, and would be in itself sufficient to preclude any claims, set up in the darkness, and founded upon the rubbish of a blind antiquity." This tendency to resurrect old titles was evident in the claim of Frederick to part of the Polish-held duchy of Pomerelia, which had been seized from the dukes of Pomerania, and to the district of the New March, which had been wrested from the dukes of Danzig.[98]

The perceptive commentator on the partition detected dire implications. Austro–Prussian cooperation in Poland may bring them ruin, he said. Poland might well be the road by which the Russians would enter Germany. Other effects included the Prussian mastery of the Vistula and the whole commerce of Poland and a blow to French influence. The dismemberment was contrary to French interest and was decided upon without the participation of Versailles; and it therefore threatened to upset the ancient German and Northern system.[99]

It was unwise for Russia to add segments of Turkey and Poland to an already vast empire of boundless and ill-cultivated areas. Possession of a part of Poland incurred disadvantages for her, as the *Annual Register* judged. Authority there had now to be divided among the partitioning powers, who would prevent Russia from retaining more than her share. A continual controversy that would keep Germany and the North in turmoil and strife was created:

> The wisest and most benevolent statesman could not have wished for a happier barrier than Poland, to prevent the clashing of the German and Muscovite empires, nor could the demon of discord have thrown out bitterer seeds of contention than it is now likely to produce.[100]

[98] XV (1772), 31.
[99] *Ibid.*, XV (1772), 4–5.
[100] *Ibid.*, XVI (1773), 3–4.

After suffering dismemberment in 1772, many Poles determined to improve their national prospects by rooting out their internal weaknesses. They were sanguine about the Constitution of 1791, which eliminated the *liberum veto* and the elective monarchy and incorporated other reforms. Burke contrasted the Polish and French Revolutions in the matter of securing liberty. While the Poles proceeded from anarchy to order, he wrote, the French went from order to anarchy. Humanity had everything to rejoice and to glory in, in the Polish Constitution, because not one drop of blood was spilled and "no studied insults on religion, morals, or manners" occurred.[101] Some Polish nobles, however, would not relinquish the old constitution for the new, and they presently formed the Confederation of Targowica. Catherine naturally supported the confederates and sent her forces into Poland in 1792 to crush resistance. Not only did Prussia—who in 1790 had signed a mutual-assistance pact with Poland—fail to come to the aid of her ally, but she joined Russia in the partition of 1793. An insurrection led by Kosciuszko captured the imagination of the nation but failed in the face of potent enemies and led inexorably to the third and final dismemberment in 1795. This time, Austria, Prussia, and Russia absorbed the remaining territories held by the Poles. A few years later they reciprocally pledged never to use a title that would even recall the existence of the republic. The long, dark night of oppression fell and the Poles could only cry out with Mickiewicz:

> From Muscovite, Austrian, and Prussian slavery
> Deliver us, O Lord.

As in the earlier divisions the Poles could expect sympathy but little assistance from other states in the great republic. The French were in the midst of their revolution, while the British could scarcely think of waging war in east-central Europe without joining either one of Poland's despoilers

[101] "Appeal from the New to the Old Whigs [1791]," *Works*, IV, 196–97.

or Revolutionary France. The great powers saw the French Revolution as an opportunity for pursuing their old ambitions, while western Europe was distracted. Catherine the Great confessed that

> I rack my brains in order to egg on the Courts of Vienna and Berlin to mix in French affairs. I want to entangle them in these concerns in order to have a free hand. I have many projects not yet completed and I wish that the two courts are occupied so that they cannot interfere with me.[102]

The distress of the friends of Poland and old Europe may be seen in Burke, who maintained that no viable choice was open except that of opposing the French revolutionaries. Before anything could be saved, the danger posed by the Jacobins—the establishment of a universal empire in the guise of fraternity and a new law of nations—had first to be overcome. Approving of neither the aggressions against Poland committed by the crowned heads of Austria, Prussia, and Russia, nor the Jacobin onslaught on the whole system of Europe, Burke chose the lesser of the evils. "No cause in the world can, as a course, be more clear in my eyes, or can have more of my warm wishes, than that of the Poles," he wrote to his son Richard. He lamented the fate of the "brave and generous Poles" but he could not entertain the idea of turning to the Jacobins for assistance in the maintenance of the European balance. There were evils greater than partition. No government could be safe as long as the revolution succeeded in France. If the balance were lost for a while, it could be recovered, he argued; but if the spirit and principles of Europe were ruined, they could not be revived.[103] When Fox proposed sending an Address to the Throne concerning the action of

---

[102] Transl. mine. Quoted in Sorel, *L'Europe et la Révolution française*, II (La Chute de la royauté), 216–17.

[103] July 29, 1792, *Correspondence of the Right Honourable Edmund Burke*, ed. Charles William, Earl Fitzwilliam, and Lieutenant-General Sir Richard Bourke, K.C.B. (4 vols., London, 1844), III, 472–74, 477.

the partitioning powers, Burke said in Parliament that it was a womanish proceeding at best, to rant without doing more; and if Britain were to do more, she would be at war with all Europe. In order to help the Poles, Britain had to be in league with France. Prudence led Burke to hold his tongue on his sentiments toward Poland. What had to be considered at the moment with respect to Britain was that "Poland might be, in fact, considered as a country in the moon." He was not blind to the ambition of the partitioning powers but considered first that the ambition of France pressed Britain. It was his hope that the partition could be made in a way not to destroy or affect in any great degree the European balance.[104] Burke told the Chevalier de la Bintinaye that he was

astonished at the blindness of the States of Europe, who are contending with each other about points of trivial importance, and on old, worn-out principles and Topics of Policy, when the very existence of all of them is menaced, by a new Evil, which none of the ancient Maxims are of the least importance in dissipating.[105]

The public crimes that despoiled the largest state in Europe outside Russia had a double aspect. They obviously victimized the Poles; like so many outrages, they debased the perpetrators; and in the process they further weakened the great republic, which—despite Burke's thunderous warnings—fell prey to revolutionary forces it could not resist in its debility.

Lost causes possess a magnetic fascination. Have not generations of Europeans and Americans been captivated by the achievement of ancient Hellas, for example, and bemoaned the tragedy of the Greeks who failed to unite? In the midst of their present discontents, they ponder the fate of the great republic and of old Poland which prized free-

---

[104] Debate on Mr. Fox's Motion for the Reestablishment of Peace with France, June 17, 1793, *Parliamentary History of England*, XXX, 1008–10.
[105] March, 1791, *Correspondence*, VI (ed. Alfred Cobban and Robert A. Smith; Cambridge, 1967), 242.

dom so dearly as to risk its existence. What would have happened, they muse, had European kings and ministers understood their real interests and had the Poles established a viable state which nurtured ordered liberty?

It may well be that great causes and powerful institutions that succeed instruct poorly; and that paradoxically what has failed in the past somehow endures because it inspires and even ennobles future generations.

# 3

# The King's Purse and the Absentee's Pocket in Eighteenth-century Ireland

## SAMUEL J. FANNING

AS A RESULT OF WHOLESALE CONFISCATIONS of the property of Catholics in Ireland in the seventeenth century and its bestowal on adventurers and soldiers in the service of Cromwell and William III, there emerged in the following century two sharply defined classes—the Protestant landowners, and their Catholic tenants. It was inevitable that a system of landownership such as this, based as it was on religious grounds, would lead to serious social and economic consequences. It was inevitable too that this system would be a contributing factor in prompting the landlord to desert his Irish property and take up permanent residence in England, for, as Lecky aptly points out, "the position of a Protestant landlord, living in the midst of a degraded population, differing from him in religion and race, had but little attraction." [1]

Whether for the reason just cited or for several others, which need not be listed, there was, in fact, a veritable

[1] W. E. H. Lecky, *A History of England in the Eighteenth Century* (New York, 1891), II, 261.

flight of the landlords from Ireland to England in the eighteenth century. Their desertion brought untold hardship to their hapless tenants and disastrous consequences to the country's finances because of the large sums of money remitted each year to the absentee landlords.

In the course of the eighteenth century, several lists were made of the absentees and the amount of money they received from Ireland. In 1729 Thomas Prior estimated that the sum remitted to absentees amounted to £350,000 a year.[2] Prior believed that the financial distress of the country was caused in great part by those "deserters" who, living abroad, "prove the worst enemies to Ireland by laying it under a continual yearly pillage to their vanity and luxury, without contributing the least farthing towards the support of the government." [3]

In 1769 (when Prior's estimate was revised and brought up to date) it was determined that the amount of money exported annually to the landowners had increased to £572,100. During his tour of Ireland in 1776 Arthur Young gathered information on the payments to absentees and arrived at the staggering annual figure of £732,000. "This total," concluded Young, "though not equal to what has been reported is certainly an amazing drain upon a kingdom cut off from the reaction of a free trade; and such a one as must have a very considerable effect in preventing the natural course of its prosperity." [4]

But the money going each year to the absentee landlords, though it was steadily increasing, was only one factor contributing toward the bankruptcy of the country. Greater threats perhaps to the country's fiscal well-being was the cumbersome and outmoded revenue system and the control

[2] *A Collection of Tracts and Treatises Illustrative of the Historical Antiquities, and the Political and Social State of Ireland at Various Periods prior to the Present Century, in Two Volumes* (Dublin, 1861), I, 233-39. Hereafter referred to as Prior.
[3] *Ibid.*, I, 252-53.
[4] A. W. Hutton, ed., *Arthur Young's Tour of Ireland* (New York, 1892), II, 116-17. Hereafter referred to as Young.

of the Irish purse by the "undertakers." Finally, it should be noted—and it is an ironic note—that the emergence of the "Patriot Party" in the Irish Parliament around the middle of the eighteenth century posed another serious threat to the country's finances.

The public revenue of Ireland in the eighteenth century was divided into three principal parts: the king's hereditary revenue, the additional duties granted for the better support of government, and the appropriated duties. The hereditary revenue was so named from its having been vested in the king, his heirs, and successors. The additional duties were parliamentary grants designed to supplement the hereditary revenue. The appropriated duties were imposed for certain particular purposes to which they were specially applied by Parliament at the time of granting them.

Prior to the reign of Charles II, the hereditary revenue was derived from a variety of sources including crown rents, port-corn rents, lighthouse duties, prizage duties on wines, casual revenue from fines, forfeited recognizances, profits of the hanaper, waifs, estrays, felons' and fugitive goods, first fruits and twentieth parts, poundage paid on imports and exports of all kinds except wines and oils.[5]

Although the list was an imposing one, the amount of money raised by these means was not very great. In the early years of the Restoration a series of changes brought about a vast increase in this branch of the public revenue. Through an "Act of Settlement and Explanation" the large number of adventurers and soldiers in the service of Cromwell who had been rewarded with grants of Irish land were obliged to pay the crown perpetual "quitrents." Subsequent enactments by the Irish Parliament between 1662 and 1666 granted to the crown forever the inland excise, the import excise, a new poundage, a hearth tax, ale licenses, wine and strong-water licenses, and alnage duties.[6]

[5] Thomas Joseph Kiernan, *History of the Financial Administration of Ireland to 1817* (London, 1930), 75–79.
[6] *Ibid.*, 83.

The net result of this legislation was an increase in the hereditary revenue from a mere £35,000 a year to £250,000.[7] This enormous increase enabled Charles II to finance the government of Ireland without any parliamentary grants of duties. Accordingly, with the lone exception of the "irregular assembly" (the so-called Patriot Parliament) summoned by James II in 1689, the Irish Parliament never met during the twenty-six-year period from 1666 to 1692. The occasion for its having been summoned in 1692 was to enact supply bills for emergencies caused by the Jacobite War which were beyond the capacities of the hereditary revenue. Thereafter it became the custom to summon the Parliament every other year for granting supplies to supplement the hereditary revenue. But even so the Parliament's control over supply bills was very negligible and its other powers were practically non-existent thanks to the ancient strictures dating back to the reign of Henry VII and the steady encroachment of the Imperial Parliament in the eighteenth century, including the Declaratory Act of 1719.

An adequate hereditary revenue at the disposal of a crafty monarch could lead to fatal consequences for the Irish Parliament. That there was to be no recurrence in the eighteenth century of the fiscal independence enjoyed by Charles II was due in part to the crippling effects of mercantilist restrictions on Irish trade and to the unwitting activities of the undertakers—the heads of the great territorial families—who, having gained personal control of the hereditary revenue, squandered it on placemen, pensioners, and court favorites rather than expend it for the general welfare of the country. "The pension list of Ireland," wrote an indignant correspondent to the *Gentleman's Magazine*

is an original of villainy and corruption, which Europe cannot equal. Does any man wish to know the traitors in that country? Let him

[7] *Ibid.*, 86.

read it. The enormous sum which appears at the bottom of this honourable and right honourable catalogue of heroes and heroines is amazing—near one hundred thousand pounds per annum. . . . The prerogative of granting pensions out of the public money, was given to the Crown that the Crown might reward merit—not prostitution of principle—to support the poor, not pamper the rich and luxurious.[8]

The one exception to this general state of insolvency was a period of marked prosperity for Ireland during and immediately following the War of the Austrian Succession which brought a sharp increase in the yield from the hereditary revenue. Between 1746 and 1754 this branch of the revenue had increased from £380,855 to £585,293, an increase of better than sixty-five percent.[9] This tremendous increase, combined with the additional duties voted by Parliament, had left the Irish treasury bulging with huge surpluses. The public accounts at Lady-day (March 25) 1749 showed a surplus of £220,240. Two years later the figure stood at £248,367 and by 1753 had increased to £318,823.[10] During these same years considerable portions of these surpluses were allocated toward the reduction of the public debt, and by 1753 the entire debt had been liquidated. But such were the vagaries of mid-eighteenth-century Irish politics and economics that this temporary prosperity and solvency, far from being national blessings, ushered in an era of corruption and extravagance which brought the country to the verge of bankruptcy.

This unusual turn of events resulted when the "patriots" in the Irish Parliament became the unwitting accomplices of the self-seeking undertakers in ransacking the country's revenues. These patriots, men such as the Duke of Leinster, Lords Charlemont and Tyrone, Sir William Osborne, James Flood, Charles Lucas, and Walter Hussy-Burgh, having caught the fever of their English counterparts

[8] Marcus, *Gentleman's Magazine* XXXXIII (Oct. 1773), 498.
[9] Kiernan, 119.
[10] *Ibid.*, 150–54.

(Cobham, Lyttleton, Granville, and Pitt), were determined to raise the Irish Constitution from the mire and muck of political jobbery and defend the ancient rights of the Irish Parliament from the steady encroachments of the Imperial Parliament at Westminster.

As a result perhaps of their patriotic fervor, these zealots regarded the immense revenue at the disposal of the crown, in the years following the Peace of Aix-la-Chapelle, as a dangerous threat to the Irish Parliament. They were well aware that a similar advantage during the reign of Charles II enabled him to dispense completely with the Parliament during his last twenty years on the throne.

Finance, consequently, became one of the chief weapons of the patriots: and the sessions of Parliament in the years following 1753 were distinguished for their preoccupation with revenue matters. Although the patriots were extremely jealous of the crown revenue, the machinations of Charles II had placed it beyond their control. It was not long, however, before they discovered an effective, if expensive, means of counteracting the threat to Parliament from the crown revenue. During the viceroyalty of the Duke of Bedford, 1757–61, a bill was passed in the Irish Parliament which granted a bounty on all corn and flour brought to Dublin by land carriage. "It is the intention and effect of this bounty," Arthur Young declared,

> to turn every local advantage and natural supply topsy turvy. We have had for several years in England, an importation of foreign corn more than proportioned (the kingdoms compared) to anything the Irish knew. If any one to remedy this, proposed a bounty on bringing corn by land from Devonshire and Northumberland, so as to give it a preference in the London market to that of Kent and Essex, with what contempt would the proposer and proposition be treated! The corn counties of Louth and Kildare in the vicinity of Dublin are not to supply that market, but it is to eat its bread from Corke and Wexford!
>
> It must also be brought by land carriage! the absurdity and folly with which such an idea is pregnant, in a country blessed with such

ports, and such a vast extent of coast, are so glaring, that it is amazing that sophistry could blind the Legislature to such a degree as to permit a second thought of it.[11]

When the Parliament first enacted this bounty it was limited to a term of years, but the patriots succeeded in persuading Bedford to have it declared a perpetuity. This marked the inauguration of a system of parliamentary bounties and premiums which in the following years was greatly expanded to include such things as canal- and road-building, harbor improvements, coal, flax-seed, fish, and many other items. When these bounties were enacted, Parliament had promised to vote funds for paying them. This was never done so that the bounties were thrown on the revenue at large. In this way they admirably accomplished the designs of the patriots: that is, to make the crown revenues insufficient for running government and thereby force the king to ask the Parliament for more money.[12]

This policy of parliamentary survival at any cost proved to be very costly indeed. Ireland, free from debt in 1753, had ten years later accumulated a new one amounting to £521,161. In 1767 it had increased to £581,964, and by 1773 had reached the staggering sum of £999,686.[13] As the debt increased the bounties continued to rise, so that the ability of the government to meet its obligations was being lessened each year. In the thirteen-year period from 1761 to 1773, the corn bounty alone had cost the government £213,939, and, by the latter year, the allotment for this one item was close to £50,000 annually. During this same period the total expenditure on corn, flax-seed, coal, and fish amounted to £354,645.[14]

It was inevitable perhaps that the country should reap

---

[11] Young, II, 179–81.
[12] George O'Brien, *The Economic History of Ireland in the Eighteenth Century* (Dublin, 1918), 311.
[13] *Journals of the House of Commons—Ireland,* App., pt. i, ix, ccccxxviii.
[14] *Ibid.*

some advantages from this lavish spending; but an empty treasury was far too high a price to pay for more homegrown corn, native coals, and unnecessary canals. One writer has aptly described this conduct of the Irish Parliament as the policy of "cutting off its own nose to spite its face." [15] A whole host of new jobs was created to administer the different bounty schemes and the expenses thereby incurred were also thrown on the revenue at large. A considerable portion of the public money also found its way into private pockets. Arthur Young, who personally witnessed many of these bounty schemes, wrote as follows about one of the navigation projects sponsored by Parliament:

> I will venture to say that if the Grand Canal was entirely complete, the navigation of it, including whatever the country towns took from Dublin, would prove of such a beggarly account, that it would then remain a greater monument of folly, if possible, than at present. Some gentlemen I have talked with on this subject have replied, "it is a job; 'twas meant as a job; you are not to consider it as a canal of trade, but as a canal for publick money"; but even this, though advanced in Ireland, is not upon principle. I answer that something has been done; fourteen miles with innumerable locks, quays, bridges, etc. are absolutely finished, though only for the benefit of eels and skating.[16]

With the coming of George III to the throne in 1760 there was to develop a new constitutional dispensation with regard to the Irish administration. In particular the young king had visions of breaking the inordinate power of the undertakers and the removal of the heavy burdens placed on the hereditary revenues by the patriots in the Irish Parliament. However, during the first six or seven years of the new reign, Ireland was perforce neglected because of domestic issues, the closing years of the Seven Years' War, and the disturbing situation in the American colonies. These troubled years witnessed a rapid turn-over in the Irish

[15] O'Brien, 311.
[16] Young, II, 129.

administration, encompassing no fewer than three actual viceroys (Lords Halifax, Northumberland and Hertford) and two viceregal designees (Lords Weymouth and Bristol) who never assumed the office though both of them had received the customary £3,000 from the Irish exchequer for their "voyage and equipage."

A cardinal point in George III's approach to Ireland was the idea of permanent residency by the viceroy. Heretofore it was customary for the viceroys to reside in Dublin only for a few months every other year during the actual sitting of Parliament and then to return to England. The first candidate whom the young king could persuade to reside permanently in Dublin was Lord Townshend, a military hero (Dettingen, Fontenoy, Culloden, Laffeldt, and Quebec) and the brother of Charles Townshend. In October 1767, Townshend arrived in Dublin to inaugurate a new dispensation. At first the new viceroy concealed his design toward the undertakers and worked harmoniously with them. He experienced a brief period of popularity when a bill limiting the duration of Parliament to eight years was enacted in 1768. Prior to this, Irish Parliaments, unless dissolved, lasted throughout the entire reign of the monarch. This had been one of the principal grievances of the patriots: consequently the so-called Octennial Bill was quite popular throughout the country. The undertakers, on the other hand, were strongly opposed to this threat to their entrenched ascendancy, and while they could not, in view of the popular clamor, openly oppose it, they never forgave Townshend for sponsoring it.

The next task to which the viceroy directed his energies was the delicate matter of increasing the Irish army. This was part of a general policy of encouraging the various colonials to provide more adequate protection for the empire. In discussing this augmentation scheme with administrative leaders, Townshend found little or no enthusiasm. The undertakers were spoiling for a chance to show their revenge for the Parliament bill. The patriots were opposed not only because of the additional expenses that would be incurred but also because of their fear that the army might be used against their fellow men in the American colonies. In an attempt to overcome the opposition Townshend lavishly bestowed peerages, places, and pensions on would-be supporters. All the same, the augmentation scheme was defeated and at the same time a money bill was rejected because it had originated in the Irish Privy Council rather than in the House of Commons. Subsequently, the House of Commons, in a manner peculiar to Irish Parliaments of the eighteenth century, reversed itself and enacted a supply bill and an augmentation scheme. This, of course, reflected no credit whatever on Townshend who by late 1769 had succeeded in permanently antagonizing both the undertakers and the patriots. During the latter years of his administration, he launched a frontal attack on the undertakers, removing many of them from their lucrative positions and greatly altering the membership in the Privy Council. His lack of appreciation for the political process as well as his almost total inability to grasp the subtleties of the Irish constitutional position, especially on money bills, made him anathema to the patriots. The end result was an insurmountable undertaker–patriot phalanx in Parliament that brought all legislation to a standstill and culminated in the recall of Lord Townshend in 1772. The power of the undertakers was bent, but not broken, and well might George III, in reviewing the administration of his first resident viceroy, have reechoed the immortal words which Shakespeare placed on the tongue of the usurper king of Scotland: "We have scotch'd the snake, not killed it."

But even though the Townshend administration had ended in failure, the king was still determined to bring about reforms in Ireland, and for a renewal of this task he now chose his old friend and tutor, the Earl of Harcourt, to succeed Townshend as viceroy. Simon Harcourt had been a prominent courtier since 1735, when he was appointed a lord of the bedchamber to George II. In addition to the tutorship he had served in a number of important posts and during the four years prior to his designation as viceroy to Ireland he had been ambassador to Paris.[17] Notwithstanding his many important posts, the earl was undistinguished in public life and possessed no conspicuous ability. All the same, Harcourt was in many respects an ideal replacement. Where Townshend had been impetuous and despotic, his successor was painstaking and conciliatory. These qualities were Harcourt's greatest assets in winning back respect for government and removing the boycotts which had lately attached to castle levees. Early in his correspondence from Dublin he told Lords Rochford (Secretary of State for the Southern Department) and North of his personal visits with such important politicians as the Marquess of Kildare, Lord Shannon, John Ponsonby, and even the fiery patriot, Flood.[18]

For his chief secretary, Harcourt selected his close friend, Colonel Blaquiere, who had been with him in Paris. Apart from debating power and a degree of skill in managing men, Blaquiere was a vain and venal man. Lord Charlemont described him as:

a man of low birth, of no property, and of weak genius, yet possessing in an eminent degree those inferior abilities which are more prized and perhaps more useful to an evil government than the greatest mental powers, the sublime faculty of exciting venality and of making proselytes to their country's ruin by corrupting individuals with the public treasure.[19]

Before his departure for Ireland, Harcourt was secretly instructed by Rochford to do his utmost to regain for the king

[17] *Dictionary of National Biography*, XXIV, 325–26.
[18] E. W. Harcourt, ed., *The Harcourt Papers* (Oxford, n. d.) IX, 45.
[19] Hist. Mss. Comm., 12th *Report*, App. X, 35.

the full control of the hereditary revenue by inducing Parliament to make good, by new taxation, the many charges that had been placed on it in the form of bounties and premiums, especially the large bounty voted in perpetuity on the inland carriage of corn.[20] In addition to the secret orders from Rochford, George III issued a long list of personal instructions to the viceroy, and in regard to the hereditary revenue he left no doubt as to the role Harcourt was to play with respect to this important matter. "We," he instructed his deputy,

> having thought fit to appoint Commissioners to manage Our whole revenue in that Our Kingdom, Our pleasure is, that you do from time to time, assist, countenance and support Our said Commissioners, and the officers employed by them upon all occasions, and as justice and Our service shall require. And you shall also take care that all Our judges, officers and ministers, more especially the Barons of Our Court of Exchequer, do give them all fitting despatch and countenance. You shall also frequently call upon them to give an account of their proceedings in the management of the Commission, and the execution of the trust We have committed to them, of which you are, from time to time, to transmit an account to Us.[21]

Although Harcourt arrived in Dublin early in December 1772, Parliament did not meet until the following October. In the meantime the crisis in the treasury continued to worsen. As already noted, the public debt by 1773 had grown to almost £1,000,000. In April of that year Harcourt informed his superiors in England that

> . . . our distresses have increased to such a degree that almost an entire stop is put to all payments whatever, except for the subsistence of the army; and at times, it has been difficult to find money even for this purpose. I have now reason to think that the arrear upon the establishment by Christmas next will not fall short of £300,000.[22]

---

[20] Lecky, IV, 434–35.
[21] Harcourt, IX, 24–25.
[22] *Ibid.*, 69–70.

During the period prior to the calling of Parliament Harcourt and Blaquiere, together with various Irish leaders, had been working feverishly on an adequate supply bill to meet this critical financial situation. This involved a great deal of compromise between the administration and different Irish interests, as a result of which it became necessary several times to postpone the meeting of Parliament. Towards the end of April 1773, however, some progress had been made, at which time the viceroy confided to North: "I have at this time, in my contemplation though not yet ripe enough to be submitted to your Lordship, several great and important matters which, I hope will put his Majesty's revenues and government of this kingdom upon a better footing." [23] A few months later Harcourt's "great and important matters" had ripened sufficiently to be plucked and placed before the North ministry. Heads of a tentative supply bill, to be presented to the ensuing Parliament, had by that time been agreed upon and Blaquiere was sent to England in August with a copy of the proposed legislation. Among the proposals submitted by the chief secretary was one to place a tax of ten percent on the rents of the absentee landlords who did not reside at least six months of each year in Ireland. Since some of the most prominent peers and gentlemen in British public life would be affected by this proposed legislation, it is readily understandable why negotiations on both sides of the Irish Sea were conducted in strict secrecy.

However unpopular this proposed absentee tax might prove to be in England, it had been for many years a popular aspiration among certain groups in Ireland. It was particularly attractive to the patriots since it would help considerably to undo the great mischief caused in part by their own folly in granting extravagant bounties, and at the same time it would serve as a chastisement for the dereliction of

[23] *Ibid.*, 70.

the absentees, many of whom were members of the English House of Commons, the enemy of the Irish Parliament. Lord Charlemont, for example, was strenuously and uniformly opposed to all of Harcourt's policies with the single exception of the absentee tax which he characterized as a popular measure. Flood, Fortescue, Pery, and other prominent patriots, besides being strongly behind the measure, also had much to do with suggesting it to Harcourt.[24]

With only a modicum of prophetic powers, it would have been possible to foretell that if the North ministry would allow the absentee tax to be brought forward in the Irish House of Commons it would be liable to be charged with political vindictiveness, since the absentees included such prominent Whig leaders as the Duke of Devonshire and Lords Rockingham and Shelburne. As shall be shown below, such a charge was indeed made by various affected absentees; but, in the interests of a more balanced view, it should be remembered that: (1) there were loyal courtiers —Lords Hertford, Upper Ossory, and several others—as well as opposition Whigs whose Irish holdings would also be affected by the tax; (2) among the Whigs themselves there was a wide variety of opinion regarding the merits of the proposed tax and the justification which the Irish had for enacting it; (3) in court circles there was little enthusiasm for the legislative proposals submitted by Chief Secretary Blaquiere in August 1773, especially for the absentee tax which George III regarded as "objectionable." [25] It would, therefore, be irresponsible to describe the controversial measure as politically motivated. It would be much closer to the truth to describe it as an unwise *quid pro quo*: in return for the eagerly desired absentee tax the Irish Parliament was to enact the necessary taxation to relieve the many burdens which had been placed on the crown

[24] Warden Flood, *Memoirs of the Life and Correspondence of Henry Flood*, 91, also Hist. Mss. Comm., Charlemont MSS, 12th *Report*, App. pt. I, 36.
[25] John Fortescue, ed., *The Correspondence of King George the Third from 1760 to December 1783* (6 vols., London, 1927–28), III, 361.

revenues—especially the large bounty on the inland carriage of corn. Lord North left no doubt in Harcourt's mind about this bargain when he warned him that:

> the parliament of Ireland, if they seriously wish to have the tax upon absentees confirmed by his Majesty, must consent to other propositions which were recommended to your Excellency in the message by Mr. Blaquiere. Nothing less than their consent to the whole of your Excellency's plan can justify us in assenting to the absentee tax, or, indeed, enable us to stand the odium of so anti-British a measure. . . . Indeed without securing the hereditary revenue from being drained by the corn bounty, all the rest of the plan will be precarious; as every addition which may accrue to the revenue by new taxes and other regulations may be swallowed up by that article alone. I do, therefore, most earnestly wish that the absentee tax may not be sent over unless the hereditary revenue is secured in this point; as no plan can be said to offer effectual relief to the government of Ireland without it.[26]

It was not until the latter part of September that the existence of this proposed tax became generally known. According to Horace Walpole, it was made known to Francis Seymour Conway, Earl of Hertford, by that Colonel Keene whose wife was Elizabeth Legge, a step-sister to Lord North.[27] As the owner of extensive property in Ireland (60,000 acres in County Antrim, where he also owned practically the entire town of Lisburne) from which, it was estimated, he was receiving an annual income in excess of £12,000 by 1773, Hertford was shocked by the news.[28] As lord chamberlain of his majesty's household and a close personal friend of the king, the distraught earl was faced with the problem of how to oppose a measure sanctioned by the ministry, but one which he resented as a gross attack on his property. At first Hertford had given some thought to a plan whereby he and his eldest son would take turns

[26] Harcourt, IX, 82–83.
[27] A. F. Stuart, ed., *The Last Journals of Horace Walpole* (London, 1858), I, 258–59. Hereafter referred to as *Walpole*.
[28] Prior, I, 311.

residing on the Irish property. He soon found a more satisfactory means of stirring up opposition to the proposed tax without absenting himself from court. He sent word of the project to his friend the Earl of Bessborough who also possessed considerable property in Ireland, but who, unlike Hertford, had no courtly obligations. Bessborough in turn forwarded the information to Lord Rockingham, then blissfully far distant from London on his magnificent estate in Yorkshire. Rockingham wrote promptly to Edmund Burke, who was to play a key role in opposing the tax, and asked him to go see Lord Bessborough for more complete information.

It was not long before all of the prominent absentees were acquainted with the threat to their properties, and there was no doubt about the intensity of the excitement that resulted. Both Rockingham and Burke felt that the proposed legislation furnished grounds for a parliamentary impeachment.[29] More violent still was the first reaction of Lord Shelburne (owner of 121,000 acres of Irish land) who, according to Horace Walpole, regarded the proposed tax as wholesale robbery and expressed the opinion that the minister who should advise it would deserve to be hanged.[30]

As indicated above there were prominent Whigs—among them the Earl of Chatham, the Duke of Richmond, and Sir George Savile—who took a more detached view of the project. Chatham's pronouncements on the tax scheme were elicited by Shelburne who distrusted his own judgment where he was so deeply interested. After weighing the matter again and again Chatham wrote as follows to Shelburne:

The operation of the bill is excessively severe, no doubt, against absentees: but the principle of that severity seems founded in strong Irish policy: which is to compel more of the product of the improved estates of that kingdom to be spent by the possessors there, amongst

[29] Burke to Rockingham, Sept. 29, 1773. *The Correspondence of Edmund Burke,* ed. Thomas W. Copeland, II (ed. Lucy S. Sutherland; Cambridge, 1960), 468.
[30] *Walpole,* I, 253.

their tenants, and in their own consumptions, rather than here in England, and in foreign parts. England, it is evident, profits by draining Ireland of the vast incomes spent here from that country. But I could not, as a peer of England, advise the King on principles of indirect, accidental English policy, to reject a tax on absentees, sent over here, as the genuine desire of the Commons of Ireland, acting in their inherent, exclusive right, by raising supplies in the manner they judge best. This great principle of the constitution is so fundamental, and, with me, so sacred and indispensable, that it outweighs all other considerations.[31]

The Duke of Richmond thought that there was considerable justification for the Irish to attempt ". . . to catch at any means of recovering some part of the money which regularly goes out of their country, and which this country will not allow them the fair chance of commerce to recover." [32]

There were serious doubts in Sir George Savile's mind regarding the injustice of the proposed imposition. "Perhaps," he wrote Rockingham,

it may be unjust, but I would not undertake to prove it so. It is a case which would on that side the water bear argument. We are two nations, not one. In money matters absolutely, in some matters hostile, for we have a separate purse. If you was to be taxed in Northamptonshire for not living there, it would be absurd: but if Northamptonshire had a separate purse, and all her landlords went and enriched neighbour counties, I don't know exactly how far I should think I might go if I were a Northamptonshire man.[33]

But in spite of whatever justification the Irish Parliament might have, both Richmond and Savile felt that it would be folly to yield to such a threat. The power lay with England, and that power should prevail. Worthy of note too was the opinion expressed by Rockingham's friend, Adam

---

[31] *The Correspondence of William Pitt, Earl of Chatham*, ed. William Stanhope Taylor and John Henry Pringle (4 vols.; London, 1838–40), IV, 299–300.
[32] *Memoirs of the Marquis of Rockingham and His Contemporaries*, ed. George Thomas, Earl of Albemarle (2 vols.; London, 1852), II, 230.
[33] *Ibid.*, II, 231–32.

Smith, whose *Wealth of Nations* was approaching completion when the controversy developed. Referring specifically to the absentee tax in his great work, Smith declared that:

> Those who live in another country contribute nothing, by their consumption, towards the support of the Government of that country in which is situated the source of their revenue. If in this latter country there should be no land-tax, nor any considerable duty upon the transference either of moveable or immoveable property, as in the case of Ireland, such absentees may derive a great revenue from the protection of a Government, to the support of which they do not contribute a single shilling.[34]

Although these dissenting opinions disappointed Rockingham, who had assumed the leadership of the opposition to the tax, they in no way impeded his determination to fight it by every means possible.

In the campaign against the tax, time was a vital factor. The Irish Parliament was not scheduled to meet until October 12, and North had advised Harcourt that if he expected the new supply bill to be enacted by the beginning of the Irish fiscal year, at Christmas, it should be in England around December 1 to allow the Privy Council sufficient time to consider it. Bessborough and Burke favored an early, prudent, and vigorous opposition before the Irish Parliament should get possession of the project. This procedure was strongly recommended to Rockingham by Burke who felt that by ". . . a proper remonstrance the Ministry, who never foresee difficulties will be more terrified about them than in reason they ought."[35] Burke, knowing of Rockingham's intention to be present at the Newmarket races in early October, had written to the marquess on September 29 and suggested that it might be expedient for him "to get on a little further" to meet his friends and make arrangements for a representation to the ministry.

---

[34] Adam Smith, *An Inquiry into the Nature and Cause of the Wealth of Nations*, ed. J. E. T. Rogers (2d ed., Oxford, 1880), II, 493.

[35] Sept. 29, 1773, *Correspondence of Edmund Burke*, II, 470.

Rockingham responded promptly to this suggestion and by October 12 was back at his London residence in Grosvenor Square, busily engaged in drafting the remonstrance proposed by Burke.

Among the things the interested landowners hoped to acquire through their protest was an official confirmation of the alarming news brought to them by Hertford, and also what stand the ministry proposed to take. If this vital information was to be obtained from North, every precaution would need to be taken in regard both to the wording of the remonstrance as well as to the rank and property of the men who should sign it. Above all they "should have weight" and be drawn from divergent political backgrounds. "In this matter," wrote Rockingham to the Earl of Upper Ossory (a courtier) on October 13,

> I shall wish to act, so as to avoid any imputation of making this matter a mere Engine of opposition. The concerns of so many are interested—of very different political general ideas, that I think the only rule of conduct should be what is equally right for all.[36]

By October 13 the remonstrance had been drawn up and was ready for the absentees of weight and substance to sign it. At this point Rockingham encountered a great deal of difficulty, caused in part by the absence from London of many of the prominent absentees. Parliament was not scheduled to meet until Christmas; the summer season was just ending, so that many of those who might have been willing to sign were not immediately available. Of those who were in London, both Lords Hertford and Shelburne, though present when the decision on the remonstrance was reached, refused to sign it when it was written. The refusal of the two peers was a serious handicap, for in addition to their political prominence they were among the largest owners of Irish property. Furthermore, since Hertford was a

---

[36] Letter to Upper Ossory, Oct. 13, 1773, Rockingham Papers deposited in Sheffield Public Library by Earl Fitzwilliam and his Trustees.

loyal courtier, his signature on the protest would have been most gratifying to Rockingham who was anxious to avoid any imputation of party. Hertford did, however, give his assurance that he would vigorously oppose the measure in the Privy Council and that he would also speak personally to North about it; but, apart from that, he thought it would be improper for him "to be in any other shape concerned." In Shelburne's case there was none of the mitigating circumstances which applied to Hertford, and for that reason as well as for his "characteristic lack of openness" it is difficult to arrive at an adequate explanation for his refusal to sign it. One explanation—though far from a completely satisfactory one—was recorded by Horace Walpole to the effect that Shelburne, when pressed on all that he said initially against the tax, "pleaded to Lord Rockingham and Lord Bessborough that Lord Chatham approved the tax and he had long determined to be governed in everything by Lord Chatham." [37]

The defection of Hertford and Shelburne reduced to five the number of those who were willing to sign the remonstrance. In addition to Rockingham, these included the Duke of Devonshire, the Earl of Bessborough, the Earl of Upper Ossory, and Baron Milton, afterward Earl of Dorchester. Although the list was small, it nevertheless realized Rockingham's ideals of property and social position. The combined annual income of these noblemen from their Irish properties was estimated at £60,000 in 1773. But more important perhaps than their property was the great influence they were capable of bringing to bear on political opinion both in England and in Ireland. By the intimate ties of intermarriage and inheritance, these peers were connected with the most distinguished families in England and Ire-

---

[37] *Walpole*, I, 253. Cf. "after consulting with Chatham, Shelburne realised that he was denying the Irish Parliament the right of taxation which he was fighting to secure for the Americans" (John Norris, *Shelburne and Reform* [London, 1963], 88).

land, and these bonds, according to Burke, "bind countries more closely together than any laws or constitutions whatsoever." [38]

Interestingly too, these five peers also represented those three social groups in eighteenth-century Ireland which Burke identified as the "native Irish," "the first races of the English," and "the new English interest." The Earl of Upper Ossory (Mac Giolla Phadruaig–Fitzpatrick) was of native Irish stock whose Catholic ancestors had learned that the surest way to maintain their property and acquire place was to forego the old religion and conform to the new. Rockingham had inherited his Irish property from his great ancestor the Earl of Strafford (Thomas Wentworth), and the Duke of Devonshire his from his mother, Lady Charlotte Boyle, a direct descendant of the Tudor adventurer, Robert Boyle, the first Earl of Cork. The inheritance of both these noblemen, therefore, had come from the "first races of the English" in Ireland—from pre-Cromwellians. On the other hand, the inheritance of Bessborough (Ponsonby) and Milton (Damer) descended from a later breed of ancestors—"the new English interest"—whose property and power were rewards for services rendered in the Protector's purge of Ireland.

As stated above, the remonstrance was completed on October 13 and was promptly signed on that date by all of the peers except Upper Ossory who, though he had planned to be present at Rockingham's home on Grosvenor Square, had been detained on his country estate at Ampthill Park in Bedfordshire by the illness of his wife. It was necessary, therefore, for Rockingham to send a special messenger to Ampthill with the remonstrance for Upper Ossory's signature. Three days later, on October 16, it was sent to North.

Though relatively short (fewer than six-hundred words)

[38] To Sir Charles Bingham, Oct. 30, 1773, *Correspondence of Edmund Burke*, II, 477.

the remonstrance has been described by Lecky as "one of the most perfect State papers of the time." [39] Going directly to the heart of the matter in their opening statement, the five protesting peers informed North that it was "publicly reported" that a project had been communicated to the "King's Ministers" for proposing in the Parliament of Ireland a tax which would particularly and exclusively "effect the property of those who possess lands in that kingdom but reside in this," and that this "extraordinary design" had been encouraged by an assurance by the administration that should such a bill be sent over it would receive the sanction of his majesty's Privy Council. As the objects of this "unprecedented imposition" the noblemen pointed out that they possessed considerable property in both kingdoms, and that their ordinary residence was in England, a residence they had not hitherto regarded "as an act of delinquency to be punished or as a political evil to be corrected by the penal operation of a partial tax." [40] Besides, many of them had their birth and "early habits" in England, some of them had an indispensable public duty, and all of them had the right of "free subjects" to live in whatever part of his majesty's dominions they considered most convenient. They were, therefore, astounded by a design to penalize them for their residence in England, the principal member of the British Empire and the residence of their "common sovereign." Protesting their ever-ready willingness to cooperate in the public service and to support his majesty's government, they expressed a cordial, though not an exclusive, regard for the rights and liberties of Ireland, a disposition in no way jeopardized but rather enhanced by their residence in "Great Britain." They regarded the tax scheme as injurious to both kingdoms: it would tend both to lessen the value of all landed property in Ireland and to

---

[39] Lecky, IV, 441.
[40] Remonstrance of the Five Peers, Oct. 16, 1773, Rockingham Papers.

separate the two kingdoms in interest and affection. In their closing statement the peers requested from North

authentic information concerning a matter in which we are so nearly concerned that, if the scheme which we state to your lordship doth exist we may be enabled to pursue every legal method of opposition to a project in every light so unjust and impolitic.[41]

On October 18 North informed the Duke of Devonshire that he had received the protest, but that no definite answer could be made until other members of his majesty's council had an opportunity to see it. Three days later, on October 21, Devonshire received a second letter from North in which he admitted that in the course of the summer the Lord Lieutenant of Ireland had sent over several propositions for restoring the credit of Ireland, among them a tax of the nature mentioned in the remonstrance. Then North informed Devonshire that his majesty's servants had advised Harcourt that "if the Irish Parliament should send over to England such a plan, as should appear well calculated to give effective relief to Ireland in its present distress, their opinion would be that it ought to be carried into execution, although the tax upon absentees should make a part of it." [42] Here now was the official confirmation the peers sought in their protest and not a minute was lost in spreading the alarm to all parts of England and Ireland. The effect on the ministry was instantaneous. On October 22, Secretary of State Rochford informed Harcourt that:

all the Lords and gentlemen in opposition here are determined to go every length to mar, if possible the absentee tax: and (but I say this in the utmost confidence) government will not support it unless the other points relative to the corn bounties and the revenue are part of the condition.[43]

[41] *Ibid.*
[42] *Ibid.*
[43] Harcourt, IX, 76–77.

A week later North was well aware that the contagion of opposition was rapidly spreading to others besides the "Lords and gentlemen in opposition." "I think it right," he wrote to Harcourt on October 29,

> to take this opportunity of informing your Excellency of the effect which the expectation of the absentee tax has in this kingdom. I always apprehended that it would cause much uneasiness: but the uneasiness which it does cause has exceeded my apprehensions. The cry is universal against it. Friend and foe, those who have and those who have not estates in Ireland, join in condemning and abusing it. In short it is nearly as unpopular here as it is popular on your side of the water.[44]

The whole letter indicates beyond the shadow of a doubt that the manifesto of the five peers had a telling effect on the ministry; and that North's frank acknowledgment of it had, indeed, as Rockingham aptly described it, got him into quite a "hobble." [45]

The prompt circulation of the remonstrance and North's two letters had inaugurated the counteroffensive of the absentees. The intelligence they had received regarding the policy which the ministry intended to pursue was indeed vital, but it would have to be used with the greatest care in order to accomplish Rockingham's objective of preventing the opposition to the government-sponsored tax from developing into a mere political issue. In view of the excitement already created it was inevitable that future negotiations between the king's ministers in England and in Ireland would be carried on in strict secrecy. This and the additional fact that so much in Irish politics depended upon "the caprice of the moment" made the position of the landlords a critical one. The Irish Parliament might strike without warning; the landlords would have to be ready to strike

---
[44] *Ibid.*, 80.
[45] Rockingham to Lady Rockingham, Oct. 28, 1773, Rockingham Papers.

back without delay. This necessitated constant vigilance and sagacious leadership, both of which Rockingham supplied to an eminent degree. From the very first knowledge of the controversial tax, Rockingham had been one of its most steadfast opponents. As the leader of a political party and a prominent owner of Irish land, the direction of the opposition to the tax in Britain had fallen naturally to him. He had been the principal mover in the proceedings that culminated in the remonstrance, and while this had been an eminently successful undertaking there remained the formidable task of transmuting what was scarcely more than the small voice of a minority of the absentees into a great national outcry both in England and in Ireland. This was the task toward which Rockingham now directed all his energies.

As noted above, Upper Ossory was unable to be in London at this time because of his wife's illness. Shortly after the signing of the remonstrance the Duke of Devonshire left London and returned to his magnificent estate at Welbeck in Nottinghamshire. It is entirely possible that neither of the young noblemen felt, in the same degree as Rockingham, the obligations of temporarily foregoing his accustomed round of pursuits in order to devote full attention to the threat against his property. That the marquess resented the tendency of some of his colleagues to shirk their responsibilities is reflected in a letter to Lady Rockingham on October 25 in which he confided that "if I don't remain at the seat of action, nothing will be done." [46]

The apparent indifference of Devonshire and Upper Ossory was more than atoned for by the exceptional vigor exerted by Rockingham in launching a concerted and systematic program of opposition against the proposed tax. On the very same day that he had written to Lady Rockingham about his inability to get away from London for a rest at

[46] Oct. 25, 1773, *ibid.*

his estate at Wentworth, he held a conference with Lords Bessborough and Milton. Here tentative plans were made for a protest meeting in London around the middle of November. Notification of the advisability of such a meeting was to be conveyed to all interested parties through a circular letter from the five peers, and additional ones were to be issued from time to time to keep the opposition informed on all matters pertaining to the controversy. To facilitate this information system a committee of correspondence was to be established under the supervision of Rockingham who was to have full authority to act for other peers.

As special messengers raced northward with news of the plans to Devonshire and Upper Ossory, there was feverish activity in London. Rockingham's home in Grosvenor Square was now, indeed, "the seat of action," and, during the balance of October and all of November, it served as the clearing-house for all information relative to the absentee tax. To the facile pen of that famous roué, William Hickey, we are indebted for an intimate, if all-too-brief, account of the intense activity at Grosvenor Square during these anxious days.

Through the recommendation of Mr. Edmund Burke, I was employed at Lord Rockingham's upon this occasion upwards of a month, attending daily from nine in the morning until ten, eleven, or twelve at night. My chief business was copying circular letters, and assisting in making them up, sealing, and directing. I sat at the same table with the Marquis, who I found to be a most affable and pleasing mannered man. During such my attendance in Grosvenor Square I had thrice the honour of dining with the before named nobleman and others who constituted the Committee. The other days my dinner was served for me in a small chamber adjoining the drawing room in which I wrote. One of the days I dined with the Marquis, I was much pleased with some delicious ale which his Lordship said had been brewed at Wentworth, (his seat in Yorkshire) upwards of twenty five years before. It was so soft and grateful that I was induced to take a second glass, upon which Mr. William Burke, who sat next to me, cautioned me to mind what I was about, the liquor I was approving of being infinitely stronger than brandy and more likely to intoxicate. Undoubtedly after drinking the second glass I felt my head rather light and giddy.[47]

Shortly after launching the work of the correspondence committee the messengers returned to London from Nottinghamshire and Bedfordshire with the information that Devonshire and Upper Ossory had approved the plan of their colleagues. Being now unanimously delegated to act for the other peers, Rockingham on October 30 signed the copies of the first circular letter which brought the absentees up to date on all that pertained to the tax and which, at the same time, cautioned them to be in readiness for future undertakings, especially the general meeting to be held in London in the near future. The actual dispatching of the letters fell to the responsibility of Rockingham's subordinates while he himself made preparations for a delayed homeward journey to Wentworth.

During his stay in Yorkshire, Rockingham was kept constantly in touch with all developments in London and Dublin. His assistants at Grosvenor Square continued to exploit every avenue of opposition. The names and addresses of absentees were assiduously sought out, and copies of the manifesto and the circular letter were sent to them. As letters of acknowledgment from the various absentees began to arrive at Grosvenor Square, their contents were summarized by clerks and recorded on tally sheets. Steps were also taken to elicit the support of various London companies (large holders of property in Northern Ireland since the reign of James I) through their governing body, "The Irish Society." [48]

Around the end of October rumors became current in London that the ministry had withdrawn its support of the absentee tax. Burke, in a letter to Rockingham on Novem-

[47] *Memoirs of William Hickey, 1749-1809*, ed. Alfred Spencer, (2d ed., 4 vols., London, 1913-25), I, 302-3.
[48] Robert Blackham, *The Soul of the City, London's Livery Companies* (London, 1931), 55-56.

ber 7, was inordinately suspicious of these rumors and readily attributed them to either "the politics of the court or the tricks of Shelburne house." His skepticism derived, of course, from his original interpretation of the ministry's part in the controversial proposal and Lord Shelburne's strange behavior in regard to the remonstrance. But despite Burke's misgivings a change was actually taking place in the ministry, and the impetus for this came from Ireland; or, perhaps more correctly, from the promptness with which the absentees in England spread the alarm among their many friends and relatives in Ireland.

The Earl of Chatham, in outlining his stand on the tax to Lord Shelburne, had declared that the proper place for opposition to the measure would be Ireland where "the exertions of all the weight of the absentees would be natural and constitutional." [49] This advice did not go unheeded. Copies of the remonstrance, North's replies, and the first circular letter were promptly forwarded to the many friends of the absentees in Ireland. It will be recalled that one of the objections to the tax which the peers incorporated in their protest allegedly derived from their fears that it would lessen the value of all landed property in Ireland. As the remonstrance was circulated throughout the country, similar fears took hold of a great many Irish landowners. Their apprehensions were increased when it was rumored that the absentee tax was in reality the first step "on the part of the English ministry to introduce a general land tax." [50] The end result was that the tax which, prior to the summoning of the Irish Parliament, had been so universally popular was now encountering considerable opposition.

As in the case of the drafting of the remonstrance, so also in the matter of polarizing opposition to the tax in Ireland, Burke's powerful pen was employed with telling effect. In a masterful letter to his friend, Sir Charles Bing-

---

[49] Taylor and Pringle, IV, 301.
[50] Harcourt, IX, 101.

ham, a member of the Irish Parliament, Burke left no argument untouched in attempting to discredit the proposed legislation. Among other things he emphasized that the tax would lead to a renunciation of the principle of common naturalization which ran through the whole empire with the result that Irishmen would be shut off from English official life, from the English peerage, from the English Commons; the bonds of human relationship such as intermarriage and inheritance would be broken. The ties of mutual love and sympathy would be severed.[51]

The absentees' greatest weapons against the tax were, of course, their extensive landed properties as well as their many relatives and personal friends in both houses of the Irish Parliament. The weight of absentee property could be brought to bear on the representatives from every section of the country. In the north were the holdings of the London companies and the Earl of Hertford; in the midlands those of Rockingham, Bessborough and Upper Ossory; and in the south those of Devonshire, Milton, and many others. Prompt steps were taken to activate this great potential influence. Early in November many counties and boroughs had already addressed their representatives on the necessity of voting against the tax. Among the actual members of Parliament were a great many close relatives of the prominent absentees. John Ponsonby, brother of the Earl of Bessborough and an uncle by marriage to the Duke of Devonshire, represented the County of Kilkenny. Brabazon Ponsonby, John's son, was a member from Cork City, while the latter's brother-in-law, Sir William Fownes, represented the Borough of Knocktopher, County Kilkenny. Two sons of the Earl of Hertford, Francis and Robert Seymour–Conway, sat respectively for the County of Antrim and the Borough of Lisburne. Francis Price, the other member from Lisburne, was Hertford's nephew. John Damer, represent-

[51] Edmund Burke, *The Works of the Right Honorable Edmund Burke* (Boston, 1877), VI, 123-34.

ing the Borough of Swords, County Dublin, was a cousin of Lord Milton. The powerful Lord Shannon, being a nephew of the third Earl of Burlington and Cork, was, therefore, a second cousin of the Duke of Devonshire. William Henry (Dawson), first Viscount Carlow, was a brother-in-law to Lord Milton, while the viscount's son, John, represented the Queen's County in the lower house. Lord Mountmorres, another strong opponent of the tax in the House of Lords, was a brother-in-law of the Earl of Bessborough.

Scarcely less significant than these powerful relatives were the many steadfast friends of the absentees in Parliament. It would be tedious to catalogue in detail the individual contributions of all of these men, but at least the names of four of them should be mentioned in passing—Lord Bellamont and Lord Carysford in the upper house, and Sir Charles Bingham and Sir William Mayne in the lower house. Mayne, in particular, played a prominent role. Throughout the whole crisis he served as the principal observer for the absentees in Dublin and his frequent letters to Rockingham kept the interested parties in England well abreast of developments in the Irish Parliament.

So effectively had the relatives and friends of the absentees in Ireland pilloried the proposed tax that by early November it appeared to have become a dead issue, and rumors were making the rounds that it might not even be brought forward in Parliament. Not surprisingly, this turn of events was no less pleasing to the ministry than to the threatened absentees. It should be remembered that at no time did the ministry ever regard the tax as other than a grudging concession for the lifting of the burdens from the hereditary revenues. Thanks now to the tumult of opposition generated by the peers and their colleagues, the ministry would be spared the odium of approving such an "anti-British" measure. On the strength of the developing opposition in Ireland, North had been assiduously advising

Harcourt on ways and means whereby the king's representative and his Chief Secretary, Blaquiere, might extricate themselves from their earlier commitments regarding the controversial measure. In a letter to Harcourt on October 29, North stated that he had received several reports that many of the principal persons in Ireland had declared against the tax, and that the patriots there would not move it. "If that be the case," he continued,

> we shall hear no more of it. The Castle party, I take it for granted, will not propose it as their measure. It cannot with propriety, originate with the servants of the Crown. Nothing indeed but the necessity of the case can justify them in adopting it.[52]

North was greatly encouraged to learn from Harcourt's reply that steps were being taken "to divert the progress of this tax for the present." Instead of being sponsored by the "servants of the Crown," Harcourt informed North that, "We mean to allow the bill to be moved in the house of Commons by a certain wild and inconsistent gentleman who has signified his intention to bring it forward. This will be sufficient to damn the measure were no other means employed against it." [53]

Apparently there was a rather obvious lack of subtlety about the manner in which Harcourt and Blaquiere sought to implement the new policy prescribed by North. The patriot leader, Charlemont, wrote with indignation of the orders from England to throw out the tax "in consequence of which administration suddenly and indecently changed sides." [54]

But if there was rejoicing in England on the part of the ministry and the absentees regarding the happy turn of events in Ireland during the first week in November, it was destined to be short-lived indeed. On November 8, in the

---
[52] Harcourt, IX, 84–85.
[53] Ibid., 93–94.
[54] Hist. Mss. Comm., Charlemont MSS, 36.

course of a budget speech in the Irish House of Commons, Chief Secretary Blaquiere mentioned the absentee tax as a possible source of revenue. To exacerbate the situation Harcourt wrote to North on November 8 and 9, and on both occasions he commended Blaquiere for his behavior in Parliament. Apparently neither of them regarded this clumsy incident as contrary to the recent instructions received from North. It is possible that since they were now in the process of scuttling the policy they had thus far so vigorously supported they felt some strange, irrational urge to mention it at least in Parliament. Whatever the explanation, this incident as well as several others in the course of the agitation over the tax pointed up the fact that simple Simon Harcourt and the blundering Blaquiere were no match for the shrewd marquess and his able colleagues. The incident also lends credence to an anecdote related to Rockingham by Burke to the effect that the friends of the "North administration who had appointed Harcourt lord Lieutenant considered him and his secretary 'as grossest bunglers'." [55]

Without delay, the alarming news of Blaquiere's speech was spread to England. Lord Hertford, from his vantage place at court, alerted Bessborough who promptly wrote to Rockingham. On the same day the speech was made Sir William Mayne wrote directly to the marquess. Apparently the letter was directed to Grosvenor Square and thence was forwarded to Yorkshire where it did not arrive until November 19. The alarmist that he was, Mayne viewed Blaquiere's speech as a clear indication that "Government" would support the tax. Rockingham was now thoroughly aroused, and on the day following the receipt of Mayne's letter he set out for London. Before his departure he wrote to Mayne informing him that he had received many reports that the ministry in England was withdrawing its support of the tax and for that reason he had postponed the calling of a general meeting. Blaquiere's speech indicated to Rock-

[55] Burke to Rockingham, Nov. 7, 1773, Rockingham Papers, R 3–148a.

ingham that the government was not quite as lukewarm as many had inferred. He told Mayne that immediately on his return to London he would set a date for a general meeting, unless he could find out definitely that Blaquiere's proposal was not being supported.

In the meantime Blaquiere's speech had caused the utmost consternation in court circles. North was so distressed by the news that he immediately forwarded to the king Harcourt's letters of November 8 and 9, accompanied by copies of the letters he had written to the Lord Lieutenant on October 29 and 30 wherein he had outlined the procedure which was to be followed in the future regarding the tax. George III was thoroughly provoked especially with Blaquiere who, despite the instructions he had received personally from North in August, as well as the latter's most recent outline of policy, was now apparently recommending "the measure as his favourite idea." [56] In accordance with instructions from the king, North wrote to Harcourt on November 20 and he left little room for the latter to doubt that the tax in any shape or form would be any longer acceptable in England. North told Harcourt that he was optimistic that some relief could be found for the country's financial difficulties without insisting on the absentee tax.[57]

Rockingham arrived in London late on the night of November 22. The next day the marquess was assured by Hertford that the ministry was opposed to the tax and that Blaquiere's mentioning it in Parliament "was indiscreet." But Hertford's assurances could persuade neither Rockingham nor Burke to abate his vigilance. Apprehensive of what the next dispatch from Dublin might bring, Rockingham put his clerks to work on a second circular letter which was sent to the various absentees on November 27. Reasons were given why the general meeting originally scheduled for mid-November had been postponed, the principal ones

[56] Fortescue, III, 33.
[57] Harcourt, IX, 96–98.

being that there was reason to believe that the government was lukewarm toward the tax and that there were strong grounds for believing that even if the project should be brought forward it would probably be rejected in the Irish Parliament. The circumstances were now altered considerably by Blaquiere's speech and accounts from Ireland that government there had taken a strong part in favor of the measure.

Though the immediate calling of a Meeting may be postponed until the fate of the Motion for this Tax which is expected to be made this Week in Ireland is known. It is thought to be highly Incumbent on us to give this Information to all those to whom we had the honour to Communicate what had already passed that they may be so far prepared, that if a Meeting is called in the course of the next Fortnight they may be able if they think it proper to come to London with the less inconvenience.[58]

But even as copies of the second circular letter were being dispatched from Grosvenor Square, couriers were racing from Dublin with the good news that the tax had been defeated. After weeks of intense anxiety, the bill was finally brought forward in the committee of ways and means on Thursday afternoon, November 25. Unbelievable as it may seem, the affair had gone off precisely as Harcourt had planned it. James Fortescue, the "wild and inconsistent gentleman," to whom the Lord Lieutenant had referred in his letter to North on November 9, opened the debate by proposing a resolution for imposing a tax in general upon the estates of absentees. Fortescue did not specify the particular sum to be levied, or the length of residence that should exempt people from the tax, or whether the impost should be applied for the support of government or to any other purposes. Furthermore he used reproachful epithets in describing the wretched state of the country.[59] His motion

---

[58] 2d Circular Letter, Nov. 27, 1773, Rockingham Papers, R3-153a.
[59] Harcourt, IX, 107.

caused great indignation among many members and his resolution was objected to as being vague, uncertain, and improper.

Apparently Fortescue had a well-deserved reputation for the wildness and inconsistency attributed to him by Harcourt, and the fact that he had early indicated his intention of introducing the measure was regarded as a good omen by its opponents. In a letter to Burke, Sir Charles Bingham declared that Fortescue's ". . . schemes are so scattered, he is such a Political Raver that I should not wish it in better hands, as any merit it may have, it will certainly lose, he being the mover." [60]

After much difficulty Fortescue was finally prevailed upon to withdraw his vague proposal. Thereupon Silver Oliver, one of the knights of the shire from County Limerick, moved the following resolution:

RESOLVED that it is the opinion of this Committee that a tax of two shillings in the pound be laid upon all the net rents and annual profits issuing out of all lands, tenements, and hereditaments in this Kingdom payable to persons who shall not actually reside in this Kingdom for the space of six months in each year, from the 25th December, 1773 to 25 December 1775 inclusive.[61]

Debate on this proposition began immediately and continued until two o'clock the following morning. It was conducted with warmth and ability by those who supported as well as by those opposed. Some of the principal speakers in support of the resolution were Mr. Flood, Leader of the House, and Philip Tisdall, the Attorney General. Notable among the opposing speakers were John Ponsonby, Edward Tighe (whose mother-in-law was a sister of Ponsonby), and Sir Charles Bingham. There were others, among them Hercules Langrishe, a close friend of Burke, who, while they seemed to support the principle of the bill, embarrassed the meas-

[60] List of Absentees and Incomes, Rockingham Papers.
[61] Harcourt, IV, 108.

ure with so many difficulties that it was impossible to determine whether they were for or against it. According to the account of the debate which Harcourt sent to North, the justice and equity of the tax was admitted on all sides, but the opposition laid their principal stress upon these points: first, that since a great variety of new taxes was to be granted for the support of government this particular one would not be necessary; secondly, that it would be impolitic as tending to irritate many people of high rank in England against this country; and finally, that the measure was in reality a design of the British government to introduce a general land tax in Ireland.[62]

At the conclusion of the long and heated debate the question was put whether the tax to be imposed should be one or two shillings. The committee divided and it was carried against one shilling by 119 to 107. Then the question was put upon the original motion made by Mr. Oliver for two shillings and was defeated by a vote of 122 to 102.[63]

Promptly Sir William Mayne dispatched the good news of the defeat to Rockingham who received it on Monday, November 29. Immediately the elated marquess put his clerks to work on a third circular letter which was to be forwarded to all absentees on Wednesday, December 1. It gave him great pleasure, he told his faithful adherents, to be able to acquaint them with the rejection of the measure, an event which reflected a great deal of credit on the wisdom and justice of the majority in the Irish Parliament. The early encouragement which the proposition had received from the ministry in England as well as in Ireland could not prevent that majority from seeing into the true nature of the measure. It was not inconceivable, he thought, that the early steps which had been taken to oppose the tax contributed in some way to final victory. Furthermore, all those

[62] *Ibid.*, 109.
[63] Lecky, IV, 447.

who opposed the measure had the satisfaction of knowing that, while defending their own property, they at the same time were "maintaining the rights of the subject and the Interest, Freedom, & Good Policy of the Whole Empire." [64]

But as copies of the circular were about to be dispatched from Grosvenor Square, Rockingham received an urgent communication from Hertford informing him that word had just arrived from Dublin that on the day following the defeat of the tax a motion was made in Parliament to reconsider it. This necessitated a postponement of the circular to the following day, December 2, so that a postscript could be added to warn the absentees about the sudden and unexpected news.

Hertford's intelligence was all too true; on Saturday, November 27 a motion was carried to reconsider the bill. A couple of hours' debate on the measure ensued after which the house adjourned until Monday. But the second attempt was no more successful than the first. After a heated nine-hour debate on Monday, November 29 in which the Attorney General, Philip Tisdall, took a leading role in support of the tax, the measure was rejected. Again it was Mayne who dispatched the news to Rockingham from the floor of the house, informing him that the tax had been withdrawn and that the matter was now finally closed.

The controversy over the King's purse and the absentees' property was, of course, a minor episode in a century memorable for great events. All the same, the controversy is not without interest to the historian. The partial picture it provides of the political jobbery and callousness which characterized the Irish administration will bring home to the reader Edmund Burke's master understatement to the effect that the land of his "birth and education" was then being "ill and impolitically governed."

In a broader context the controversy provides interesting insights into the evolution of two of Britain's revered insti-

[64] 3d Circular Letter, Dec. 1, 1773, Rockingham Papers, R 3-156.

tutions—the monarchy and the landed aristocracy. It was folly for the ambitious young George III to attempt to turn back the clock and rule as well as reign in Ireland—if not in Britain. But this was visionary in the extreme, not merely because it went counter to long-established precedents and demonstrated at the same time little appreciation of the intricacies of the Irish establishment, but especially because it entailed a costly compromise of the interests of the landed aristocrats who were still riding the flood tide of English polity.

But the shadows that had already overtaken the monarchy were moving slowly but inexorably toward the landed aristocrats. Their victory in 1773 was in many respects their last one, and while the battle itself was fought in Ireland the strategy and tactics which carried the day were admirably devised and directed in England by Lord Rockingham and his fellow-aristocrats. Time, however, was running out on the landed gentry and by a curious coincidence exactly seventy-three years after 1773 the "House of Landlords" would disintegrate like a house of cards beneath an anti-corn-law avalanche. This was a battle fought on home territory, but by an ironic reversal of the plan of campaign of 1773, it was an Irish weapon—the dreadful famine—that gave Bright and Cobden the psychological advantage which enabled them to prevail in 1846.

# 4

# The Role of Prudence in Burke's Politics

## PETER J. STANLIS

FOR THE PAST CENTURY or more perhaps the most common single error of writers on Edmund Burke has been the failure to understand the nature and function of "prudence" in his political philosophy. Nineteenth-century utilitarian and positivist writers on Burke—Henry Buckle, John Morley, William Lecky, and Sir Leslie Stephen—understood Burke's principle of prudence as the basis of his political "expediency," as an empirical, rational, and pragmatic principle, wholly unrelated to religion or ethics. In Morley's words Burke's expediency overthrew "the baneful superstition that politics . . . is a province of morals."[1] Morley and his utilitarian contemporaries assumed that Burke's prudence made "expediency" or "the standard of convenience," rather than an appeal to normative ethical and legal principles, the ultimate foundation of his politics. Thus, Burke's principle of prudence was separated from ethics and law, and set in opposition to traditional morality and jurisprudence. Burke's own explicit words, that "the principles of true politics are those of morality enlarged," were completely ignored.

The path charted by Morley's interpretation of Burke's

[1] John Morley, *Edmund Burke: A Historical Study* (London, 1867), 152.

principle of prudence was followed, with some slight variations, by a whole host of Victorian and twentieth-century writers in the liberal tradition of politics. At the beginning of the twentieth century Charles E. Vaughan, a learned authority on Burke, applied the usual Benthamite antithesis between "natural rights" based on a normative view of human nature, and "expediency" based on pragmatism and the general welfare of society, and concluded that in Burke's politics "the last appeal is not to Rights but to expediency." [2] Vaughan noted that Burke's "expediency" differed from that of Hume and Bentham, because it was qualified by "higher principles" and "a tissue of moral and religious ideals," but like Morley he never doubted that Burke made "expediency the ultimate principle of politics." In 1913, John MacCunn, an excellent Burke scholar, also assumed that Burke was a utilitarian in politics, and concluded: "To Burke, as to Bentham, all rights . . . are not ultimate but derivative." [3] Elie Halévy supplied a variation on this theme in 1928: "From a utilitarian philosophy Burke deduced an anti-democratic political theory. . . . The utilitarian morality led Burke to social views which were profoundly different from those to which it led Bentham." [4] In 1934, Lois Whitney, a noted eighteenth-century scholar, contended: "Priestley, Burke, and Bentham are in harmony in their utilitarianism, Burke developing the doctrine in the form of a philosophy of expediency." [5] John Herman Randall, Jr. also stated in 1940 that Burke's political philosophy rested ultimately upon utility and pragmatic expediency,[6] and during the 1940s other writers repeated this

[2] Charles E. Vaughan, *Studies in the History of Political Philosophy Before and After Rousseau* (London, 1925), II, 5.
[3] John MacCunn, *The Political Philosophy of Burke* (London, 1913), 193.
[4] Elie Halévy, *The Growth of Philosophical Radicalism* (London, 1928), 158, 161.
[5] Lois Whitney, *Primitivism and the Idea of Progress* (Baltimore, 1934), 196–97.
[6] *The Making of the Modern Mind* (Boston, 1940), 432.

commonly held conviction that Burke's principle of prudence was utilitarian and expedient.

Unfortunately, even writers who believed that politics is a branch of practical morality were led to accept the utilitarian and positivist interpretation of Burke's principle of prudence. Late in the nineteenth century Lord Acton, whose early interpretation of Burke was filled with praise of his moral wisdom in politics, came to accept Morley's utilitarian view of Burke as valid, and condemned Burke for having separated politics from ethics. As late as 1953 this same error was repeated by Richard M. Weaver who noted that Burke frequently employed "the argument from circumstance" when he was "at grips with concrete policies," and that Burke's strict regard for circumstances was proof that he believed, with the utilitarians and positivists, that empirical observation and rational analysis were sufficient as a basis for politics, and that therefore Burke's politics was wholly separated from any normative ethical or legal principles. Like the utilitarian and positivist writers to whom they were strongly opposed, Acton and Weaver identified Burke's "prudence" with the intellectual calculation of utilitarian expediency.[7] They failed to understand that Burke's insistence upon taking all circumstances into account, in dealing with politics, was not a denial of general principles of morality and law, but rather an insistence that through

---

[7] In a letter to Mary Gladstone (Oct. 16, 1887), after noting that "The great bulk of cultured men in our day do not believe that politics are a branch of Moral Science," and expounding on instances in which political actions have been separated from ethics, Acton commented: "Above all, this is part of the teaching of Burke, and from him Morley has adopted it" (*Letters of Lord Acton to Mary Gladstone*, 2d ed. [London, 1913], 180–81). For further comment on this point, see Lionel Kochan, *Acton on History* (London, 1954), 46–47 and 85. For detailed explications of the changes in Acton's estimate of Burke's politics between 1859 and 1877, see also Gertrude Himmelfarb, *Lord Acton: A Study in Conscience and Politics* (Chicago, 1952), 69–75, 82, 143–44, 170, 204, 208, 216, and *passim*; see also G. E. Fasnacht, *Acton's Political Philosophy* (New York, 1953), 190–97 and 200. Richard W. Weaver, *The Ethics of Rhetoric* (Chicago, 1953), 58.

prudence the general principles of ethics and law could find their practical realization in all the concrete circumstances of man's social life. In brief, both the utilitarian and positivist critics of Burke (and many of their opponents as well) failed to understand in Burke's political philosophy the vital connection between his principle of prudence and the normative principles of morality—derived from Christianity and the natural law—and the normative principles of law, derived from English common law.

Undoubtedly, one of the chief reasons for this common misunderstanding of Burke's principle of prudence is that in his discussions of how changes should or should not be made in civil society he frequently appealed to history. Therefore, an understanding of Burke's conception of history is essential to an understanding of his principle of prudence. The relationship between history, prudence, and politics in Burke's total philosophy is summarized by Burke as follows:

My principles enable me to form my judgment upon men and actions in history, just as they do in common life, and are not formed out of events and characters, either present or past. History is a preceptor of prudence, not of principles. The principles of true politics are those of morality enlarged; and I neither now do, nor ever will, admit of any other.[8]

History is primarily a descriptive account of man's past, and as such it does not supply men with their normative moral principles; indeed, normative ethical principles are applied in judging men and events in history. Clearly, such principles derive from a source that transcends the ordinary temporal events of politics and history. For Burke there

[8] *The Correspondence of Edmund Burke,* ed. Thomas W. Copeland, II (ed. Lucy S. Sutherland; Cambridge, 1960), 282.

were two sources of transcendent normative principles—the revelations of Christianity and religion, and the natural law. In addition, the English common-law tradition provided Burke with legal norms for judging the political actions of Englishmen. Yet if history differs from religion, ethics, and law in not providing general normative principles in morals and law, as imperatives for man's personal and social conduct, nevertheless there are lessons, even moral lessons, to be learned from history. Burke was an Aristotelian in his philosophy, and he perceived transcendent normative moral principles as immanent in the temporal affairs of men. Moral laws do not exist only in general laws, abstracted from men in civil society; the principles of morality and law are embodied in practice in systems of religion and law, and therefore they are perceived in the great patterns of historical change and continuity. Through its specific examples history teaches the precepts of moral prudence, of temperance and restraint, as political virtues. Prudence was for Burke the first of political virtues because it was the link between politics and ethics, between the specific actions of men in history and the general laws of ethics and law. Prudence was the virtue which made it possible for "the principles of true politics" to be "those of morality enlarged."

To Burke history itself could not be understood simply as a matter of empirical observation of human events understood through rational analysis and synthesis. This was how the *philosophes* of the Enlightenment and English utilitarians and positivists viewed history. Unlike them, Burke saw history as involving the will of God as well as the will, reason, and actions of men. So far as history reflected transcendent normative principles embodied in the temporal events of mankind, it was to Burke a secondary form of revelation. History supplemented through concrete examples, empirically perceived and rationally understood —all that was revealed to man by faith through religion and by "right reason" through the natural law. To understand what Burke meant by history as "a preceptor of prudence" it is necessary to understand the role of God in Burke's view of history.

At the core of Burke's view of history was his belief that a transcendent God is concerned with the temporal events of mankind. This belief occurs frequently throughout Burke's writings, and it cannot be dismissed as idle rhetoric, since it rests at the base of some of his most important political arguments. Burke regarded the great social institutions of mankind, such as church and state, as instruments given to man by a concerned and benevolent God to be used for man's spiritual and temporal self-fulfillment. In the *Reflections* (1790), he explicitly states that God is the ultimate cause of the state: "He who gave our nature to be perfected by our virtue willed also the necessary means of its perfection: He willed, therefore, the state." In the *Appeal from the New to the Old Whigs* (1791), while advancing his argument that the duties of men in civil society are not voluntaristic, Burke asserted that "the awful Author of our being is the Author of our place in the order of existence," and that He marshals and disposes "us by a divine tactic, not according to our will, but according to His." Burke also affirmed that the general course of a nation's life is "the known march of the ordinary providence of God." In all such statements Burke was a world removed from the *philosophes,* utilitarians and positivists, whose view of man in history was based wholly upon empirical observation and rational analysis and synthesis.

Burke's view of history included the divine will of God, acting directly, or indirectly through man's reason and will, to determine temporal events. The direct intervention of God into human affairs was very rare, according to Burke, and could be ascertained with reasonable confidence only in those enormous changes which alter the whole course of history. In his entire writings Burke mentioned only two such events: the migration of the Teutonic tribes into the Roman Empire, and the French Revolution. In *An Abridgment of English History* (1757), Burke described the invasions of the Teutonic tribes as a "resistless inundation" of "most cruel barbarians." As an historian examining this event, Burke wrote:

We are in a manner compelled to acknowledge the hand of God in those immense revolutions by which at certain periods He so signally asserts His supreme dominion, and brings about that great system of change which is perhaps as necessary to the moral as it is found to be in the natural world.[9]

Thirty-four years later, in a famous passage that Matthew Arnold praised as the finest example of magnanimity in the entire eighteenth century, Burke wrote at the close of *Thoughts on French Affairs* (1791):

If a great change is to be made in human affairs, the minds of men will be fitted to it, the general opinions and feelings will draw that way. Every fear, every hope, will forward it; and then they who persist in opposing this mighty current in human affairs will appear rather to resist the decrees of Providence itself than the mere designs of men. They will not be resolute and firm, but perverse and obstinate.[10]

Where God's mysterious ways were manifested in events that baffled Burke, and contradicted his most cherished convictions, he accepted a wisdom and power that transcended his own. Yet Burke continued to oppose the direction and methods of the French Revolution to his dying day, because given his convictions it was part of his role in history to oppose it to the last.

Burke believed that, although many events in history could be explained by observation and rational analysis, not

[9] *The Works of the Right Honorable Edmund Burke* (12 vols.; Boston, 1877), VII, 232.
[10] *Ibid.*, IV, 377.

all historical causes or effects spring from the mind and will of man. Burke was aware of "those accidents which so frequently interpose to the disgrace of human wisdom, and which demonstrate that she is far from being the sole arbitress." [11] Beyond human reason and will and chance there were causes in history which could not be explained by science and scholarship, and these Burke attributed to God:

It is often impossible, in these political inquiries, to find any proportion between the apparent force of any moral causes we may assign and their known operation. We are therefore obliged to deliver up that operation to mere chance, or, more piously, (perhaps more rationally,) to the occasional interposition and irresistible hand of the Great Disposer.[12]

According to Burke, the ultimate cause of decisive historical events is God, acting rarely directly, most commonly acting indirectly through the agency of leaders in civil society. Burke saw no conflict between the omnipotence of God in man's temporal events and the freedom of man's will and reason in shaping his historical destiny. Those events which fall within the explanations of empirical observation and rational analysis, "in their proximate efficient cause," are "the arbitrary productions of the human mind." Burke was not an historical determinist; he believed that the "arbitrary" or free will and reason of individual men and of corporate bodies of men acting through institutions determined to a great extent the events and destiny of nations.

Although the ultimate cause of man's historical destiny is in the mind and will of God, the proximate efficient causes are to be found in all the circumstances surrounding the temporal conditions of men, in geography, climate, past history, the inherited laws, customs, habits and basic institutions of a people, their nature, intelligence, temper, energy, feelings, prejudices and interests, their leadership, and their

[11] *Annual Register*, II (1759), 38.
[12] *Works*, V, 235.

state of affairs at a particular time. These are the "internal causes which necessarily affect the fortunes of a state," and even these, Burke noted, "are infinitely uncertain," "obscure," and "difficult to trace." In studying the events and courses of history, Burke believed that the historian should follow the methods of scientific scholarship, and approach history inductively, through a close and thorough examination of the empirical evidence contained in documents and monuments of the past, and through a rational analysis of all the available records. The following two paragraphs, from the "Preface" to the second edition of his *A Philosophical Inquiry into the Origin of Our Ideas of the Sublime and Beautiful* (1757), summarize respectively Burke's historical method and his deep skepticism that men can arrive at ultimate truths through the study of history:

The characters of nature are legible, it is true; but they are not plain enough to enable those who run, to read them. We must make use of a cautious, I had almost said, a timorous method of proceeding. We must not attempt to fly, when we can scarcely pretend to creep. In considering any complex matter, we ought to examine every distinct ingredient in the composition, one by one; and reduce everything to the utmost simplicity; since the condition of our nature binds us to a strict law and very narrow limits. We ought afterwards to re-examine the principles by the effect of the composition, as well as the composition by that of the principles. We ought to compare our subject with things of a similar nature, and even with things of a contrary nature; for discoveries may be, and often are made by the contrast, which would escape us on the single view. The greater number of the comparisons we make, the more general and the more certain our knowledge is likely to prove, as built upon a more extensive and perfect induction.

If an inquiry thus carefully conducted should fail at last of discovering the truth, it may answer an end perhaps as useful, in discovering to us the weakness of our own understanding. If it does not make us knowing, it may make us modest. If it does not preserve us from error, it may at least from the spirit of error; and may make us cautious of pronouncing with positiveness or with haste, when so much labor may end in so much uncertainty.[13]

[13] *Ibid.*, I, 70–71.

Perhaps even more than David Hume, Burke was aware of the uncertainty of man's temporal knowledge, and skeptical that empiricism and reason were sufficient instruments for establishing the causes and effects of truth:

> That great chain of causes, which, linking one to another, even to the throne of God himself, can never be unravelled by any industry of ours. When we go but one step beyond the immediate sensible qualities of things, we go out of our depth. All we do after is but a faint struggle, that shows we are in an element which does not belong to us.[14]

Clearly, Burke was so aware of the unknown and mysterious factors which constantly operate in human affairs that it was impossible for him to have a formula or system or method of procedure to explain fully the temporal affairs of men. In light of these convictions, it is not surprising that Burke had no philosophy of history, and that he was skeptical of all claims that politics was or could ever be an exact science.

Burke's view of history as a reflection of the will and reason of God and man is perhaps most clearly illustrated in his conviction of how sovereign political power is legitimately exercised by each generation under its inherited constitution. Each generation of Englishmen was for Burke not the master of the constitution under which it lived, but its creature at the latest point in history. The sovereignty of constitutional law always supersedes the exercise of present political sovereignty, for present rulers are themselves under the law which they have inherited and administer. Even when their executive or legislative acts depart from past positive laws, they do not so much break precedents as make new precedents for the future. To make the will of the present generation absolute and supreme over the constitution, as Dr. Richard Price, Thomas Paine, and others advocated, was in effect to destroy the constitu-

---

[14] *The Sublime and the Beautiful,* IV, i; *ibid.,* I, 209.

tion and to make the present convenience of each generation the supreme source, test, and end of political power. Burke strongly condemned such an *ad hoc* conception of sovereignty. In the *Reflections* he wrote that "The temporary possessors and life-renters" in the nation, "unmindful of what they have received from their ancestors," invariably become as unmindful "of what is due to their prosperity." History is a preceptor of moral prudence because, among other things, it teaches men reverence for the enduring achievements of mankind, and links the generations of man. Without a sense of man's achievements in history, "the whole chain and continuity of the commonwealth would be broken; no one generation could link with the other; men would become little better than the flies of a summer." [15] When men expunge out of their minds the achievements of their ancestors, in order to rebuild society out of their private speculative theories, they are guilty of an insane kind of pride and arrogance: "I cannot conceive how any man can have brought himself to that pitch of presumption, to consider his country as nothing but *carte blanche,* upon which he may scribble whatever he pleases." [16] Without reverence for history as the embodiment of what God has willed and man has achieved over many centuries, men despise prudence and become fanatical ideologues in their methods of changing society: "Rage and frenzy will pull down more in half an hour than prudence, deliberation, and foresight can build up in a hundred years." [17] By placing a check upon the arbitrary will of men, prudence conserves the best achievements of each generation and transmits them unimpaired to the future through the continuity of history.

Burke did not believe, however, that the "retrospective wisdom" of history should itself ever be made the basis of

[15] *Ibid.,* III, 357.
[16] Reflections, *ibid.,* III, 440.
[17] Reflections, *ibid.,* III, 455.

speculative theory in determining the practical decisions of present politics. History does not provide statesmen with political principles on how to rule in the ever-changing circumstances of the present. Burke believed that statesmen should "enter into the most ample historical detail" of a problem, in order to understand the particulars of practical wisdom. The chief concern of the statesman is the sum total of what constitutes "the business before him," in its particular and inherent character. Historical analogies are of very dubious and limited use as guides in solving current political problems, and metaphysical speculations based upon history were as suspect to Burke as similar speculations based upon abstract philosophy or mathematical logic.

As a preceptor of prudence history taught that politics is the practical art of governing, not a theoretical science. To Burke no pure theory was a sufficient guide in practical politics, because theory as such could never supply the practical wisdom of prudence, and, by making claims for some abstract truth, theory often ignored the particular and contingent in concrete situations, and at times even prevented sound political practice. Burke insisted that not abstract truth but circumstances give "to every political principle its distinguishing colour and discriminating effect." In contrast to knowledge of the general principles of politics, Burke wrote that "The science of constructing a commonwealth, or renovating it, or reforming it, is, like every other experimental science, not to be taught *a priori*." [18]

The distinction between false theory and sound practice in politics was probably even more important to Burke than the appeal to history, because appeals to history were themselves only useful examples of the past habits of political wisdom exercised by men, or of the dire consequences of imprudent actions.

---

[18] Reflections, *ibid.,* III, 311.

Burke's lifelong intense antagonism against rational speculations and "metaphysical" theories of society springs directly from his view of history as a preceptor of moral prudence. In opposing metaphysical abstractions in politics he invariably appealed to history and moral prudence as valid alternatives to the plausible delusions of speculative theorists. Burke denied that through the study of history men could derive any general infallible laws by which to govern society: "But as human affairs and human actions are not of a metaphysical nature, but the subject is concrete, complex, and moral, they cannot be subjected (without exceptions which reduce it almost to nothing) to any certain rule." [19] From this it follows that the leaders of nations cannot possess the means to reach a single remote goal toward which the state moves the nation, because the final goal either does not exist for man, or if it does cannot be known. Since the laws which govern civil society are too complex and mysterious to be known by human reason, no metaphysical or political speculations can supply the formulas or means to shape the state to preconceived ends. Burke illustrates this point by describing how the states of Europe have grown through history:

The states of the Christian world have grown up to their present magnitude in a great length of time and by a great variety of accidents. They have been improved to what we see them with greater or less degree of felicity and skill. Not one of them has been formed upon a regular plan or with any unity of design. As their constitutions are not systematical, they have not been directed to any peculiar end, eminently distinguished, and superseding every other. The objects which they embrace are of the greatest possible variety, and have become in a manner infinite. In all these old countries, the state has been made to the people, and not the people conformed to the state.[20]

---

[19] Report from the Committee of the House of Commons, Appointed to Inspect the Lords' Journal in Relation to Their Proceedings on the Trial of Warren Hastings, Esquire (1794), *ibid.*, XI, 69.

[20] Three Letters to a Member of Parliament on the Proposals for Peace with the Regicide Directory of France, Letter II, *ibid.*, V, 373.

In short, Burke believed that nations are not formed according to any theory; rather, theories are drawn from studying the evident structure of the state. Nations change and grow by at once adhering to the design evident in old establishments, and by alterations made within the inherited structure of laws and customs. These changes are determined by past experience and present necessities, and even by happy chance which improves the design even as it seems to depart from it. Human reason and free will aid the growth of the state by preserving inherited institutions and adjusting them continuously to changing circumstances and needs.

Burke's view of the general continuity of history and of how social changes occur within history is most evident in his statements on the constitutional development of England. The English constitution was not the result of a theory of ideal government, but of a long series of solutions to particular problems and crises, a process that Burke called "working after the pattern of Nature":

> The institutions of policy, the goods of fortune, the gifts of Providence, are handed down to us, and from us, in the same course and order. Our political system is placed in a just correspondence and symmetry with the order of the world, and with the mode of existence decreed to a permanent body composed of transitory parts,—wherein, by the disposition of a stupendous wisdom, moulding together the great mysterious incorporation of the human race, the whole, at one time, is never old or middle-aged or young, but, in a condition of unchangeable constancy, moves on through the varied tenor of perpetual decay, fall, renovation, and progression. Thus, by preserving the method of Nature in the conduct of the state, in what we improve we are never wholly new, in what we retain we are never wholly obsolete.[21]

Through constitutional changes made from generation to generation, the "chain and continuity of the commonwealth" is maintained. The evolved constitution at the furthest

[21] Reflections, *Works,* III, 275.

point in history is "a deliberate election of ages and generations," in harmony with "the peculiar circumstances, occasions, tempers, dispositions, and moral, civil and social habitudes of the people, which disclose themselves only in a long space of time." [22] The changes in the constitution of England not only reflected the corporate character of the English people, but in their direction through history extended to all its citizens the natural and civil rights to life, liberty, and property which were the chief objects of all good government.

From Burke's view of history it should be evident that his political philosophy was not and could not be a speculative science dealing with abstract truth, but that politics was for him the practical art of governing men through moral prudence, and that the state was a moral instrument for giving order, justice, and civil liberty to all its subjects. The politician, by Burke's definition, was "the philosopher in action," and no prudent politician–philosopher could ever assume a priori knowledge of principles that would enable him to attain exact mathematical certainty in the consequences of his decisions. Politics was a part of practical reason, not of theoretical reason; it was concerned with the good, not the true. The nature and actions of men are indeed under general laws of moral necessity, Burke believed, but because the will of man is free to obey or defy the moral law, and because his social circumstances are infinitely varied, in contingent matters and details there can be no general laws of politics. Although justice must always be maintained, the determination of what is just in each particular instance, under the different institutions and conditions of mankind, must always vary in its means, according to the infinite variations of men's temporal circumstances. The common social nature of man is infinitely modified by climate, geography, history, religion, nationality, and race;

---

[22] Speech on a Motion Made in the House of Commons, May 7, 1782, *ibid.,* VII, 95.

by institutions, customs, manners, and habits; by all the civil circumstances of time, place, and occasions, which cut across and qualify, but do not impair, the different means by which the great moral ends of society are fulfilled. Prudence is the principle that links the divine will, as evidenced in the changing patterns of history, with the concrete practical affairs of men. "The progressive sagacity that keeps company with times and occasions," Burke wrote, "and decides upon things in their existing position, is that alone which can give true propriety, grace, and effect to a man's conduct. It is very hard to anticipate the occasion, and to live by a rule more general." Burke's view of history and principle of prudence made his political philosophy as far removed as possible from any theory of politics based on metaphysical speculations applied deductively as an exact science.

To Burke, "no moral questions are ever abstract questions." Prudence was for Burke a moral virtue, not an intellectual virtue, and as such it was the best corrective and positive alternative to the errors of rational metaphysical abstractions in politics:

Nothing universal can be rationally affirmed on any moral or political subject. Pure metaphysical abstraction does not belong to these matters. The lines of morality are not like ideal lines of mathematics. They are broad and deep as well as long. They admit of exceptions; they demand modifications. These exceptions and modifications are not made by the process of logic, but by the rules of prudence. Prudence is not only the first in rank of the virtues political and moral, but she is the director, the regulator, the standard of them all.[23]

Burke always maintained that "the exercise of competent jurisdiction in politics is a matter of moral prudence," be-

[23] An Appeal from the New to the Old Whigs, *ibid.,* IV, 80–81.

cause "moral necessity is not like metaphysical, or even physical." Tyranny was a more common abuse in government than usurpation, Burke believed, because even under legitimate legislatures, "if the rules of benignity and prudence are not observed" oppressive actions would result. Prudence, or a strict regard for circumstances, is not merely a matter of empirical observation and intellectual calculation; it is morally imperative to regard circumstances, because otherwise political action could mortally injure those whom the statesman wishes to serve.

Burke's conception of prudence as a moral virtue is well illustrated in his attempted economical reform of 1780. In his speech (on February 11, 1780), he distinguished between his principle of prudence and mere moral weakness or equivocation:

... it is much more easy to reconcile this measure to humanity, than to bring it to any agreement with prudence. I do not mean that little, selfish, pitiful, bastard thing, which sometimes goes by the name of a family in which it is not legitimate, and to which it is a disgrace—I mean that public and enlarged prudence, which, apprehensive of being disabled from rendering acceptable service to the world, withholds itself from those that are invidious.[24]

Burke's remark, "if I cannot reform with equity I will not reform at all," and his statement, "I am not possessed of an exact measure between real service and its reward," provoked from Jeremy Bentham the sarcastic reply: "Except Edmund Burke, no man is thus ignorant." Bentham's willingness to compute the ratio between public service and its reward illustrates one of the great differences between Burke's principle of prudence and the utilitarian idea of "expediency." To Burke, prudence is the general regulator of social changes, including the reforms of abuses in society, according to the legal norms of the constitution and the moral principles of the natural law. As such, prudence is

[24] *Ibid.*, II, 268–69.

the cardinal political virtue because it supplies the practical means by which natural-law principles are fulfilled in the various concrete circumstances of man's social life. Burke's prudence is not the utilitarian computation of circumstances, an intellectual calculation of how far political power might be utilized before provoking opposition. Nor is Burke's prudence merely the social virtue of tact. To Burke, prudence is part of God's "divine tactic" fulfilled through man's moral temperance and political tact. Prudence is the principle that checks the impetuous will and speculative reason of man by subordinating man's reason and will to the mysterious reason and will of God, as manifested in the unfolding pattern of historical events, and in accordance with revealed normative laws. Understood in this profoundly Aristotelian sense, Burke's principle of prudence is nothing less than the universal, eternal, and unchangeable moral law, applied in a variety of ways in practice through politics to each particular man, at every moment and in all circumstances, under the constitutional sovereignty of various nations. Since "the situation of man is the preceptor of his duty," prudence tells us when we should "abate our demands in favor of moderation and justice, and tenderness to individuals." Prudence is not intellectual calculation, but the moral discretion which enables men to live by the spirit of natural law and constitutional law.

The claim of utilitarian writers that Burke belongs to their political camp has obscured the absolute difference between their conception of utility and his principle of prudence. Burke had a principle of utility, but he was no utilitarian. In the "Tract on the Popery Laws" (1765), Burke indicated that he derived utility from Cicero's principle of moral equity, which was based upon "original justice." It was a utility "connected with and derived directly from our rational nature; for any other utility may be the utility of a robber." [25] Many years later, in his attack

[25] *Ibid.*, VI, 322–23.

on Warren Hastings' "system of corruption," Burke noted the governor's "attempts to justify it on the score of utility," and added, "God forbid that prudence, which is the supreme guide, and indeed stands first of all virtues, should ever be the guide of vices." Burke distinguished carefully between a true and false adherent of moral prudence: "Our love to the occasionalist, but not server of occasions." In any conflict between merely utilitarian convenience and law, his stand was clear: "What the law respects shall be sacred to me. If the barriers of law should be broken down upon ideas of convenience, even of public convenience, we shall have no longer any thing certain among us." When rulers follow true moral prudence they are perfectly in accord with natural law and constitutional law, from which men's true natural and civil rights are derived. Burke believed that when claims to individual "rights" conflicted with moral expediency or prudence, they were not really "rights" —not, as Morley and the utilitarian critics of Burke said, that they were personal rights but had to yield to public expediency.

Late in life Lord Acton came to interpret Burke as a utilitarian, and charged that "Burke loved to evade the arbitration of principle." Burke did indeed refuse often to engage in speculative theories of a metaphysical nature, particularly when such theories contributed nothing but heat toward the solution of a practical political problem which did not require an appeal to ultimate moral principles. But apart from Acton's failure to distinguish between principles or political policy, which are subject to arbitration, and basic moral principles, which are beyond arbitration, Burke's whole practical political career is the best answer to Acton's misinterpretation. Burke's loyalty to the Rockingham Whigs, and his moral and intellectual guidance of Whig policies for almost three decades, in the face of strong administrative opposition, is but one sustained instance of his deep personal integrity. He gave up his seat for Bristol rather than support an iniquitous economic and religious policy against Ireland. For years after most of his colleagues would have liked to have quietly dropped Hastings' trial, Burke made himself unpopular because of the moral zeal with which he pursued a just decision for India. He broke lifelong friendships and stood alone for several years, rather than give approval of the French Revolution. Goldsmith's famous line is literally true: Burke was "too fond of the right to pursue the expedient." Because of his refusal to be bought by the crown, Burke spent most of his political life with the loyal opposition. All these factors in Burke's political life show that neither in practice nor in theory did his principle of prudence cause him "to evade the arbitration of principle." Acton should have read Burke more carefully than to identify his principle of prudence with the calculated expediency of utilitarian self-interest.

Burke once described prudence as "the god of this lower world." Professor Leo Strauss has wisely seen fit to note that "Prudence and 'this lower world' cannot be seen properly without some knowledge of 'the higher world'—without genuine *Theorie*." [26] Religion and the natural law were for Burke the basis of his moral principles in the higher world of political philosophy, just as English common law supplied the legal principles for his politics. As a practical means of applying the principles of natural law in "this lower world" of civil society, prudence was supreme, because only through prudence could statesmen give full regard to men's differences, have reverence for local loyalties, and take into account all the circumstances involved in a problem. Through the ethical norms of natural law and the legal norms of the common law and political prudence, Burke united ethics, law, and politics within a vast framework that included religious mysticism concerning the divine intent in human history, and the immediate desires, needs, and objectives of men in their concrete practical

[26] *Natural Right and History* (Chicago, 1953), 321.

affairs. Burke's ability to combine the natural law and prudence made his political philosophy thoroughly consistent, yet almost wholly unsystematic. Religion, the natural law, English common law, and prudence, all operating together in history, enabled Burke to fuse to the limit of their valance the most sublime moral precepts and the most concrete empirical facts, details and circumstances, so that political theory and practice were one: "A statesman," wrote Burke, "never losing sight of principles, is to be guided by circumstances; and judging contrary to the exigencies of the moment he may ruin his country for ever." This is the key statement behind Burke's definition of the politician as "a philosopher in action." As a philosopher, Burke drew his ethical principles from religion and the natural law; as a politician, he applied his principles in the concrete, with a full regard to historical circumstances, through his principle of moral prudence.

For Burke, history is "the preceptor of prudence" because it reveals "the known march of the ordinary providence of God." History was for Burke a secondary form of divine revelation, supplementing Scripture and the "right reason" of the natural law. History taught practical ethics, not directly through moral principles, but indirectly, by inculcating the spirit of morality through temperance and moderation: "Our physical well-being, our moral worth, our social happiness, our political tranquillity, all depend on that control of our appetites and passions, which the ancients designated by the cardinal virtue of Temperance." Burke believed that "the restraints on men are to be reckoned among their rights." In civil society, the moral law alone was insufficient to restrain the passions of men. The most immediate restraints on men come from the established institutions and legal processes of society, regardless of its political structure. In every just social order, sound ethical norms are embodied in its established laws and institutions, so that in ordinary cases, within "the ordinary providence of God" which constitutes the historical process, society provided the practical means of solving its political problems by political and legal norms, in harmony with the moral law. Since for Burke "the actual and the present is the rational," prudence was a sufficient guide in the ordinary political problems of men. It was not necessary to appeal to transcendental moral standards in every political conflict; such appeals were reserved for extraordinary violations of the moral law, as in the cases of British misrule in Ireland and India, and the Jacobin tyranny in France. But for "the ordinary providence of God" which constitutes human affairs in history, prudence is indeed "the god of this lower world."

5

# The British Career of a New York Federalist

## JOSEPH F. X. McCARTHY

IN THE SWIRLING POLITICAL CURRENTS that accompanied the rupture of the British Empire and the establishment of American independence, few individuals underwent more sudden and dramatic changes in role than did Henry Cruger, Junior. He entered the New York State Senate as a Federalist in 1792, only two years after he had relinquished a seat in the House of Commons, where he had been distinguished as one of the two American-born Members of Parliament sitting during the years of the Revolutionary War.[1]

The Crugers had been a prominent New York family throughout the eighteenth century, and had achieved equal distinction in provincial politics and commerce. The first John Cruger in New York, grandfather of the Member of Parliament, entered the Common Council of the city as early as 1712.[2] Members of the Cruger family held influential

---

[1] Cruger's status as an American-born M.P. has drawn occasional attention in such works as H. C. Van Schaack, *Henry Cruger, the Colleague of Edmund Burke in the British Parliament* (New York, 1859), and Lewis Einstein, *Divided Loyalties* (London, 1933), 245–66.

[2] William Smith, *The History of the Late Province of New-York* (New York, 1830), 190

posts in the city and in the provincial government of New York continuously from 1712 to the outbreak of the Revolutionary War, supporting their political position—or vice versa—through the conduct of an extensive export–import business which was based in New York, but which included correspondents in various Caribbean and European locations.[3]

Henry Cruger Junior was the second son of his father, and was selected for an important family duty, representing its interests in Britain. The New York affairs were handled by his father and his uncle, the second John Cruger, while his elder brother was given a business apprenticeship in Jamaica before joining the elder Crugers in New York commerce. Henry Cruger Junior, after a period as a member of the first class to study at King's College, turned to business affairs also.[4] In 1757, at the age of only eighteen, he left New York to take up residence and business in Bristol.[5]

As the principal British correspondent of his family business, Cruger had an excellent foundation for his own Bristol business, which expanded to include trans-Atlantic trade, not only with New York merchants, but with business connections in New England and the West Indies as well. The Cruger family followed a similar pattern with each of the younger Cruger brothers of the revolutionary generation: Nicholas Cruger became a merchant and landholder in St. Croix, and Telemon Cruger established himself in Curaçao.[6] As a result, the family possessed a network of intercon-

[3] Cf. Bentley Hassell, *The Cruger Family in America* (New York, 1892) and the typescript copy of family Bible of Henry Cruger, Sr., in New York Genealogical and Biographical Society Library.

[4] Thomas Jones, *History of New York During the Revolutionary War* (New York, 1879), I, 417.

[5] A Cruger connection with Bristol existed prior to the arrival of Henry Cruger Junior. It is asserted that the young man arrived in 1757 to take over his family's office in Bristol by Bryan Little, *The City and County of Bristol: A Study in Atlantic Civilization* (London, 1954), 177.

[6] Evidence of the interconnections among the Cruger houses can be seen in the Waste Book of Henry and John Cruger, Manuscript Collection, New-York Historical Society.

nected, independent, but mutually supporting houses, located in New York, Britain, and the West Indies—three corners of a highly lucrative North Atlantic "triangular trade."

Henry Cruger Junior gave every indication that he regarded Bristol as his permanent home. He became a freeman of the city shortly after arrival,[7] and soon thereafter joined the Merchant Venturers, an organization of Bristol businessmen engaged in overseas trade.[8] Baptized an Anglican, the former student at King's College became not only an active communicant in Bristol, but a warden of the church of St. Augustine-the-Less. In 1770, he indicated his interest in the parish by the very substantial gift to it of a new organ.[9]

Cruger's social position in Bristol was solidified by marriage, in 1760, to Hannah Peach, daughter of one of Bristol's wealthiest men. Samuel Peach had a background as a slave trader, but was best known as a linen draper and banker. The Cruger–Peach connection was one of the most important in Cruger's active career. Despite the early death of Hannah Peach Cruger, the elder Peach remained a close political and business ally of his son-in-law; a dramatic indication of the connection is the fact that Cruger's eldest son assumed the family name "Peach," and inherited his grandfather's extensive possessions.[10]

Cruger first became prominent in Bristol, not because of his connection with the Peach interests, but because of his personal and business identification with America. The Stamp Act controversy created a crisis in Bristol, and in this crisis the American-born Cruger emerged as a leader

[7] G. E. Weare, *Edmund Burke's Connection With Bristol* (Bristol, 1894), I

[8] John Latimer, *History of the Society of Merchant Venturers* (Bristol, 1903), Appendix.

[9] Churchwarden's Account Book, Church of St. Augustine-the-Less, Bristol, 1728–92.

[10] Hassell.

of opinion. In 1766 the Merchant Venturers dramatized Bristol's opposition to the Stamp Act, and became one of the many organizations in Britain that petitioned Parliament for the repeal of the act. Cruger was selected as one of the two members of this association deputized to present the petition to Commons, and on his return shared the honors at a public testimonial dinner.[11]

Political prominence followed rapidly for the expatriate New Yorker. He was selected sheriff in 1766, and that same year was designated a life member of the Corporation of the City, in effect an aldermanic position.[12] Further honors from the Merchant Venturers attest to his continued prominence, for in 1768 he was elected one of the two "wardens" of that organization.[13]

Despite the growing public role he assumed, Cruger must have undergone difficult days in his business during the Stamp Act crisis. His business was largely dependent on exporting British manufactured goods and textiles to America and on placing insurance on these and other shipments, including those of his American correspondents; the import phase of his business involved direct imports on his own accounts, and the commission sale of consignments from America: tropical produce from the West Indies; lumber, foodstuffs, iron, and even complete vessels produced in the mainland colonies.[14] When American merchants, for patriotic or personal reasons, cut off payments to England as a protest against the Stamp Act, Henry

[11] C. M. MacInnes, *A Gateway of Empire* (Bristol, 1939), 273.
[12] John Corry, *The History of Bristol, Civil and Ecclesiastical* (Bristol, 1816), I, 4–5 and 10.
[13] Latimer, 197 and Appendix.
[14] Evidence of Cruger's trading activity is drawn from the Bristol Presentments, manuscript volumes of export–import information; the Waste Book of Henry and John Cruger in New-York Historical Society; and widely scattered individual commercial papers. The most useful published source is devoted to parts of Aaron Lopez' commercial records published as *The Commerce of Rhode Island*, W. C. Ford, ed. *Collections*, Massachusetts Historical Society, Seventh Series, IX; this work must be supplemented by the Letter Books of Aaron Lopez in the Newport Historical Society Library.

Cruger Junior found himself in an extremely precarious position: he had virtually uncollectable credits from American correspondents on his books, but his own accounts showed him with considerable debts to British suppliers who were close at hand to insist on payments.

In this crisis, the family connection of the Crugers came to his rescue. Bills of exchange belonging to his relatives went to Bristol for collection and remission, thus providing a temporary cover for his British accounts. This gesture gains impact when it is considered that such bills served virtually as currency in America. A more direct aid was extended by the New York members of the family. Aaron Lopez, a prominent merchant–speculator of Newport, R.I., was deeply in debt to Henry Cruger Junior. When a Lopez ship arrived in New York, it was simply attached by the New York Crugers, who sold it and its cargo, remitting the proceeds to their Bristol relative. The hapless Lopez could hardly argue: he was swamped in debts to Cruger, and the New York members of the family who helped him wash out the debts were in positions of impregnable power. Uncle John Cruger was Speaker of the New York Assembly; father Henry Cruger was a member of the Governor's Council; and elder brother John Harris Cruger was Chamberlain (principal tax collector) for the City of New York. As a matter of fact, relations between Lopez and Cruger remained reasonably cordial despite the liquidation activity.[15] This financial crisis and the unusual means taken

[15] Lopez, a prime factor in the spermaceti trade and in general one of Rhode Island's chief merchants, had been a correspondent of the Cruger house in New York before beginning trade with Henry Cruger Jr. He had insisted on the senior Cruger's guarantee of his son's performance of orders, and on the right to draw against proceeds of shipments immediately after sending them to England. In the crisis of the Stamp Act period, Lopez overdrew his accounts with Bristol, and found himself near bankruptcy; the elder Crugers not only liquidated his ship in New York, but through their Jamaica and St. Croix connections assisted him in becoming solvent once more and continuing in business: the West Indian houses had access to specie badly needed in Rhode Island and New York.

by the Cruger family to solve it provided an object lesson on the need for a reliable system of credit and debt collection—both to become vital parts in later Federalist politics.

The years following repeal of the Stamp Act were not marked by peaceful consensus in British politics. Parliamentary opposition had been reduced to dangerously ineffective levels, and the experience of successful moves out-of-doors by means of petitions against the Stamp Act led to other instances of public discontent in British cities and towns. The controversy surrounding the Middlesex election of John Wilkes, and the action of the House of Commons in excluding him from a seat became the *cause célèbre* and the touchstone of anti-government activity.[16]

Protest meetings were held in many parts of England, protesting the exclusion of Wilkes and proclaiming the rights of electors. Wilkes had become the symbol of the rights of electors to be represented by men of their own choosing, which was a matter of opposition to the government on which most factions could agree; he was also a symbol of the most extreme political ideas of the day, and a rallying point for Britain's radicals. Thus, the protest meetings in the Wilkes affair drew together both those who opposed the government's policies as a matter of principle, and those who would advance radical notions of government itself. Because of its status as Britain's second city, Bristol's protest meeting was an especially important one: rumors were spread that participants in a pro-Wilkes meeting might be summoned to Westminster, to the bar of the House of Commons, and jailed for contempt. Defying such real or imagined threats, there was a large meeting in Bristol in support of Wilkes; it was held at the Guildhall,

---

[16] The question of seating Wilkes was tied very closely to opposition to the Government in Commons; supporters of both Chatham and Rockingham spoke for Wilkes' seating, the principal proponents being Sir George Savile and Sir William Meredith.

and presiding at it was the American-born Bristol merchant, Henry Cruger Junior.[17]

Cruger's political position in Bristol became even more prominent in 1769, when the Guildhall was the setting for a meeting of Bristol's discontented merchants. Richard Champion and Joseph Harford, later to be among Edmund Burke's chief friends in the city, took part in the meeting, as did Cruger and his father-in-law Samuel Peach. The assemblage voiced discontent with the way in which Bristol's two Members of Parliament were behaving, and a petition was prepared, addressing to them the viewpoint that Members should follow the wishes and directions of their constituents. This concept of "instructing" Members was at the time one of the more radical notions in British politics; it became a major interest of the "Independent Society" established in the aftermath of the 1769 Guildhall meeting as a new organization in Bristol politics. Two of the founding members, and prominently active participants in the Independent Society, were Samuel Peach and Henry Cruger.[18]

The work of the Independent Society centered on developing and pushing the petition to the sitting Members for Bristol, Lord Clare and Matthew Brickdale. Peach himself was the principal proponent of the petition, and a considerable number of signatures were secured by his personal solicitation; eventually fifteen-hundred Bristol signatures were collected. At the same time, Cruger appears to have been forming opinions about the political prospects of the Members. In one of his long friendly letters to Major Horatio Gates (later the American hero at Saratoga), Cruger made both an observation and what might well become a campaign slogan: "Our member B——— loses ground in ye estimation of the generality of his Constituents.

[17] John Latimer, *Annals of Bristol in the Eighteenth Century* (Bristol, 1893), 391.
[18] Weare, 15.

We lament his Want of Spirit, to supply his Want of Knowledge." [19]

The politics of reform, or at least of dissent, continued to enlist the attention and interest of Henry Cruger Junior. Together with his father-in-law and Sir William Codrington, Cruger formed a committee to invite Wilkes to a great reception in Bristol. At the Bristol testimonial dinner for Wilkes, given on January 2, 1772, Cruger was once again prominent as a major sponsor of the event.[20] His connections with prominent dissenters were not merely political: one of his favorite drinking companions during the years after his first wife's death was Col. Isaac Barré, and, as noted above, Horatio Gates was an intimate and concerned correspondent.[21]

By the early 1770s, the Cruger business had expanded sufficiently to warrant its conversion into a partnership. John Mallard, his longtime clerk, was taken into the business, probably at least in part to release more Cruger time for political activity.[22] In an effort to consolidate his connections with American merchants, Cruger made an extensive visit to America during 1773 and 1774, spending considerable time in his home town of New York, and visiting Boston, Philadelphia, and Portsmouth as well.

Parliamentary elections were drawing near by the time Cruger returned to Bristol. The old "joint interest" which resulted in uncontested elections and the return of one nominal Whig and one presumed Tory for Bristol was certain to be challenged by the well-connected Cruger, and

---

[19] Cruger to Gates, Nov. 3, 1769, Gates Papers, Box 7, 210, New-York Historical Society.

[20] P. T. Underdown, "Henry Cruger and Edmund Burke," *William and Mary Quarterly*, Third Series, XV (Jan. 1958), 16.

[21] Cruger to Gates, July 6, 1770, Gates Papers, Box 3, 46, New-York Historical Society.

[22] Broadside, July 1, 1770, New-York Historical Society.

at least some of Cruger's friends had considered it wise to put forward two condidates in opposition to Clare and Brickdale, the two incumbents, whose "interest" seemed to be crumbling. Dr. Wilson had in fact already made overtures to Edmund Burke, and there can be little doubt that Wilson represented at least part of the Crugerite interests in Bristol.

It is interesting to consider the description Wilson offered to Burke of the local candidate, Henry Cruger. In his first letter to Burke, Wilson described the candidate to be offered by the Bristol opposition as a man "who certainly has a very great influence and a large family connexion, and a man of spirit and understanding in commercial affairs." [23] In the following letter, written a day after Cruger had called on Wilson while enroute to London, Wilson identified his candidate by name, adding that he had no question of Cruger's carrying the election, and that Burke could "confide in his secrecy, honour, and integrity." [24] A somewhat more complete description was provided by Richard Champion, who was not a member of the group for which Wilson had approached Burke:

> He [Cruger] is a Merchant of the first Consequence here. A generous good natured man but one that has not only given himself a loose in the youthful follies of life but has at the same time preserved no appearances. This in a City whose Inhabitants devoted chiefly to trade have a severe case of manners has subjected him to great Disadvantages. He is besides Young and being only on a par with the other Merchants of the town a great degree of envy has arose.[25]

Cruger was not especially anxious to take part in a four-cornered election contest. He approached the 1774 election from a position of strength, with his own election considered virtually certain by both Wilson and Champion, a man of

[23] Wilson to Burke, June 26, 1774, *The Works and Correspondence of the Right Honourable Edmund Burke* (London, 1852), I, 231–32.
[24] Wilson to Burke, July 11, 1774, *ibid.*, I, 233.
[25] Champion to Burke, Oct. 1, 1774, Champion Letter Book, New York Public Library.

obviously different tastes and acquaintances. In view of his own strength and the high expense of a contested election, it is easy to understand Cruger's reluctance to encourage the entry of another candidate, even one so eminent as Burke. However, Cruger sought out Burke shortly after he returned to England from his American journey, perhaps as much on New York business as in search of a joint interest in the Bristol election. In his letter suggesting a meeting, Cruger's tone was friendly, but reserved and noncommittal on the question of the election; by contrast, the opening of his letter, dealing with New York affairs, seems considerably more cordial.

Dear Sir:

On my arrival last week at Bristol I had the pleasure of forwarding to you a letter from the Committee of Correspondence at New York. I hope it got safe to your hands. Those gentlemen were desirous of my having a little Conversation with you on the subject of American Affairs, but really, Sir, I do not know what more can be said on that head of sufficient Consequence to put you to the least inconvenience. I must confess, however, I should be extremely glad myself to see You, purely for the satisfaction & honor of a personal Acquaintance with you, having long admired & respected the Character of Mr. Burke.

Pray Sir, do you expect to be in London soon, and if so, when will be the earliest day? If you do not come to town before Friday s'ennight, I will wait upon you (for an hour) that Day on my return to Bristol. In the interim, I shall be much obliged to you to favor me with a line directed to French & Hobson's, London.

Dr. Wilson intimated a desire, that *if* I should be happy enough to meet you I would say a few Words on the Subject of the late letters that have passed between you & him—

I have the Pleasure to remain with respectfull Regard—

    Sir, your most ob't Hble St.

        HEN. CRUGER[26]

[26] Cruger to Burke, July 13, 1774, Wentworth–Fitzwilliam MSS, Bk 332, Sheffield Central Library.

There was no solid political commitment of cooperation as a result of the brief meeting between Cruger and Burke. In fact, when the opposition Whigs held their meeting at Bristol's Guildhall, the suggestion that Burke's name should be endorsed was shouted down by cries of "Cruger only!"

The story of the 1774 election campaign has been told in detail by both G. E. Weare and more recently by P. T. Underdown.[27] Both writers have demonstrated that, even after Lord Clare withdrew as a candidate for re-election, and Burke entered as a candidate, there was not a unified Cruger–Burke campaign, but rather two Whig campaigns aimed at winning the two seats separately. Events at Bristol were highly distasteful to Government, for the doom of Clare's candidacy apparently came as a surprise. Lord North described the situation to King George III as "The worst news that has been received today . . . that Lord Clare has declined the Poll of Bristol, & made room for a hot Wilkite & American Patriot, Mr. Cruger. . . ."[28] The chief contribution of Cruger's supporters to the Burke campaign seems to have been the fact that some of their second votes were cast to Burke's credit; even so, 895 Cruger supporters did not do so, and Cruger's margin over Burke was 858 votes. In a hot and bitter contest, Burke came in second, thereby winning Bristol's second seat and retiring Matthew Brickdale to private life.[29]

At the conclusion of the poll, both candidates followed the custom of addressing their constituents. Cruger, speaking first, took the occasion to point out the "legality and propriety of the people's instructing their representatives

[27] In addition to the works cited by these two authors, Underdown covered the field of the 1774 election and its political antecedents in the unpublished Ph. D. thesis, "Edmund Burke as Member of Parliament for Bristol, 1774–1780" (University of London, 1954).

[28] No. 1518, North to George III, Sept. 1774, John Fortescue, *The Correspondence of King George III from 1760 to December 1783* (6 vols. London, 1927–28), III, 137.

[29] *The Bristol Poll Book* (Bristol, 1775).

in Parliament." [30] Cruger's remark was chiefly notable for the fact that it gave Burke the occasion for one of his most widely quoted public speeches, on the nature and functions of representatives in Parliament.[31] This public difference between the newly elected colleagues obscured three other points made by Cruger: first, that he intended to do all he could to conciliate the differences between Britain and the colonies; second, that he would use his position to work for Bristol's local interests; and third, that he took pride in being simply a "merchant" and "honest man," "as uninfluenced as unsupported by great men." [32]

The aftermath of the election provided a certain amount of insight into the proceedings themselves. Brickdale, of course, challenged the entire election. He tried to have Burke's election set aside because Burke had not been a candidate when the polls opened; Brickdale's petition was aimed also at overturning both elections (Cruger's and Burke's) on the ground of corrupt practices in purchasing the freedom of Bristol for well-disposed but impecunious residents. Champion approached Mallard about the possibility of a joint defense against the charges, but the defenses were conducted like the election—separately. In reporting his negotiation to Burke, Champion noted that Mallard had admitted providing purchase money for "freedoms" to new voters and added, drily, "The Relation, had I been Mallard, I would have kept as quiet as possible . . . with respect to us, I am certain he is wrong and indeed know nothing about the matter." [33]

Arrived in the capital, however, Cruger seemed anxious to cultivate Burke, and even asked his new colleague for an introduction to the Marquess of Rockingham, which Burke could easily have arranged. Burke refused to do so, on the

---
[30] Weare, 79.
[31] *Works and Correspondence of Edmund Burke*, III, 235–36.
[32] Weare, 79.
[33] Champion to Burke, Nov. 28, 1774, Champion Letter Book.

grounds that Cruger had given no indication of supporting the principles of the Rockingham Whigs, and that such an introduction to a party leader was usually arranged only after a pledge of support from the new member. Cruger then requested that Burke escort him into Commons and introduce him, a gesture that Burke also declined to provide, for he thought it a novel and unusual procedure. Furious at these rebuffs, Cruger had himself escorted into Commons by Sir William Meredith, Member for Liverpool, and an erstwhile supporter of the Rockingham group who by 1774 was acting consistently with government.[34]

Cruger had apparently made up his mind neither to antagonize nor to support the North ministry very enthusiastically. Writing to his kinsman Peter Van Schaack, he indicated that he would try to impress North with his maiden speech, especially since someone had already persuaded North that he was "all gunpowder." In the same note, Cruger commented, "I shall not oppose government for *the sake* of opposition, but will join Lord North whenever I think him right." He added that he planned his maiden speech to be both "moderate and modest."[35]

The maiden speech hardly measured up to his expectations. Already a curiosity because of his American birth, he chose the debate on Army estimates to read Parliament a lecture on American affairs on December 16, 1774. After praising the American love of liberty, and describing the good relations that existed between colonies and mother

[34] Meredith had several points of contact with Cruger; like Cruger, he had been prominent in support of Wilkes' seat in Commons; like Cruger he sat for a prominent commercial city, and during the 1774-80 session they acted together in opposition to liberalizing trade restrictions on Ireland, receiving jointly the thanks of Liverpool merchants. Meredith, who had for some time earlier acted with the Rockingham Whigs, became a royal placeman as Comptroller of the Household and a Privy Councillor in 1774. Burke's explanation of the events surrounding Cruger's entry into Commons is found in his letter to Champion of Jan. 5, 1775 in the Champion Letter Book, New York Public Library.

[35] Henry C. Van Schaack, *The Life of Peter Van Schaack* (New York, 1842), 31.

country before the Stamp Act, Cruger turned to the matter of imprudent legislation concerning the colonies since that unfortunate turn of events. He took the position that most Americans would accept parliamentary supremacy, but that the key problem facing Commons was a constitutional one, to be worked out before passing any new laws. As to the government he was trying to impress, Cruger described North as a capable minister who simply had poor judgment in American affairs: "Though an American, I applaud his jealousy for the dignity of Parliament, and think the impolicy and inexpediency of the late measures may reasonably be imputed to the difficulty of the occasion, and the unsettled and undefined nature of the dependence of the colonies on the mother country." [36] There was no indication that North's opinion of the new Member for Bristol changed appreciably: government censors still copied Cruger's personal correspondence for study, and Cruger was complaining to Van Schaack a month later that he could get no information about the Privy Council, for he had no connection with government.[37]

If Cruger's standing with either the ministry or its principal opposition was in doubt in 1774, there was little question about his status with his New York relatives. His support and good offices were sought by Governor William Tryon, about to re-embark for his shaky government in New York. Cruger wrote with a tone of unmistakable authority to his father, uncle, and elder brother about this meeting, and even added a postscript to one document containing political intelligence bearing on New York, questioning whether the De Lanceys, apparently New York's leading political family and the group with whom the Crugers acted, should be informed of his advice from England.[38]

---

[36] *The Parliamentary History of England,* XVIII, 67.
[37] Van Schaack, 43.
[38] Manuscripts of the Earl of Dartmouth, II, #1244, Stafford, William Salt Library.

Cruger's Americanism left him in a very isolated position early in 1775. He tried to pressure Edmund Burke to act more forcefully in an effort to get the Remonstrance from New York accepted by Commons as a basis for peaceful relations between America and Britain. His vitriolic analysis of Burke as "crafty . . . selfish . . . cunning" ended with the bitter remark, "May such deep Jesuits soon die." Although intended for Van Schaack's eye, it must have provided interesting political intelligence for government, whose spies dutifully transcribed it for Lord Dartmouth and posterity.[39]

Equally bitter expressions used in Commons led to Cruger's being silenced by the Speaker during a Commons debate. One Major Grant had insinuated that the Americans would not, indeed could not, put up a serious fight against the British, and Cruger railed at Grant and became personal in attacking the major while defending the valor of Americans.[40] The question of conciliation with Americans occupied the center of Cruger's remaining public speeches, although he engaged in a good deal of work in behalf of Bristol commercial and local interests during sessions. In 1776, Cruger faced a hostile house to warn that victory in the war would itself be ruinous because of the bitterness engendered by the quarrel: he argued that liberty-loving Americans had been driven into revolution by Britain's refusal to accept their remonstrances, but that it was still possible to settle the war by negotiation.[41]

Cruger's last major speech during his first term in Commons was brought about by discussions of British reversals in the war. In this 1780 address, Cruger again reminded the house of the New York Remonstrance, which he still regarded as a basis for peace negotiations. He pointed out that the war had not been prosecuted effectively, merely

[39] *Ibid.*, II, #296.
[40] *Parliamentary History*, XVIII, 227-28.
[41] *Ibid.*, 1148-54.

brutally; and that British arms had subdued, not the American army, but the remnants of American affection for Britain. His remarks about the "barren and useless" war effort must have removed any doubts as to his political future, if government could control it.[42]

Cruger's private correspondence and his behavior out of the public eye, however, indicate that there was another side to his interest in the American Revolution. Charles Jenkinson, generally regarded as one of the confidants of George III, seems an unlikely partner or correspondent for an outspoken critic of royal policies. Yet there is evidence that Cruger did correspond with Jenkinson, passing on to him certain documents that Cruger had received from American correspondents. The earliest such transmittal to survive in the Liverpool Papers is covered by a note from Cruger in which he remarks that "You have been peculiarly obliging to me. I am sensibly grateful." [43] On another occasion, he transmitted a letter from his "intelligent agent" with the comment that it was "agreeably to my promise & your permission." [44] Examination of extracts from the enclosures, and a third document presumably from 1778,[45] indicates that the information transmitted to Jenkinson—and presumably therefore to the government—included economic intelligence, dealing primarily with the impact of the war on the price structure in America and with the currency crisis brought on by the issuance of continental paper money; and with political intelligence, dealing primarily with the morale of Americans and the viewpoints of Loyalists in the New York area.

It may be argued that the intelligence contained in the extant letters is of a minor nature, and quite probably could have been had from other sources in Britain. It may

[42] *Ibid.*, XXI, 579.
[43] Cruger to Jenkinson, May 11, 1777, Liverpool Papers, Brit. Mus. Add. MSS 38,209, F. 120.
[44] Cruger to Jenkinson, June 8, 1778, *ibid.*, 38,210, F. 59.
[45] "Extract of a Letter rec'd from Mr. Cruger," *ibid.*, 38,209, F. 178.

also be that Cruger transmitted those documents in an effort to protect his own and his family's business interests, for questions of price control and currency valuations were involved; quite possibly, too, they represented on a personal level the split that the Cruger family itself was experiencing, with sympathies on both sides: the elder Cruger brother, John Harris Cruger, was a Loyalist officer, while at least one of the younger brothers, Nicholas Cruger, was affiliated with the American cause. It seems unlikely, in any case, that the Jenkinson correspondence is totally divorced from a £500 pension to Mr. Cruger that was extinguished when he went out of Parliament.[46]

As the war continued in America, Henry Cruger's influence in Bristol suffered a marked decline. His public position was odd: an American by his own description as much as by his opponents' charges, he marked his place in Commons not so much as a spokesman for Bristol as for New York. While Cruger's business slipped badly during the wartime crisis of Atlantic commerce, his Bristol foes drew financial strength from the government itself, which poured a thousand pounds into an effort to remove the American from Parliament.[47] The fact that Cruger had hoped to avert the war, and that he had clearly traced the dangers in attempting a military solution to the imperial crisis, was of little help in Bristol in 1780, when patriotism became an anti-Cruger campaign weapon.

The mercantile interests that had supported Whig candidates in 1774 had seen their profits disappear as the war

[46] W. T. Laprade, ed., *The Parliamentary Papers of John Robinson, 1774–1784* (London, 1922), 50.
[47] Cruger himself stayed successfully in business during the war, but his partner Mallard went bankrupt. The government, meanwhile, spent in addition to £1,000 in the actual election, a total of at least £6,500 between 1774 and 1780 to support anti-Cruger (and anti-Burke) candidates. Laprade, 37 and 75.

continued. Moreover, the split between Cruger and Burke had been dramatized by their respective factions among the Whigs, so that by 1780 there was no possibility of a united Whig interest. Burke recognized the situation as an impossible and expensive one, and withdrew from the hopeless contest, citing Whig disunity as his chief reason. Cruger, on the other hand, faced two candidates alone until it became perfectly obvious that over a thousand Whigs would not appear at the polls to vote for him.[48]

The excitement of the 1780 election had scarcely ended before a by-election became necessary on the death of the new Member, Sir Henry Lippencott. This by-election of 1781 pitted Cruger against George Daubeny, and was one of the most unpleasant in Bristol's history. Actual bloodshed resulted when a swivel gun aboard one of the ships in the harbor was turned on a pro-Cruger crowd on the waterfront.[49] Crugerites attacked Daubeny's French ancestry, his remarks favoring an absolute maximum wage for workers, and his desire for an uncontested election that would have deprived Bristol's electorate of an exciting activity. Daubeny's friends continued the 1780 program of referring to "Doodle-Ooo" Cruger as a "Yankee" and a "Compromiser." The same combination of interests that had defeated him in 1780 left Cruger in 1781 as a private citizen with leisure to rebuild his diminished business.[50]

His status as a defeated foe of government did not keep Cruger from turning once more to his correspondent Jenkinson. The occasion was the military career of his elder brother John Harris Cruger, whose defence of Ninety–Six had given the royal forces one of their few moments of glory in the 1781 campaigns. Henry Cruger drew Jenkinson's attention to these exploits, and with great candor

---

[48] Election Broadsides, Bristol Public Library, 1774–90, and Einstein, 260–61.
[49] Latimer, *Annals of Bristol*, 447.
[50] Election Broadsides, Bristol Public Library, 1774–90.

asked Jenkinson to arrange for a royal reward in these words: "I hope I may, without offence, remind Mr. Jenkinson that it is more Common for his Majesty to reward, than to overlook, such distinguished merit." [51] The request was fruitless, for Jenkinson pointed out that such requests could not be made by him, but by Lord George Germaine.[52] However, the fact that so direct an intercession by one brother was made for another indicates the continuing strong family loyalty that marked the Crugers.

Business and political power in Bristol were replenished during the next few years. During 1781, the hard core of Cruger's support in Bristol itself re-emerged, and he was elected both Mayor of Bristol and Master of the Merchant Venturers.[53] A second office of the Cruger firm opened in London, and as soon as military affairs in North America seemed to have been concluded, Henry Cruger was off on an extended business trip to his homeland. On this trip, he sought both to re-establish his own contacts with former customers, and to look into Cruger family business interests in New York. He solicited new and old American business, stressing his speeches in Commons as a spokesman for American liberty, interests, honor, and courage.[54]

While still in America, Henry Cruger was re-elected to Parliament in the general election of 1784. It is morally certain that he never stopped campaigning after the 1780 election, and the Whigs in Bristol no longer had a serious Burke question on which to split. Further, Cruger's attitude toward conciliation with America was no longer anathema. Perhaps his chief asset in the campaign was his brother

---

[51] Cruger to Jenkinson, Oct. 31, 1781, Liverpool Papers, Add. MSS 38,217, F. 108.
[52] Jenkinson to Cruger, Nov. 5, 1781, *ibid.,* 38,308, F. 195.
[53] Latimer, *Merchant Venturers,* 197.
[54] Henry C. Van Schaack, *Memoirs of the Life of Henry Van Schaack* (Chicago, 1892), 99–100. An example of Cruger's fence-mending epistles can be seen in his letter to John Hancock, Mar. 1783, *New England Historical and Genealogical Register,* XXVIII (Jan. 1874), 52.

John Harris Cruger; that gallant and personable officer was on hand as the candidate's representative, and supplied a crushing response to attacks on Cruger's British patriotism; Colonel Cruger was one of a very few genuine war heroes produced on the British side by British America.[55]

Henry Cruger's actions during his second term were less prominent than those of his first term as a Member of Parliament. His time was chiefly devoted to the local interests of Bristol's businesses, and in only one instance did this interest impinge on a major issue in Commons. The beginnings of the movement to abolish the slave trade elicited a strong response from Bristol, one of the principal centers for that traffic in human misery. As the Member for Bristol, representing merchants who had supported him, like Samuel Peach, as well as those who had opposed him, like George Daubeny, Cruger took the floor to oppose the unequivocal abolition of the slave trade.

During debate on Wilberforce's resolutions to terminate the slave trade, Cruger rose to defend the commerce against charges that it was unduly cruel and oppressive: "from his own knowledge, and the evidence which would be laid before the House, he could venture to pronounce the picture over-charged." He pointed out that any such abolition would be economically disastrous to those active in that branch of commerce, and of honor presumably to the whole country on humanitarian grounds (which he questioned as well); from this, Cruger deduced that the country as a whole should compensate its merchants whose business would be destroyed by an action taken for the good of the whole country. He suggested that a fund of at least 60- or 70-millions of pounds sterling would be needed for this compensation. "Otherwise, gentlemen might be justly con-

[55] Election Broadsides, Bristol Public Library, 1774–90. John Harris Cruger issued a devastating defense of his brother against a charge that the M.P. had sworn allegiance to the United States in New York: at the conclusion of the poll, John Harris Cruger was "chaired" in his brother's place during the Crugerite celebration; *vide* Weare, 167.

sidered as liberal, or even ostentatious, in their sacrifice to the cause of humanity, at the expense of others." [56] Cruger concluded his argument by suggesting that there might at best be a limited effort to mitigate the alleged abuses of the slave trade, with gradual abolition perhaps as the ultimate objective to be attained in concert with other nations; meanwhile, Cruger suggested that the development of the arts and sciences of civilization among the Africans would lead to the abolition of slavery in Africa itself, thereby ending the slave trade naturally.

Curiously enough, the names of Cruger and Burke are linked in the public record on this loathsome issue at the end of Cruger's career as a Member of Parliament just as they were linked at the start of Cruger's Commons career. Burke took the floor immediately after his erstwhile colleague to demolish Cruger's argument, just as he had followed Cruger's speech on accepting the 1774 election with a lecture on the nature of a representative's duties to his country and to his constituents. In Burke's opinion, 'the African trade was no legitimate business but an "absolute robbery," and, "as for the West-India merchants being reimbursed what they might lose by this abolition, it was totally against every principle of legislation." After pointing out the fact that these merchants enjoyed their profits only because of government's past active protection of the business, Burke asserted that the merchants, and the planters as well, had no claim for compensation if Government ceased to countenance the slave trade. Burke concluded by pointing out the preposterous nature of expecting the Africans to develop "civilization" while the source of their degradation, the slave system, remained; his conclusion removed the argument from the merely commercial to the moral field; "Africans have that claim on our humanity which could not be resisted, whatever might have been ad-

[56] *Parliamentary History*, XXVIII, 95–96.

vanced by an hon. gentleman in defence of the property of the planters." [57]

Cruger's political philosophy seems to have been formed largely by his background as a merchant, and by his interests as an exponent of liberalizing reforms in the election laws and procedures of Britain. More frequent elections and a view of representatives as agents of their constituency appear as among his interests; likewise, there is a plain indication that government should support and protect business and property rights, even when these are involved in repulsive aspects of business.

Henry Cruger's interests became centered more and more in the new United States during the later 1780s. He had failed of re-election in 1780 largely for being too American, and his victory in 1784 had not provided him with the scope he seems to have desired for his political talents. Meanwhile, his business seems to have grown, especially as regards American commerce.[58] He became a benefactor of the New York Hospital,[59] a member of the arbitration committee of the New York Chamber of Commerce,[60] and speculated in continental land warrants.[61] In at least one instance, he arranged for a skillful English mechanic to evade laws prohibiting emigration, and introduced the man in New York to William Duer and Alexander Hamilton, in an effort to set up machinery in America similar to Arkwright's equipment in England.[62]

[57] *Ibid.*, 96–97.
[58] The Cruger firm in London, listed as "Cruger, Lediard & Mullet," appears in the 1791 publication of W. Loundes, *London Directory* (London, 1791).
[59] Bryan Little, 179.
[60] *Earliest Arbitration Records of the Chamber of Commerce of the State of New York* (New York, 1913), 97 and 110.
[61] Erastus C. Knight, *New York in the Revolution as Colony and State* (Albany, 1901), 65 and 212.
[62] Joseph Stancliffe Davis, *Essays in the Earlier History of American Corporations* (Cambridge, Mass., 1917), I, 401.

By 1790, Henry Cruger had determined on a change of permanent residence. His eldest son, Samuel Peach Cruger, dropped the surname and remained in Bristol as a second Samuel Peach. Together with the rest of his family, Henry Cruger left Bristol permanently, after formally declining any interest in the 1790 elections. Settling in New York in a household staffed by three slaves, he continued his business interests in overseas trade, land speculation, government bonds, and the infancy of American manufacturing. These interests, together with his political background and his contacts with Hamilton and John Jay, led him almost immediately into New York politics. He was a Federalist candidate for the New York State Senate, winning election in 1792.[63]

Cruger's career in the New York State Senate lasted only four years; but the period was a turbulent one, and the Senate was closely divided. The gubernatorial election of 1792 hinged on acceptance of returns from four counties in which Federalists expected victory. The Republican majority voted to refuse the returns from the four disputed counties.[64] Cruger found himself in a minority again, in the voting to restrict the salary to be paid to Clinton after that Republican had managed to get himself declared Governor.[65] On the other hand, the bitterness of the 1792 campaign did not prevent him and his friends from proposing higher salaries for State Senators than the Republi-

[63] Henry Cruger held two parcels of land in New York City by 1793, worth £2,200 in appraised valuation; this and his family establishment data are derived from the "Taxpayers of the City and County of New York, 1793" Manuscript in the New–York Historical Society, and *Heads of Families at the First Census . . . New York* (Washington, 1908), 116. Political data on Cruger are found in Edgar A. Werner, ed., *Civil List and Constitutional History of the Colony and State of New York* (Albany, 1886), 114, and on a more personal level in his personal letter to Peter Van Schaack, Apr. 20, 1792, in Miscellaneous Manuscripts, Chicago Historical Society.
[64] *Journal of the Senate of the State of New York,* Sixteenth Session (New York, 1793), 24 and 81.
[65] *Ibid.,* 61.

cans would accept.[66] In 1795, for probably the only occasion in a legislative career that spanned two continents, Cruger found his vote to be a crucial one in a 12–11 majority that sent Rufus King to the United States Senate.[67]

Insight into Cruger's own scale of values may be found in his positions during the 1796 session, when New York's criminal code was revamped. For instance, he voted with a tiny non-party majority to retain the death penalty for both burglary and buggery,[68] but with a bipartisan majority to eliminate arson, counterfeiting, and statutory rape as capital offenses.[69] He strongly opposed the principle of double jeopardy, not only voting to prevent acquittal by a jury from being a complete bar to further prosecution, but voting against a milder version of the Assembly's position, which was close in wording to the guarantee in the United States Constitution.[70]

At the end of the 1796 session, Henry Cruger returned to private life. His interests were wide: foreign commerce, manufacturing, real estate. His background of over thirty years in England provided him with strong predilections toward secure commercial arrangements, sound currency, and peaceful mutual acceptance by Great Britain and the United States. These and his personal friendships with leading New York Federalists made him a convinced and influential member of that party in New York.

[66] *Ibid.*, 63.
[67] *Ibid.*, Eighteenth Session (New York, 1795), 15.
[68] *Ibid.*, Nineteenth Session (New York, 1796), 27–29.
[69] *Ibid.*
[70] *Ibid.*, 38 and 86.

# 6

# The Whigs and the Invasion Crisis of 1779

## JAMES E. BUNCE

DURING THE YEARS OF HER WAR with the American colonies, Britain's political landscape was dominated by a series of political crises stemming in part from the intervention of foreign states in this basically civil conflict, and in part from the chronic instability of a government almost paralyzed by the blunders of its principal officers and the loss of nerve in its chief, Lord North. Each of these incidents served as well to test the political capacities of the parliamentary opposition, whose aim was always to rally the public to effective resistance against a ministry beset (as they saw it) by corruption and an almost criminal inefficiency. The challenge was especially prolonged and severe in 1779, when England was faced with the dual peril of disintegration within her government and the threat of foreign invasion along her coasts.

The events which precipitated the political crisis within North's ministry are well known. In the gloomy winter of 1778–79, William Eden and Alexander Wedderburn, restless and ambitious figures in the administration, began to harass North with extortionate demands for pensions and advancement, as the price of their continued support.[1] Others prominent in the government, particularly Lord Carlisle and Lord Gower, joined them in undermining confidence in a colleague, Lord George Germain, whose conduct at the Colonial Office they blamed for most of England's failures in the war.[2] The death of Lord Suffolk, who had been the patron of Eden and Wedderburn and leader of the Grenvillite remnant in the government, caused these pressures to mount. By the spring of 1779, North was so afflicted by indecision that all responsibility for running affairs had fallen on the shoulders of the "men of business," the indefatigable Charles Jenkinson and John Robinson, who joined in urging George III to resist the unreasonable demands of their colleagues.[3] The king, who had greater fortitude than North, resolved to make no concessions; he pursued a firm course with Wedderburn (who was the most persistent in his attacks), and finally convinced him that in the interests of his professional advancement he should continue to support the government with "vigour and effect." [4]

Such dissidence within the ministry seemed to strengthen the resolution of opposition to proceed with decision and unity in their attacks. When North proposed that the Duke of Grafton and Lord Camden, former partisans of Lord Chatham, should join his government, they insisted on consultation with their ally, Lord Shelburne; and all three replied that they could not negotiate "till such time as proper application can be made to Lord Rockingham and

[1] Herbert Butterfield, *George III, Lord North, and the People* (London, 1949), 29–33; Grey Cooper to Eden, n.d., British Museum, Add. MSS 34,416, f. 498; Hist. Mss. Comm., Carlisle MSS, Fifteenth *Report*, App., Pt. VI, 419.

[2] The King to North, Feb. 11, 1779, *Correspondence of King George the Third*, ed. Sir John Fortescue (London, 1927–28), IV, 272.

[3] Jenkinson to the King, May 15, 1779; the King to North, May 17, *ibid.*, IV, 342–43.

[4] The King to North, July 2, 1779; Robinson to the King, July 4, *ibid.*, 386–87.

the Duke of Richmond, to know their sentiments."⁵ This proposal to introduce Rockingham into the affair was contrary to North's purpose of dividing opposition, and completely unacceptable to the king, who observed tartly: "Opposition, as I expected, when they talk of coalition, mean to dictate."⁶ The incident nonetheless demonstrated that a rapprochement was taking place between the two principal branches of opposition; it promised that the chief critics of North's ministry would be united when England was menaced by Spanish intervention in the war.⁷

In Parliament, the opposition mounted a war of nerves against the government, exploiting fully the acquittal of Admiral Keppel at the court martial instigated by his subordinate, the courtier Sir Hugh Palliser.⁸ Soon they launched an attack on what they professed to be a potent source of ministerial influence, the presence of government contractors in the House of Commons. North regarded the bill as a reflection on his personal integrity, and insisted that his opponents were seeking to force his resignation. The king, however, was imperturbable and took occasion to lecture his minister on the need for indifference to the whims of Parliament:

> I am convinced this Country will never regain a proper tone unless Ministers as in the reign of King William will not mind being now and then in a Minority particularly on subjects that have always carried some weight with popular opinions; if it comes to the worst the Bill will be thrown out in the House of Lords.⁹

Possibly with a view to reducing the vehemence of the opposition's assaults, the ministry resumed negotiation with

⁵ *Autobiography and Correspondence of Augustus Henry, Third Duke of Grafton*, ed. Sir William Anson (London, 1898), 306–7.
⁶ The King to North, Jan. 29, 1779, *Corres. Geo. III*, IV, 263.
⁷ Grafton, 307–8.
⁸ David F. Wells, *The Keppel–Palliser Dispute, 1778–1779* (Atlanta, 1964), 23–24.
⁹ North to the King, Feb. 12, 1779; the King to North, Feb. 12, *Corres. Geo. III*, IV, 275–76.

opposition leaders, although it is not clear which side took the initiative. Jenkinson informed the king that Grafton and Rockingham had offered the leadership of a new administration to Gower, but it is difficult to suppose that they would have made such proposals, unless first approached by some member of the government. The end of the negotiation is as obscure as its beginning; its only result was to inspire North with renewed hope of escaping distasteful and burdensome duties.[10] But George III was equally intransigent in insisting that his chief minister stay by him, and in refusing "to treat with opposition as a party." [11] He warned North:

. . . before I will hear of any Man's readiness to come into Office, I will expect to see it signed under his hand that He is resolved to keep the Empire entire and that no troops shall be consequently withdrawn from thence, nor Independence ever allowed.[12]

The king could do little to stiffen the will of his minister: North continued to be gripped by a pusillanimity and lassitude which severely crippled England's capacity to wage a world-wide war and command the obedience of her restless subjects. The ministry indeed had long been enfeebled by his unwillingness to exercise a firm control over his subordinates—a weakness which North seemed to regard as a virtue. In the fall of 1779, he would write to the king of his relations with his colleagues: "I have never interfered in any of their departments. I have never clashed with their views—but have promoted their interest as much as lay within my power on every occasion." [13] And in the following year he complained:

[10] Jenkinson to the King, May 29, 1779, *Corres. Geo. III*, IV, 344–46; North to the King, June 15, *ibid.*, 355–56; "Minutes of Arrangements" June 11, *ibid.*, 352–53.
[11] The King to North, June 16, 1779, *ibid.*, 368–69; the King to Robinson, July 2, Add. MSS 37,834, f. 103.
[12] The King to North, June 22, 1779, *Corres. Geo. III*, IV, 369–70.
[13] North to the King, (Nov. 1779), *ibid.*, 493–95.

I have without reluctance, at all times, sacrificed my interest to that of every one of my brother ministers; I have hardly ever asked and seldom received any mark of friendship from any of them. Why then are they out of humour of me? [sic][14]

In spite of North's ineffectualness, the king was too satisfied with his loyalty, his faithful adherence to commands, and his capable management of the Commons, to release him from his service. Yet North caused endless concern to Robinson and Jenkinson; by the early summer of 1779, Robinson found that the administration was "totally disjointed," and he gloomily predicted that the whole edifice of government must "blow up" if this state of things endured.[15]

This breakdown in the effectiveness of North's government occurred at a critical moment in the war, when Great Britain was endangered by new perils in her relations with the Bourbon powers. Since the latter part of 1778, the British had declined several offers from Spain for mediation, for they believed her biased in favor of France and America, and objected to any foreign intervention in the settlement of their colonial problems.[16] The King of Spain reacted by recalling his ambassador from the Court of St. James, and by issuing a manifesto in which he insisted that he had been acting in good faith; he further charged the British with violating Spanish rights in North America and Honduras and on the high seas. By the 17th of June, a virtual state of war existed between England and Spain; the

---

[14] North to Dundas, June 14, 1780, William L. Clements Library, Melville Papers.
[15] Butterfield, 60–61.
[16] Copies of much of the correspondence which preceded the Anglo–Spanish rupture is in the Bancroft Transcripts at the New York Public Library. See especially Weymouth to Grantham, Oct. 27, 1778; Paper of Mediation, Dec. 5, 1778; Florida Blanca to d'Almodovar, Jan. 29, 1779; Ultimatum proposé aux Cours de Paris et de Londres par celle de Madrid, Apr. 19, 1779; Weymouth to Grantham, May 4, 1779. See also the account in John Adolphus, *The History of England from the Accession of George the Third* (London, 1810), III, 140–47.

government communicated the Spanish manifesto to Parliament, seeking from each house the customary addresses of loyalty and support.[17]

The opposition prepared fully to exploit the ministry's maladroit handling of the crisis and charge it with lack of vigilance in failing to anticipate the emergence of a new adversary. In the House of Lords, their principal line of attack was embodied in the Duke of Richmond's amendment to the address, which demanded "a total change of that system which has involved us in our present difficulties in America, in Ireland, and at home . . . prudent œconomy, and a due exertion of the forces of a free and united people." [18] Richmond singled out Lord Sandwich for his possibly criminal negligence in ignoring the information that twenty-eight French ships of the line had sailed from Brest on June 3, which had resulted in the joining of the Bourbon fleets. The climax of his speech was an appeal "to abandon the American war, at least for the present, to collect the great military force now doing nothing there, and employing it [sic] instantly against our enemies [he meant Spain] both in North and South America." [19]

The ministers offered surprisingly little defense against these charges, probably certain that they had the votes needed to defeat Richmond's amendment. But he received formidable support from Lord Shelburne, who heaped ridicule on all the men responsible for a disastrous colonial and foreign policy, and sarcastically characterized North:

This phantom of a real minister had led the country gentlemen into a war; he had buoyed up their expectations; he had led them into a French war; he had lately inspired them with hopes of once more recovering America; and finally, he had led them into the calamitous situation of being obliged to go to war with the whole House of

---

[17] *Parliamentary History*, XX, 876-79.
[18] *Ibid.*, 882.
[19] *Ibid.*, 882-84.

Bourbon allied with the subjects of a third part of the British empire.[20]

In calling not only for the dismissal of North, Germain and Sandwich, but the overthrow of the whole political system in which they were only "the ostensible actors," Shelburne hinted at the operation of a secret government, by this time a well-tried opposition device. He demanded the destruction of "that baleful, wicked, and absurd system of politics which had pervaded our councils for the last 18 years"; but he also launched into the familiar Chathamite attack on party which was always the insuperable obstacle to any real union of both branches of opposition: "There ought to be but one party in this country, who should distinguish themselves solely in its defense, with a warm, resolute, and spirited zeal for its honour." [21]

Although the Lords defeated Richmond's amendment by a vote of 57–32, the debate of June 17 provided occasion for one of opposition's most severe attacks on the ministry. Yet that evening, Lord Rockingham, who has frequently been accused of a lack of passion and force in his political conduct, reflected on the day's events in a letter to Richmond:

My Mind is not at Ease in regard to what has passed today—I fear *we* took too temperate a Line in the Course of *our* debate. I felt inclined to speak, but I durst not trust myself. The conduct of the Ministers, in saying *nothing,* and the Futility and presumption of the *only* speaker in their *behalf,* really affected me with indignation.

He found Shelburne's speech "sufficiently personal" but felt that effective action against the government required not "*mere personal* attack . . . but an attack on their general systematic Conduct which has drawn on this Country,

---
[20] *Ibid.,* 886.
[21] *Ibid.,* 887–90.

all the evils which are now falling upon it." [22] Rockingham had evidently paid little attention to Shelburne's remarks on the "baleful, wicked, and absurd system," or did not consider these as bearing sufficiently upon the ministers' general conduct.

The opposition's attack on the government was not abated by the dangers attendant to Spain's entry into the war: the juncture of the Bourbon fleets and the exposure of the British Isles to the threat of invasion. Britain was ill prepared to parry this threat, for her navy was neglected, undermanned, and dispersed over the globe. The service was rent by political faction, centering on Admiral Keppel, who had resigned his command after his acquittal, and no one but the aged, ineffectual Sir Charles Hardy was available to take charge of the Channel Fleet. Caution rather than vigor was the counsel that animated the Admiralty, and Hardy's principal instructions were to avoid action with the enemy. England was fortunate that the French and Spanish fleets were also inefficient, beset by petty squabbles, and ravaged by disease among their seamen.[23]

But the British government could not be certain in advance of their unmerited good fortune; they had to reckon with the possibility of a full-scale invasion, while their land forces, undermanned, poorly trained, and ill-equipped, were scarcely better prepared than the navy to check the enemy. North thought his difficulties might be solved by doubling the number of men enrolled in the militia, and he shortly asked Parliament to authorize this policy. Opposition speakers in both houses insisted that this belated measure revealed the ministers' lack of preparedness, and would interfere with recruitment into the regular services. The alternative they preferred was to accept the offers made by many noblemen and gentlemen to raise military compa-

[22] Rockingham to Richmond, June 17, 1779, Sheffield City Library, Wentworth–Fitzwilliam MSS, R 140–29.

[23] A. T. Mahan, *The Major Operations of the Navies in the War of American Independence* (Boston, 1913), 97; Butterfield, 47–53.

nies at their own expense. Government indeed was inclined to discourage such proposals on the grounds that the companies would not be ready in time, would compete with regular units, and would interfere with the seniority of experienced army officers, since their well-to-do patrons were seeking military commissions for themselves and their friends.[24] Lord North insisted that "the doubling the militia was found to be the most practicable mode of having a large army on foot in a short time, and therefore it was adopted in preference to receiving the offers made to government by several individuals."[25] Later in this debate, Charles Fox suggested that since the government had earlier accepted the offers of a number of Scottish noblemen, their present refusal must be imputed to "the remains of that miserable partiality to the Scotch, which had so long disgraced this country"; he further charged that Lord Derby had been singled out for persecution owing to his family connection with General Burgoyne.[26]

The militia debate provided the opposition with new opportunities to indulge their invective and to cast suspicion on the good faith of ministers. With characteristic vehemence, Thomas Townshend affirmed his belief "that there was something about the court and the cabinet that bought and sold"; while Alderman Sawbridge declared that treachery must be the underlying principle of the North administration, since "indolence, neglect, or incapacity" were not sufficient to explain the misfortunes of the country.[27] Such remarks were irresponsible and politically unwise, for no evidence was offered in support of them, nor could any have been produced; North correctly attributed them to "the administration's having pursued such measures as had not met with the support of the hon. gentlemen and their

[24] A. Temple Patterson, *The Other Armada: The Franco–Spanish Attempt to Invade Britain in 1779* (London, 1960), 107–13.
[25] *Parl. Hist.*, XX, 921.
[26] *Ibid.*, 934–39.
[27] *Ibid.*, 918–19, 922–23.

friends." [28] Such hysterical attacks on the honor of ministers whose real failing was incompetence earned for opposition the reputation for factiousness which helped to keep an otherwise undeserving government in office until 1782.

By the time the bill reached its third reading in the Commons, opinion among the members was divided and confused regarding the best manner of augmenting the military forces of the country. An effort to simplify the situation was made by Lord Beauchamp who submitted an amendment authorizing the raising of volunteer companies. Disorganization on the government side was revealed when North was obliged to ask Sir Grey Cooper to withdraw a motion limiting the new forces to 15,424 men. Altering the position he had taken earlier in the progress of the bill, North assured the House "that if the force wanted was procured by independent corps, companies, or new regiments, the end would be answered." [29] With the Beauchamp amendment, then, and still including the provision for doubling the militia, the bill passed the Commons by a unanimous vote on June 24th.[30]

The success of the militia bill in the House of Commons did not discourage the opposition peers from preparing a vigorous campaign against it in their house. Lord Rockingham conveyed to the Duke of Grafton his fears that "attempting to force fresh Ballots or to the forcing the Counties to the extra Expense of double numbers of Substitutes, will be a measure which will create much disturbance," and with Lord Shelburne he urged the Duke to come up to London at once and take part in the debates.[31]

The onslaught against the bill in the upper house was led by Rockingham and Richmond, who attacked the ministry

[28] *Ibid.*, 925.
[29] *Ibid.*, 959.
[30] *Ibid.*, 962.
[31] Rockingham to Grafton, June 22, 1779; Shelburne to Grafton, (June 22, 1779), West Suffolk Record Office, Grafton MSS.

for their delay in introducing a bill which to be effective should have been enacted into law at a much earlier date. Richmond predicted that any provision for compulsory service would provoke popular resistance; he preferred that new forces be raised by private initiative, and rebuked the government for its coolness toward offers which he and the Duke of Rutland had made to raise their own companies. The Duke also objected to using the militia as a regular army force, for he regarded it as a weapon of local defense which should encourage "local affections" among the men, while as a Lord Lieutenant he opposed moving militia regiments from their home counties to distant areas where they were unfamiliar with the terrain and local conditions. Doubling the militia would be an expensive measure, but Richmond observed that this seemed to be in keeping with the maxim adopted by government "that the security of the public must inevitably be great if the cost were large." [32]

When he turned his attention to an accompanying measure which authorized impressment into the navy, Richmond was perhaps not speaking as a disinterested observer. He was especially concerned with the effect impressment would have on ships engaged in the coal trade, which, he conceded, "concerned the public materially, but . . . concerned him most materially." Interference with this trade would seriously harm London and the manufacturing towns, and strike at his own fortune which was derived in large part from a one-shilling duty on each chaldron of coal sent from Newcastle. Richmond insisted that apprentices on colliers' ships be totally exempted from liability to impressment, and rejected Lord Sandwich's amendment which made men in the coal trade subject to impressment for one month only.[33]

At the end of these debates, the Lords passed the im-

[32] *Parl. Hist.*, XX, 969–72, 978–85.
[33] *Ibid.*, 987–88, 997–1000. Alison G. Olson, *The Radical Duke* (Oxford, 1961), 1.

pressment bill, 51–20, but recommitted the militia bill and subjected it to radical surgery. These alterations were proposed by a government peer, Lord Gower, who called for removing the provision for compulsory service, and for giving each county the option of raising 150 or 200 men for the regular army, or balloting for additional militia. When the Commander-in-Chief, Lord Amherst, conceded that efforts at recruiting into the regular army had lately yielded few men, Gower observed that the reserve of manpower should not be further diminished by conscription into the militia. At a stroke, the peers cut through the problem by eliminating all provision for augmenting the militia: North's original bill from the Commons was swept away, leaving only Beauchamp's amendment. It was a surprising moment, which found many members of the government—Gower, Weymouth, Stormont, and others—aligned with the opposition; the latter now found themselves, as the *Annual Register* wryly noted, in the unaccustomed position of being in the majority. They would not enjoy the experience again for many months.[34]

The government reluctantly accepted the authority to raise volunteer companies which this statute conferred; several of the offers which had been referred to in the debates were now taken up. The press reported that such men as Lord Bute, Lord Winchelsea, Lord Chewton, and Sir Thomas Egerton were active in raising men on their estates or in districts where they were prominent.[35] None of these men was politically hostile to the government, but the king disliked such exertions of individual initiative (legal though they might be); he favored other modes of strengthening the national defenses, such as armed associations of gentlemen and popular subscriptions to supplement bounty

---

[34] *Parl. Hist.,* XX, 1008; *Parliamentary Register* (ed. John Almon), XIV, 564–72; *Annual Register,* 1779, 171–72. The Duke of Grafton in endorsing Rockingham's letter of June 22, which urged his return to London, sounded a jubilant note: "I did go up, and we defeated the measure." Grafton MSS.

[35] *Lloyd's Evening Post,* July 12, 13, 15, 17, 1779.

payments.³⁶ Private subscriptions of this type were being raised in many places to support military and naval companies, and even to underwrite the ordinary expenses of government. Edmund Burke suggested to Lord Rockingham some of the varied purposes of these subscriptions:

In some places they vote the money to the Marine Society; in others they vote Bounties to Seamen; in some they vote additional recruiting money for the general recruiting service; in one place they propose a new Corps of regulars, in another additional Militia; in a third Troops of horse and foot for local service to support legal Government.³⁷

County meetings were generally summoned to open the subscriptions; a typical resolution was passed by the Surrey meeting at Guildford:

We, the Custos Rotolorum, Chairman, Magistrates and other Gentlemen of the County of Surrey, taking into our serious Consideration the present critical Situation of the Country, do agree to pay the several sums of money set against our respective Names, to be paid and applied at such Times and in such Manner as the Committee herein after named shall direct, for the purpose of raising men for the Sea Service, or for such other Purposes as the Exigency of the State may require, under the Direction of the said Committee, and subject to the Controul of the Majority of the Subscribers.³⁸

The county meetings which were called for the raising of subscriptions were often rent by bitter partisan debate and provided a new forum for attacks on the government. The impact of politics on the invasion crisis was notably felt at

---

³⁶ Patterson, 117–19. The arming by gentlemen of their servants had been advocated by Lord Townshend in the Lords debate on June 28. *Parl. Hist.*, XX, 995.

³⁷ Burke to Rockingham, Aug. 8, 1779, Wentworth–Fitzwilliam MSS, Bk 1–808, printed in *The Correspondence of Edmund Burke*, IV, ed. John A. Woods (Cambridge, 1963), 112–14.

³⁸ *Lloyd's Evening Post*, July 19, 1779. Thirty men of the county, headed by Lord Onslow, pledged sums of 20 to 300 pounds, and the list was extended later in the summer. *Ibid.*, July 29, Aug. 2, 1779.

Bristol, where friends of opposition attempted to amend an address of loyalty to the king by adding a petition that he give the direction of affairs to men more trustworthy than the present ministers. Many believed that there was a clear majority for this measure, but Richard Champion reported that it was defeated by the fears of "moderate men" who disliked "dictating to the Sovereign" and believed that it was more prudent to allow the king to make changes on his own initiative.[39] The city subsequently voted a thousand pounds for the public services and offered additional bounties to men entering the regular army and the marines.[40]

Champion, who was a leading member of the opposition forces in Bristol, attempted to analyze for Lord Rockingham the political situation in that city. The Whigs he found complacent and slothful; some willfully ignored the losses which England had suffered at the hands of the French; some were despondent with doubts that any effective moves against the government were possible; there were former court Whigs too obstinate to come forward to oppose measures which they had once supported. The Tories, on the other hand, while "convinced of the futility and danger of their system," would not countenance a change of ministry. Champion found their union so firm that "they would risque every danger, and trust to accident for relief, than pursue the most salutary and certain measures of obtaining it, at the hands of a Whig Administration." He believed that the Tories in Bristol aimed at maintaining local military forces under their control, while totally excluding the Whigs. They proposed a regiment to guard the French prisoners in the city, in which their own adherents would enjoy a monopoly of the commissions with a Scottish merchant as colonel. He lamented to Lord Rockingham:

---

[39] *London Chronicle,* July 3–6, 1779; Champion to Rockingham, Aug. 13, 1779, Wentworth–Fitzwilliam MSS, R 1–1842.
[40] *London Chronicle,* July 3–6, 1779; *Lloyd's Evening Post,* July 31, 1779.

There never was a time when England saw so formidable, so patriotic an opposition, as that of which your Lordship is the illustrious head; yet with the purest Intentions, the highest Capacity, and the greatest Powers that Family, Fortune, and Abilities can possibly combine in opposition, it has failed at a time of the greatest Necessity, whilst on occasions of comparatively small importance, a much less opposition to Government has been successful. Complaint is now become of little avail, and we must undergo severe Trials, before the People can be brought to reason.[41]

The ministry received further support at the Nottingham meeting of July 22, when the men of the county voted a subscription for "strengthening the hands of Government . . . to be applied to increase his Majesty's bounty to volunteers."[42] The Duke of Newcastle,[43] Lord Lieutenant of the County, pledged a thousand guineas; but the Duke of Portland, another great landowner and a Whig, was convinced that only the "Doubts, Delicacies and Absence" of a few gentlemen prevented the defeat of the subscription. Some notables, such as Lord George Sutton, were prepared to contribute only if the subscription were restricted to raising volunteer companies under the recent act of Parliament. Portland sensed great resentment in the county against the high-handed conduct of Newcastle, who had not troubled to attend the meeting, and whose salary and profits as Auditor of the Exchequer would have easily yielded the entire sum of the subscription. Yet Portland himself and many of his friends had stayed away from the meeting, although he was convinced that an assembly which fairly represented the county could have passed an address "representing the Calamitous State of the Country and giving good advice to the Crown."[44] He later grumbled:

[41] Champion to Rockingham, Aug. 13, 1779, R 1–1842.
[42] *Lloyd's Evening Post,* July 27, 1779.
[43] Henry Pelham-Clinton, second Duke of Newcastle-under-Lyme and ninth Earl of Lincoln, was the nephew and successor of the famous minister of George II, Thomas Pelham-Holles, first Duke of Newcastle.
[44] Portland to Rockingham, July 29, 1779, Wentworth-Fitzwilliam MSS, R 1–1839.

"I don't like to complain, but I am every day more and more satisfied that if our Friends had attended the Duke of Newcastle's meeting there is nothing they could have proposed that might not have been carried triumphantly." [45]

The opposition had more reason to be pleased with the Hertford meeting of August 2, where the sense of the assembly opposed offering assistance to the crown, perhaps because Lord Cranborne, the Lord Lieutenant, failed to make any specific proposals for action.[46] One supporter of opposition charged that, in view of the danger of invasion, the ministers deserved hanging for failing to convene Parliament, which had been prorogued scarcely a month before. He suggested that the government "had no other view than to create a separate and undue interest for the King in the country independent of the controul of Parliament." The opposition men, despite their success in facing down the ministerial motion, hesitated to bring forth one of their own. William Baker wrote to Burke that they were "victorious without victory," [47] but conceded that "The carrying of other questions would have been problematical, certainly it could not have been done without much opposition, and the adverse party would always have had it in their power to put injurious construction on our conduct." [48]

At the Nottingham and Hertford meetings some men had questioned the legality of raising new militia companies by subscription. Their doubts were shared by Rockingham, who was disturbed because the ministers had persuaded the House of Lords to omit from the militia bill an amendment providing that in any county where three or more volunteer companies were raised, these might be formed

[45] Portland to Rockingham, Aug. 8, 1779, R 1–1841. Rockingham replied: "I don't think by the subscriptions—names—that there is much demonstration of Court zeal in Nottinghamshire." July 29, 1779, University of Nottingham, Portland MSS.
[46] *Lloyd's Evening Post,* Aug. 4, 1779.
[47] William Baker to Burke, Aug. 4, 1779, Wentworth-Fitzwilliam MSS, Bk 1–805, printed in *Correspondence of Edmund Burke,* IV, 108–10.
[48] William Baker to Burke, Aug. 9, 1779, Bk 1–809.

into regiments or battalions. He was convinced that only parliamentary authorization could make legal the raising of regiments by public subscription; without the sanction of law, ministers had no other basis for their acts than "a supposed prerogative arising out of state necessity," and Rockingham regarded this as inadequate justification for their policy.[49] In the same way, the Secretary at War was directing militia colonels to fill up vacancies in the ranks of their regiments. (Such vacancies had been deliberately left unfilled for the purpose of maintaining a contingency fund.) Rockingham doubted whether counties could be required to replace men who had already been legally raised and discharged. He insisted that he had no desire to place obstacles in the way of stronger forces at a time of national peril; but he told the Secretary: "I cannot readily concur in adopting plans wherein I may doubt the legality or the wisdom of the policy."[50] These last words are perhaps the best clue to the marquess' thoughts: when he disagreed with the political wisdom of a measure, he was not easily convinced of its legality.

Burke agreed that subscriptions were of dubious legality, and reinforced the argument by charging that the correct measures lacked real effectiveness. He wrote to Rockingham:

For a plan of defense, which is neither legal or vigorous, can have little said in its favour. Nothing seems to be more wild, and ridiculously unsystematical, than the subscriptions now on foot. They are calculated to cheat the people of their money, and can answer no other purpose.... I confess, I am not very fond of any volunteer modes of raising money, for publick Service. They must all be, from

---

[49] Rockingham to Burke, (Aug. 7, 1779), Bk 1-807. The *Journal of the House of Lords* does not indicate that this amendment was removed by ministerial action, but states merely that on July 1 it was "disagreed to by the House." XXXV, 812.

[50] Charles Jenkinson to Sir George Savile, July 24, 1779, Public Record Office, W.O., 4/767, 283-84. Rockingham to Jenkinson, (post Aug. 7, 1779), Wentworth-Fitzwilliam MSS, R 81-150.

their nature, loose and ineffectual in the application, more or less. They cause improper emulations; lead to invidious comparisons; and lay, under the appearance of being voluntary, more unequal Burthens on men than could be done by almost any compulsory Tax. It would be impossible to prevent their one way or other becoming a sort of Test of particular attachments; and would be used to create influences in the Country, for those, who have the contribution, in part; and in the whole, the raising and management of so much money out of the ordinary Course.[51]

This view that the subscriptions might be used as a political test echoed a dominant theme in the correspondence of many Whig politicians in the summer of 1779: fear that this campaign was a Tory device directed against opposition. Edmund Burke's excitable kinsman, William, smelt a Tory scheme when citizens of London covenanted to maintain domestic peace and Bristol formed its association to guard the prisoners of war held there. To the Duke of Portland he confessed a paranoid fear that such volunteer groups in their zeal might capture "quite some other sort of Prisoners than the Enemys of England."[52] Edmund Burke likewise regarded conditions in Bristol as a reflection of the court-party's partisan impulses:

The steady Tories consider the fate of the Ministry to be their own; and as they expect some time or other, that the publick indignation may break out in some violent way, they are resolved, if they can be beforehand with it;—to accuse the opposition party of a disposition to rebel,—and on that Colour to arm themselves as they think fit, and to tyrannize in a manner agreeable to their nature and principles.[53]

He believed, however, that such measures were less formidable than their authors intended, and suspected that the names of many important merchants had been placed on

[51] Burke to Rockingham, Aug. 8, 1779, Bk 1-808, printed in *Correspondence of Edmund Burke,* IV, 112–14.
[52] William Burke to Portland, Aug. 12, 1779, Portland MSS.
[53] Edmund Burke to Champion, Aug. 13, 1779, Bk 1-811, printed in *Correspondence of Edmund Burke,* IV, 114–17.

the London list without their knowledge or consent.[54] But that opposition lieutenants like the Burkes indulged in such fantasies without evident reproof from their party leaders suggests that years of parliamentary opposition had not matured the political judgment of Lord Rockingham's friends.

Burke regarded the private voluntary corps as a measure which the government had devised to prevent the whole people from enlisting in the defense of their country. He found further evidence for this view when the authorities rescinded an order to distribute pikes among the men of the countryside; for Burke this was an indication of the ministers' "extreme dread of any Method which could tend to make the people know and feel their own Force." Yet he thought that arming the people with pikes was in any case an unwise measure, which would tempt them to "some irregular and contemptible Hostilities." He viewed subscriptions as designed not "to strengthen the Nation, but to strengthen their Faction," and to Champion he described them as a propaganda device:

I observe that they are totally indifferent about the quantity, the application or even the payment of the Money. They want nothing but Names, in order to pass as a sort of proof, that they possess the Confidence of the Country which they have ruined; that our last Stake is thought safe in their hands; that after all the delusions which have been put upon us, our Eyes are still shut; and that we still put our Trust in their Integrity, Vigilance and Wisdom.[55]

Burke advised his friend to promote concord between Whigs and Tories at Bristol, but not to cooperate with the court party if they insisted on monopolizing the leadership in any military organization formed there. He warned

---

[54] *Ibid.* Lord Rockingham agreed with Burke in observing that the London subscriptions were "in general laughed at and disappointed." Rockingham to Portland, Aug. 13, 1779, Portland MSS.

[55] Burke to Champion, Aug. 22, 1779, Bk 1-815, printed in *Correspondence of Edmund Burke*, IV, 122-25.

Champion against the "libels" circulated by the Tories, which imputed cowardice and disloyalty to men in opposition; he suspected that these rumors were intended to drive Whig gentlemen out of military service—"the only part of the publick Service in which they have been permitted to have a Share." The people could do little for the security of England until they inquired "how the preparations of our Enemies came to be so neglected, that at length their fleets domineer in our Seas and anchor in our havens." Burke persisted in the Whig habit of imputing the basest motives to the ministers, for, he wrote, "believe me, it is not the force of France and Spain, but the treachery of our own administration, denying our danger, to palliate their Neglects in not providing against it, that has brought us into our present Condition." [56]

The Whig criticism of the government's defense measures appears to a considerable degree as a partisan attack; but this need not suggest that they were indifferent to the perils faced by England in 1779. Frequently their disagreements with official policy were based on honest differences of opinion. Thus the Duke of Richmond, on the basis of his experience in commanding the Sussex militia, attacked the royal proclamation of July 9 which ordered the evacuation of livestock in case of invasion. He wrote to Portland:

The order for driving the Cattle and Country is general to all officers civil and Military, under no Regulation without Limit, and without Places being appointed to which the Cattle is to be driven; all is left to everyone to do as he pleases, which must produce nothing but Confusion.[57]

[56] *Ibid.* Later, Burke continued in the same vein to Champion: "It certainly cannot be right to arm in support of a faction, though it is most laudable to arm in favour of our Country. Those who confine their military arrangements to one set of men mean evidently to crush the others; and not to defend the whole." Aug. 29, 1779, Bk 1–817, printed in *Correspondence of Edmund Burke,* IV, 126.

[57] Richmond to Portland, July 18, 1779, Portland MSS; for the proclamation, see *London Chronicle,* July 10, 1779.

At the Sussex assizes, Richmond expressed publicly his disapproval of the proclamation, and called on the magistrates of the county to refuse their cooperation in enforcing it. The king was outraged by Richmond's stand, which he deemed grave disobedience of military orders, and threatened to remove the duke from the lord lieutenancy of Sussex.[58]

When John Paul Jones threatened the eastern coasts of Britain in the autumn of 1779, Lord Rockingham in his capacity of High Steward of Hull made a hasty journey to that town, one of the chief ports of the Yorkshire coast. He found the town alarmed and defenseless, for there were scarcely more than a few decayed guns in the local fort to defend it against an enemy from the sea. The Corporation was impatiently awaiting replies to the letters it had dispatched to the Admiralty and the Board of Ordnance, asking for additional armaments; a burgess wrote to Rockingham: "All we have to trust to is the blunders of our Enemies, which we [hope] will keep pace with our own."[59] Rockingham called a meeting of the townsmen at which he attempted to rally the inhabitants to their own defense and at the same time warn them of the futility of relying on the government. Describing the meeting to his wife, he wrote:

> I made them an *omnium gatherum* speech *rather confused* but my chief object was to persuade them—that *Government* had *neglected them* and perhaps that they themselves had been too *flattering* and too *Courtly* in their late address.[60]

He felt that there was slight danger of Jones's landing men on the coast, but was nonetheless distressed to find the

[58] The King to North, Aug. 5, Sept. 1, 1779, *Corres. Geo. III*, IV, 407-8, 418.
[59] William Hammon to Rockingham, Sept. 23, 1779, R 12-5.
[60] Rockingham to Lady Rockingham, [Sept. 25, 1779], R 1-1849. Lady Rockingham was evidently mistaken when she told Burke that her husband had gone to Hull as "Admiral of the Coasts" in her letter of Sept. 23, 1779, Bk 1-820 (printed in *Correspondence of Edmund Burke*, IV, 128-29).

meeting unwilling to mount ships' guns in the fort or to accept his offer to underwrite the cost of a new battery, for "It was said—It must not be done without the Consent of Government." But Rockingham's own efforts to rouse the authorities at Whitehall to action were finally successful, and he later received a letter from the king commending his conduct during the emergency.[61]

By the time Jones had appeared off the coast of England, the danger of a Franco–Spanish invasion had receded, for, after an indecisive brush with Hardy on August 31, the combined fleets, paralyzed by the same caution which crippled the British Admiralty, had started back to Brest. The danger was past, but Britain's crisis in the summer of 1779 had offered to opposition a chance for effective political maneuver, which they had foregone largely by default. They had faced the challenge with real advantages— the renewed political alliance of Shelburne and Rockingham, the exultation following Keppel's acquittal, the ministry's blundering diplomacy in Spain. But their attacks in Parliament were marred by clumsy and unconvincing overstatement, while their conduct in the Nottingham and Hertford meetings suggests that they were not yet ready to seize the political initiative. In the aftermath, they had the leisure to reflect on their standing in the country and their prospects for rallying the people. In every part of England, the Whigs seemed to be crippled by the same handicaps which, according to Richard Champion, had weakened their numbers in Bristol; in that city, he noted, they lacked firmness of principle, owing to "a Languor which does infinite discredit, and is productive of very injurious consequences to their Party." He attributed this apathy among the Bristol Whigs to their traditional support of the house of Hanover, which had lulled them into a false sense of loyalty and pre-

[61] Rockingham to Trinity House, Hull, n.d., R 12–19; Rockingham to Col. John Harvey, n.d., R 12–52; Rockingham to Burke, [Nov. 2, 1779], R 140–9, printed in *Correspondence of Edmund Burke,* IV, 159–64; *Lloyd's Evening Post,* Oct. 1, 1779.

vented them from "appearing in public with the warmth and decision necessary at this alarming crisis." [62] In the same way, William Burke was concerned that the great magnates of his party did not feel compelled "by their personal dignity no less than by their Country's dreadful Situation" to express their alarm at the condition to which the ministers' incapacity had brought the nation. He implored the party leaders to come out of their political retirement and point the way for the people in the event of an enemy invasion; Lord Rockingham, especially, must be persuaded "that the people are looking to him, and waiting for him, not . . . to waste his Authority and Understanding in vain watchings to follow those whom he is born and qualified to lead and direct." [63] But Rockingham's adventure at Hull did not suggest that the people of England waited with great expectancy for their natural leaders to point the way. Although William Burke later urged the Whig leadership to emulate the late Lord Chatham by capturing the loyalty of the public and compelling them to "look up to one man," he acknowledged that the chief men of his party had neither the style nor the disposition to adopt such a stance.[64]

In any case, these entreaties proved needless: the invasion did not materialize, and the Whigs failed to come up with any grand scheme of action. Another chance would come when Parliament convened in the late autumn, and William Burke continued vainly to urge the magnates to arrive early in London to concert their plan of action. Extending Lord John Cavendish's pithy comment that the party was "a snug chaste corps," Burke expressed doubts that they were "much liable to be concepted by power." [65]

Edmund Burke was a more realistic political observer than his mercurial kinsman: conceding that there was grow-

[62] Champion to Rockingham, Aug. 13, 1779, R 1–1842.
[63] William Burke to Portland, Aug. 20, 1779, Portland MSS.
[64] W. Burke to Portland, Sept. 4, 1779, *ibid.*
[65] W. Burke to Portland, [ante Sept. 22, 1779], *ibid.*

ing political discontent in England, he saw no sign of its drawing popular esteem to opposition. He felt that the Whigs had deserved the respect of the people for their "consistency, candour, and sincerity," and for their "total want of false profession, and . . . of political mountebanking," but admitted that these qualities were not sufficient to command a national following. Burke was compelled to charge his colleagues with "a little dilatoriness . . . a weakness which appears much more decisively from our attempting nothing, than it could from our being defeated in any attempt." He was comforted only by the reflection that if the Whigs were less popular than they deserved to be, the government was "perfectly odious." [66] Lord Camden shared the Burkes' concern that the opposition members were out of power and out of favor, but saw no remedy except a passivity—which, "if well conducted, might have a stronger operation than the vain repetition of those feeble efforts that have hitherto been made in Parliament by perpetual wrangle, personal animosity, abuse or bad language. . . ." [67]

The analyses of Champion, the Burkes, and Camden all pointed to the necessity of opposition's finding an issue sufficiently urgent to galvanize the nation into effective resistance to government, and to shake the ministry's hold on the independents in the House of Commons. They had not found such an issue in the invasion threat, but in the months immediately following, they would seize the opportunity when the Yorkshire movement launched its crusade for economy in public expenditures and reduction of the influence of the crown.[68]

[66] Edmund Burke to Portland, Oct. 16, 1779, *ibid.*
[67] Camden to Grafton, Sept. 16, 1779, Grafton MSS, printed in Grafton, 308–9.
[68] See James E. Bunce, "Rockingham, Shelburne and the Politics of Reform, 1779–1780," *Studies in Modern History,* ed. G. L. Vincitorio (New York, 1968), 155–92.

# 7

# The Forces of the Crown in Ireland, 1798

## WILLIAM D. GRIFFIN

"ON WHAT DO THE DESTINIES OF EMPIRES HANG!" mused Napoleon at St. Helena. "If, instead of the expedition of Egypt, I had made that of Ireland . . . what would England have been today? And the Continent? And the political world?"[1] Considering that the Corsican was so little inclined to admit mistakes, it is curious that historians have neglected to develop his line of speculation. The great errors of his Spanish and Russian involvements have been debated endlessly, and even the Egyptian alternative which he chose in 1798 has received abundant attention. To be sure, an invasion that actually took place doubtless deserves more examination than one that did not; but while Napoleon's conquest of the Mamelukes was ultimately pointless and profitless, the conquest of Ireland, as he himself finally realized, could have brought about the collapse of Britain and the unchallenged French domination of Europe.

Historians have not, of course, ignored the strategic significance of Ireland, set athwart Britain's western approaches and threatening her trade and security.[2] Research

[1] E. A. D. Comte de Las Cases, *Mémorial de Sainte–Hélène* (4 vols., Paris, 1823), II, 355.
[2] See, for example, E. Guillon, *La France et l'Irlande pendant la Révolution* (Paris, 1888).

in French archives has revealed the extent of the Directory's interest in Ireland.³ The spread of revolutionary sentiments among the Irish people has been chronicled amply, if not always impartially.⁴ Yet a basic question remains unanswered: could Ireland have been conquered? Napoleon obviously thought that twenty-thousand veteran troops under his command could sweep aside all resistance. Admiring his self-confidence and acknowledging his military genius, we must nevertheless recognize three obstacles to his potential success: (1) the difficulty of the transportation of his forces to Ireland and their maintenance there; (2) the reaction of the Irish people to a French "liberation" of their country; (3) the opposition offered by British military forces in Ireland. It is with the last of the three that this essay is concerned.

With regard to the first obstacle, it need only be remembered that prior to 1800 Britain's vaunted "command of the sea" was far from absolute. An indecisive Admiralty had vitiated numerical superiority by wide dispersal of ships; elderly, unimaginative officers like Bridport and Colpoys clung to their commands despite repeated failures; the fleets were plagued by mutinies, and the blockade of key ports like Brest was careless and ineffectual. Although the French navy lacked the firepower and the morale for a full-scale sea battle, its captains had learned how to baffle the British by stealth, craft, and evasion, as demonstrated by the success of the Hoche expedition in reaching Bantry Bay in December 1796. In 1798 two separate squadrons under Savary and Bompard were able to break through to Ireland, and in the same year Bruix eluded Bridport completely in getting into the Mediterranean and back again.

[3] French invasion projects are discussed in E. Desbrière, *Projets et tentatives de débarquement aux Iles Britanniques* (4 vols., Paris, 1902), and in L. D. Woodward, "Les projets de descente en Irlande sous la Convention," *Annales historiques de la Révolution Française*, No. 115 (1931), 12–45.

[4] The classic, though biased, account is R. R. Madden, *The United Irishmen, Their Lives and Their Times* (5 vols., Dublin, 1858).

Even Nelson was unable to prevent Bonaparte's departure for Malta and Alexandria. Clearly the French could have carried an army to Ireland and kept it supplied with whatever necessities the country itself did not offer.[5] As to the second consideration, most Irishmen eagerly awaited a French landing as the means of attaining their freedom, and there is no reason to doubt that an Irish "sister republic" under French auspices would have emerged to aid Bonaparte in the humbling of Britain.[6] But any discussion of such possibilities must be highly subjective, and could easily degenerate into an Irish Jacobin fantasy. The third "obstacle" affords an opportunity for an objective evaluation of British "preparedness." Before we can answer the question "could Ireland have been conquered?" we must determine what forces actually would have been opposed to Napoleon had he made the "expedition of Ireland." What exactly was the state of Ireland's defences in the crucial year 1798, of which Lecky writes: "never perhaps in the history of England had there been a period when the peril was so great"?

Despite the attention which they devote to the dramatic events of 1798, it is impossible to obtain an accurate statement of the crown forces from the principal historians of eighteenth-century Ireland: Lecky's figures are much too high,[7] and those of Froude much too low.[8] Nor are more recent studies particularly illuminating. Curtis, for instance, touches both extremes, underestimating the regular forces and overestimating the irregulars.[9] Troop strengths ranging

[5] The relative strengths of the British and French navies at this period are analyzed in A. T. Mahan, *The Influence of Sea Power on the French Revolution and Empire* (2 vols., Boston, 1897). For the Bantry Bay expedition, see E. H. Stuart Jones, *An Invasion that Failed* (Oxford, 1950).

[6] On the prospects of an "Irish Republic," see F. MacDermot, *Theobald Wolfe Tone* (London, 1939), 287–290.

[7] W. E. H. Lecky, *A History of Ireland in the Eighteenth Century* (5 vols., London, 1903), IV, 420.

[8] J. A. Froude, *The English in Ireland in the Eighteenth Century* (3 vols., London, 1886), III, 406.

[9] E. Curtis, *A History of Ireland* (6th ed., London, 1950), 338.

from 20,000 to over 100,000 have been cited by a variety of authorities.[10] These discrepancies arise largely from an indifference to definition of terms and a failure to distinguish between real and paper strengths.

Although Ireland in 1798 was a separate kingdom, with a separate Parliament, there was, strictly speaking, no Irish army. Instead, the Irish Exchequer paid and equipped certain regiments which composed "the army on the establishment of Ireland." [11] The peacetime establishment had been 15,000 men, of whom 12,000 formed the home garrison, the remainder being available for foreign service. When, in February 1793 the Irish Parliament voted an augmentation of the establishment to 20,000 men, it stipulated that the original 12,000 must still be left in Ireland, while the new balance of 8,000 was at the disposal of the crown in the war against France. These Irish "regulars," therefore, were really British regiments supported out of Irish taxes. Only a few of them were raised in Ireland (e.g., the Royal Irish Artillery) or had local associations (e.g., the four dragoon regiments which, from long being quartered in the kingdom, were known collectively as the Irish Horse). The regular infantry in Ireland consisted as a rule of ordinary British regiments recruited indiscriminately from all parts of the British Isles and placed on the Irish Establishment in rotation. No special effort was made to garrison Ireland with "native" regulars, such as the 18th "Royal Regiment of Irish" or the 27th Inniskillings, and during the entire war neither of these units paid more than a brief visit to its place of origin while on service in the British Isles.[12]

The regular troops in Ireland were supplemented by

[10] G. P. Gooch (in the *Cambridge Modern History*, IX, 701) speaks of "only 15,000 British troops in Ireland."

[11] The greater part of the material on the Irish Establishment in this essay has been drawn from the Kilmainham Papers (headquarters records of the British forces in Ireland) and the Melville Papers (correspondence of Henry Dundas, secretary at war), both in the National Library of Ireland.

[12] D. A. Chart, "The Irish Levies During the Great French War," *English Historical Review*, XXXII (1917), 507ff.

auxiliary cavalry and infantry regiments known as "fencibles." A product of the war with France, they were enlisted only for the duration of the conflict and could not be sent overseas. Although they were in other respects supposed to be indistinguishable from regular regiments, their lack of experience and special circumstances of recruitment and origin placed them in a lower category of reliability. The rapid growth of the United Irish conspiracy, with its ominous links to Jacobin France, had prompted the London government to dispatch eighteen English and Scottish fencible infantry regiments to Ireland in 1795, another two in 1796, and a further five—as well as five cavalry regiments—in 1797. The only fencible units actually raised in Ireland were Lord Roden's Horse and Lord Glentworth's Fencible Cavalry, both dating from 1795.[13]

The third category of military forces in Ireland was composed of the thirty-seven battalions of foot embodied by the Militia Act of 1793. Coming immediately after the Relief Act, and manifesting the same willingness—or political need—to trust the mass of the population, the Militia Act gave Catholics the right to bear arms for the first time in over a hundred years. But it was expected that they would use their muskets as well as their votes under the direction of their landlords. Each county and city was assigned a quota of men, to be raised and officered by the local gentry. The original call for 16,000 men had gradually been raised to over 26,000, nearly all of whom—except in some Ulster battalions—were Catholics, though commanded by Protestants.[14]

The fourth class of armed manpower available to the crown, although it has often been included in the figures

[13] J. W. Fortescue, *History of the British Army* (13 vols., London, 1899–1930), IV, App. E gives details as to dates of formation, etc. of fencible regiments. See also G. A. Hayes–McCoy, "The Fencible Corps in Ireland," *The Irish Sword*, II, no. 6, 140ff.

[14] For the origins and organization of the militia, see Henry McAnally, *The Irish Militia, 1793–1816* (London, 1949), 9ff.

quoted for the Irish "army," was not properly a military body at all, but rather a volunteer police. The yeomanry originated in the "local associations" formed by the "comfortable classes" to counteract the threat of revolutionary agitation. Beginning in 1796, the government extended official recognition and support, and supplied arms, equipment, and uniforms. Scattered in hundreds of local companies of cavalry and infantry, the yeomanry provided an illusion of strength, and, being generally Protestant and Orangeist, its fidelity was unquestioned. It would be misleading however, to classify the yeomanry as anything more than an extremely amateurish home-guard corps.[15]

Such were the distinct components of the British armed force in Ireland. Any realistic assessment of the Irish military situation must take these distinctions into account when weighing the overall quality and capability of that force. Imprecision of definition has caused a number of writers to equate fencibles with regulars, and to count yeomen as troops of the line.

An even more fertile source of confusion is the numerical strength of the king's army in Ireland. Here even contemporary documents vary, and "secondary authorities" have accepted one or the other without any attempt to reconcile the variations. The following figures for 1798 are based upon a careful comparison of official establishment strength with the Muster Master General's records, regimental returns, and the estimates of senior officers.[16]

---

[15] The genesis of the yeomanry is described by one of their number in W. Richardson, *History of the Origin of the Irish Yeomanry* (Dublin, 1801). A great deal of material on "loyalism" is contained in Hereward Senior, *Orangeism in Ireland and Britain, 1795–1836* (London, 1966).

[16] The figures upon which these calculations are based are derived from the Melville Papers (MSS 54A, 135); various entries in the Kilmainham Papers (MSS 1110–1113); a "memoranda book" of Deputy Muster–Master General Mathew Handcock (now in private possession; extracts printed in G. A. Hayes–McCoy, "The Government Forces which Opposed the Irish Insurgents of 1798," *The Irish Sword*, IV, no. 14, 16ff); regimental returns in the Public Record Office of Ireland (extracts printed in D. A. Chart, *op. cit.*); J. F. Maurice, ed., *The Diary of Sir John Moore* (2 vols., London,

On paper, the regulars numbered 6000 horse and 6000 foot; the fencibles 200 cavalry and 14,000 infantry; the militia 26,000 foot, and the yeomanry 35,000 in all, of whom about two-thirds were infantry, while the rest provided their own mounts. In addition, there were about 1500 gunners of the Royal Artillery and Royal Irish Artillery, some 500 German mercenary cavalry, and 600 "Invalids." Though properly classified as regulars, these corps were usually counted separately. This gives a nominal strength of 81,600, or, if we subtract the yeomanry, a first-line force of 46,600 men who might with some accuracy be called soldiers.

The actual number of men "present and fit for duty," however, was considerably smaller. Although nine regiments of regular infantry had their headquarters in Ireland, some of these had just returned from serving abroad, where they had been reduced to mere skeletons. Four of the nine had fewer than 100 rank and file. One, the 68th, was down to 28 privates. The depleted regular battalions of foot, in theory the mainstay of the British regime in Ireland, could provide little more than 1600 muskets.[17] The regular cavalry was in somewhat better state, though also below strength. The nine regiments of horse, plus the Hompesch Dragoons, should have mustered about 6500 sabres; their returns, however, total some 4000.[18] Among the fencibles, too, the infantry—4000 men short of its 14,000 paper strength—was in worse state than the cavalry, whose seven regiments had close to the authorized 2000 troopers.[19] The militia returns show scarcely more than 22,000 men.[20]

Thus, the effective, as distinguished from the paper,

---

1904); H. Pearse, *The Life of Viscount Lake* (London, 1850). Troop strengths are for May 1798 (the month in which Bonaparte launched the "expedition of Egypt").

[17] Regimental returns (Infantry), P.R.O.I.
[18] Regimental returns (Cavalry), P.R.O.I.
[19] Regimental returns (Fencible infantry and cavalry), P.R.O.I.
[20] Regimental returns (Militia), P.R.O.I.

strength of the army was approximately 40,000 men. But the field force amounted to even less. It had been officially calculated as recently as 1797 that soldiers detached as baggage guards, officers' servants, etc., as well as those on sick list or on garrison duty would, at any given time, total around 10,000.[21] Allowing for this deduction, the force left to defend Ireland against invasion included little over 30,000 men, exclusive of the yeomanry, who had never been intended for battlefield duty.

No attempt was made to compensate for the numerical weakness of the British army in Ireland by a prudent disposition of the force available. Careless dispersal of troops had long been a characteristic failing of the Irish high command. Two days after the French had anchored in Bantry Bay in 1796, there were fewer than 2000 men to oppose them between Bantry and Cork, with only two pieces of artillery and no provisions.[22] John Beresford, the politically puissant First Commissioner of the Revenue, had described the situation candidly:

> No landing was made. Providence prevented it; if there had, where was a stand to be made? it is clear that Cork was gone; who would answer afterwards for the loyalty of the country, then in possession of the French? Would the Northern parts of the country have remained quiet? Not an hour.[23]

The government's response to this embarrassing challenge was to shift the bulk of its army to the south of Ireland. By 1798, a good half of its regulars, fencibles, and militia were stationed in Munster, being concentrated especially along the comparatively short line from Limerick to Waterford which an enemy coming from the southwestern bays would have to cross.[24] With its gaze firmly directed toward

[21] Melville Papers, MSS 54A, 136.
[22] Jones, 165.
[23] John Beresford to William Eden, Jan. 25, 1797, *The Journal and Correspondence of Lord Auckland,* ed. the Bishop of Bath and Wells (4 vols., London, 1862), III, 376.
[24] Chart, 508.

the site of the earlier invasion threat, the high command was unwilling to credit the French with sufficient imagination or initiative to strike in the West or the North, where the defenses were correspondingly weakened.

Whatever advantage might have been gained by allocating more men to a particular region was irretrievably lost by the unsound contemporary practice of placing the troops in small detachments here and there throughout the country. The yeomanry, designed for local service, were of course assigned to their own areas of residence. But loyalists demanded additional protection, and the government, yielding to pressure from local magnates and desiring to enforce the disarming of "restless" districts, reinforced the yeomen by splitting the regulars, fencibles, and militia into companies and half-companies, and scattering these detachments in dozens of towns and villages. Thus an overall defensive strategy was impossible. With the regiments dispersed in "penny packets," the country's military posture was little improved from that of 1796. It was estimated in April 1798 that not more than 6000 men could be assembled for action in four or five days if an enemy appeared either in Bantry Bay or at the mouth of the Shannon, and it would require twice that time to bring together 10,000 men.[25] The import of these figures is clear when one recalls that by generally accepted calculation an invading force could march from Cork to Dublin in ten days and from Galway to Dublin in six.[26] By dividing up the Irish army to better defend the homes of Ascendancy supporters against domestic enemies, the government seriously crippled the defense of the kingdom against overseas enemies.

The lack of quality, both absolute and relative, indicated by the preceding figures might have been offset to some ex-

[25] Maurice, ed., I, 288; Melville Papers, MSS 54A, 137.
[26] Lieutenant General Sir H. S. Keating, *The Defence of Ireland* (Dublin, 1795), 48. (This book—actually a brief "tract for the times"—was intended to call attention to the defects of Ireland's defenses. It did not have much of an effect.)

tent by quality. Had the troops in Ireland possessed the steadiness, experience and *esprit de corps* of elite veteran units, they might have held their own against the armies of the French Republic, despite unfavorable odds. But the overwhelming mass of evidence shows that indiscipline was universal, infecting regular as well as auxiliary regiments. Continual subdivision of units and their employment on constabulary duties could not but destroy military spirit and moral fibre. The shock of the United Irish rising in 1798 proved too much for the majority of the regular cavalry regiments. Panic and ignominious flight before the insurgents crowned a multitude of offenses and caused the disbanding of two regiments; four others, thoroughly demoralized, were shifted to England.[27] Their conduct in the face of Napoleon's veterans could hardly have been much better.

Their prolonged service on relaxed, easy-going garrison duty in Ireland had particularly bad effects on the regular cavalry. Discipline in the scattered contingents of a few dozen men and a subaltern at provincial market towns was usually lax. The habit of idleness which the Irish Horse had acquired during long peaceful decades was not easily shaken off, despite the threat of invasion. It had long been the custom for officers to take six or seven months' leave at a stretch, and for the men to receive extended furloughs. Assembled as regiments only once a year for drills and reviews mixed with balls and galas, the regular cavalry was endowed with all the social graces, but little fighting capacity. The 5th Light Dragoons, for instance, had been in Ireland since 1714 without ever hearing a shot fired in battle; its nine troops of horse were spread across the country from the far north to the extreme south; one of them deserted *en masse* during the insurrection and others became so insubordinate that the regiment had to be dissolved.[28] Though the regular infantry regiments had not

[27] Fortescue, IV, 593, 595–97.
[28] Charles Ross, ed., *Correspondence of . . . Cornwallis* (3 vols., London, 1859), II, 421–22.

suffered the same deterioration through prolonged inactivity in Ireland as had the cavalry, repeated subdivision and drafts for service abroad (especially in the West Indies) had not only reduced some of them to minimal strength, but also sapped the morale of the few men who remained.

The fencibles, who had been enlisted only since the beginning of the war with France, obviously had not experienced the same deleterious effects of prolonged inactivity. But their very newness meant that they lacked even a nucleus of veteran officers and sergeants, and while employed on morale-destroying police work they had little chance to learn their proper trade. Contemporary observers deplored the fencibles' "most wretched discipline" and complained of "the most dishonourable sentiments and ignorance" among all but a few officers.[29] Several of the Scottish battalions were notoriously riotous,[30] and one Welsh unit, the "Ancient Britons," embarrassed even the Irish Government by its brutality toward the peasantry.[31] Regiments like the Loyal Durham Infantry, whose gallantry at Arklow turned defeat into victory during the insurrection, were evidently the exception.

The militiamen who made up such a large proportion of Ireland's defensive force were regarded by the government as its least reliable element. Although unwilling to admit their fears publicly, the senior officers of the crown tended to accept the inflated claims of United Irish propaganda, and anticipated mass desertions in the face of a rising or an invasion. In fact, although the United Irishmen did their best to win over individual soldiers or even whole detachments, the actual subversion of men whose sympathies presumably lay with the Catholic peasantry from whom they were drawn was minimal. While defections did take place

---

[29] James Gordon, *The Rebellion in Ireland in the Year 1798* (London, 1810), pref., xxv.

[30] J. R. Western, "Formation of the Scottish Militia," *Scottish Historical Review*, XXXIV, no. 117 (Apr. 1955), 8.

[31] Lecky, IV, 41, 275, 343.

during the rebellion in 1798, they were far fewer than had been feared, and in most cases represented spontaneous decisions rather than planned treachery. In some cases, such as that of the North Cork battalion, whose excesses in Wexford helped provoke insurrection there, the militia went out of its way to demonstrate "fidelity" to the regime by terrorizing the peasantry. Nonetheless, the government could never be sure of the Catholic majority of its troops, and only the Ulster battalions of Down, Cavan, Fermanagh, Monaghan, and Armagh, each of which incorporated a lodge of the Loyal Orange Order, were considered "safe." [32]

Censure of the militia on the familiar ground of slackness was more generally justified. Sir John Moore, fresh from active service with regular British troops when he was assigned to an Irish command, found his militiamen "extremely undisciplined," and "as ignorant and as much a rabble as those who have hitherto opposed us." [33] Lord Castlereagh, Chief Secretary of the Irish Government, and a former militia officer, while praising their "determined spirit" and denying that they had shown "the smallest disposition to fraternize" with the masses, admitted that the militiamen were "defective in many instances in subordination." [34] The usual bad practice of dividing and subdividing was extended to the militia with the usual bad results. In order to make them a more trustworthy police force, the government took care to send battalions as far away from their native districts as possible, the Kerry Militia, for example, being stationed in Armagh, and western contingents like those of Galway and Sligo in the extreme southeast.[35] Fraternization was thus discouraged, but morale was not notably improved, and transportation problems were multiplied. Furthermore, the influx of raw recruits, replacing the

[32] Senior, 57.
[33] Maurice, ed., I, 294, 302f.
[34] Lord Londonderry, ed., *Memoirs and Correspondence of . . . Castlereagh* (8 vols., London, 1848), I, 219.
[35] Kilmainham Papers, MS 1112, f. 39ff.

men whose four-year service time under the Militia Act had just expired, weakened the county battalions at the very moment when trained manpower was most needed. The Irish militia, which had been raised as a national defense force, was incapable of sustaining that function against any sort of determined assault.

The fourth major component of the crown forces, although also purely Irish, was under no such cloud of suspicion as enveloped the militia. The yeomanry was overwhelmingly Protestant, drawn from the landlord class, their retainers, and those who had a stake in preserving their ascendancy. Its members had volunteered in order to hold in check the Catholics, and, by maintaining the English Conquest, secure their own property and interests against revolution. Hence the yeomanry was regarded as the "sheet anchor" of the administration.[36] But the motivation and methods of the yeomen limited their effectiveness. Raised and maintained locally, preoccupied with local fears and local feuds, they were of some use to the government for holding rural districts in awe. As soldiers, they were worthless. While the numerous bands of "loyal subjects" were invariably added to the total of troops available, no realistic commander took them seriously as a force capable of putting down a general insurrection, much less repelling an invasion.

To the quantitative and qualitative deficiencies of the army in Ireland there must be added the shortcomings of antiquated tactical training and equipment. Prevailing British military doctrine considered cavalry solely as an attacking force. The whole of mounted drill was designed to secure maximum shock against the enemy front by exact alignment of each squadron's two parallel ranks. Cavalry regulations virtually ignored the use of cavalry as skirmishers or mounted infantry. There was no training for patrol work, and, in the words of a dragoon officer, "to attempt giving

[36] Lecky, IV, 100.

men or officers any idea . . . of outpost duty was absurd."[37] Foreign observers were unimpressed by the British cavalry: General Foy dismissed them as useless for irregular warfare or scouting, and, despite their "showy evolutions" on the parade ground, weak in the assault.[38] Another French general, Exelmans, commented that "the British cavalry officer seems to be impressed by the conviction that he can dash or ride over everything, as if the art of war were precisely the same as that of fox-hunting."[39] The broken ground, treacherous bogs, hedge-crossed fields, and walled-in farmlands of Ireland were particularly ill-suited to drill-book maneuvers and headlong charges. They offered ideal conditions for partisan activities and demanded the use of scouting parties—but for these tasks the British cavalry was totally unprepared. Trained solely for shock tactics, the troopers were all equipped with sabers, but too few firearms were allocated to each regiment to permit effective dismounted fighting.

Infantry tactics, too, adhered to rigidly prescribed patterns. Sir David Dundas's drill book of 1788 had introduced the Prussian system of three ranks drawn up one behind another, in place of the two-rank array used in the American war. As a fighting formation, the three-rank line presented serious practical difficulties: firing over the shoulders of file leaders and manipulating muskets in the complicated steps of reloading was so awkward that the third rank often could not fire at all. By 1801 the shortcomings of the triple-line arrangement were to become so apparent that many commanders would ignore regulations and return to the double line. The Irish infantry of 1798, however, would have faced the French battalion columns that had swept everything before them on the Continent with its firing power diminished by one-third by obstinate adher-

[37] W. Tomkinson, *Diary of a Cavalry Officer,* 135. Quoted in Hayes-McCoy, "Government Forces," 24.
[38] *Ibid.,* 24.
[39] R. H. Gronow, *Reminiscences and Recollections* (London, 1889), 110.

ence to an unrealistic, discredited tactical principle. As with the cavalry, little thought had been given to any sort of training but the most fundamental parade-ground drill. The "street-firing" prescribed for use in built-up areas was a purely mechanical maneuver, and the use of cover in combat, despite the lessons of America, was ignored by the instructors. A few commanders appeciated the value of light infantry as skirmishers, and even taught such troops to fight as individuals; but such innovations were the exception, and far ahead of the prevailing tactic of erect and perfect alignment in the open field. The triple-ranked foot soldier of 1798 was still equipped with the venerable "Brown Bess" musket and bayonet. While this flintlock was more accurate than the standard French firearm, the superior marksmanship of which the British army boasted was not characteristic of the poorly trained regiments in Ireland. The virtues of the rifle were only just being grudgingly accepted by army leaders, and but a single unit of riflemen was available in Ireland—the 5th battalion of the 60th Foot, comprising 400 "Jaegers" drafted from Hompesch's Hessian regiment, placed on the Irish Establishment on April 20, 1798.[40]

British artillery did not enjoy the same superiority in range and accuracy over French as did their small arms. Most contemporaries agree that there was little difference between British and French performance at this period, though the presence of an artillerist of Bonaparte's genius would certainly have given the advantage to his gunners. But if the Royal Artillery had made technical advances in recent years—lighter gun carriages, howitzers, mobile field pieces ("battalion guns") attached to infantry units—the Irish Establishment was deficient in this arm as in others. Guns, ammunition, and equipment were kept in a poor state of repair and readiness. There were no permanent supply or transport arrangements, necessitating the hiring of civil-

[40] Fortescue, IV, 916ff; Hayes–McCoy, "Government Forces," 25–27.

ian horses, drivers, and vehicles "on the spot," whenever an emergency should arise. Even the two six-pounders allocated to each infantry battalion were without horses, and since the scattered detachments were scarcely ever brought together, no one had any idea of how much transport would be required for an "army" in the field.[41]

Ireland's disordered and defective defenses accurately reflected the archaic confusion of her military administration. The army's nominal head was the "Commander-in-chief in Ireland," a senior British officer with headquarters at Kilmainham, on the outskirts of Dublin. He was assisted by "the Staff in Ireland," which included an adjutant-general, a quartermaster-general, a judge-advocate-general, a medical board, and various other categories of officials, some military, some civilian—all with their deputies and aides, most of them ornamental rather than useful. But Kilmainham was obliged to share control over essential army services with four distinct departments of the civil administration at Dublin Castle: the ordnance office, the commissariat, the barrack board, and the muster-master-general's office. Moreover, the lord lieutenant, though prior to June 1798 invariably an English politician with little knowledge of Ireland and none of military affairs, was entitled to intrude on the commander-in-chief's sphere, and while such intrusions might be confined largely to matters of patronage, they involved a great deal of correspondence back and forth. Such communications passed through a section of the chief secretary's office known as the Military Department, though it was often confusingly referred to as the "war office" and the undersecretary in charge designated as "the secretary at war." Although some half-hearted attempts were made by the "war office" to coordinate the activities of the "staff" and the four civil de-

---

[41] Maurice, ed., I, 271; Keating, 90; Hayes–McCoy, "Government Forces," 27.

partments, it was ill suited to liaison duties, and little real collaboration resulted.⁴²

Under the outmoded and irrelevant organizational system which placed "mechanical" matters in a separate category from the affairs of cavalry and infantry, the artillery, the engineers, the munitions laboratory, and all stores and supplies pertaining to them were subordinate to the Master–General of the Ordnance. Though usually held by a military man, this office was regarded as a political sinecure, and rapidly passed from hand to hand. The Marquess of Drogheda had been replaced in 1797 by the Earl of Carhampton when that extremely unpopular general was dismissed as commander-in-chief. Carhampton, negligent and usually absent, was supplanted in 1800 by the Honorable Thomas Pakenham, M.P., a captain in the Royal Navy. Though the second-ranking post in the department, Lieutenant–General of the Ordnance, was customarily given to a veteran officer (Pakenham had held it from 1797 to 1800), the five remaining "patentee" (or executive) positions in the office were invariably occupied by members of Parliament, who spent little time on the job. Such work as was done, therefore, was left to some twenty-five clerks and "store-keepers."

Provision of food and forage for the army was the responsibility of the commissariat, a duty which its establishment of seventy clerks and assistant commissaries carried out adequately, though not without much delay and corrup-

---

⁴² A brief outline of Irish military administration is contained in R. B. McDowell, *The Irish Administration, 1801–1914* (London, 1964), 15–19. This, of course, is a mere retrospective sketch, since most of the distinctively Irish military institutions were abolished after the Union. There exists no substantial study of eighteenth-century Irish military administration (or, indeed, of eighteenth-century Irish administration as such). Most of the information on the administration contained in this essay was derived from Rowley Lascelles, ed., *Liber Munerum Publicorum Hiberniae* (Dublin, 1852), and James L. J. Hughes, ed. *Patentee Officers in Ireland, 1173–1826* (Dublin, 1960). In addition, various contemporary directories, notably *The City and Country Calendar, or Irish Court Registry* (Dublin, annual), were consulted.

tion, in peacetime. But the "wagon train" of nearly a thousand "conductors," drivers, smiths, and farriers which had been attached to the commissariat in 1789 had not been kept up to strength. It is doubtful that, lacking purposeful professional direction, the commissariat could have stood the strain of supplying a large force in the field in a rapidly changing military situation.

Housing for the troops in all parts of Ireland was supervised by the barrack board, which also functioned as the "board of works" and was responsible for various government buildings in Dublin. The seven "Commissioners and Overseers of the Barracks" (only one of whom had any direct experience of military life or knowledge of barrack requirements) presided over several dozen patentee officers, clerks, and provincial barrack-masters. The whole department was notorious for "general disorder and abuse," with the inspecting officers collecting travel allowances, though never leaving Dublin, and the barrack-masters falsifying accounts and making illicit profits on stores and repairs. Widespread neglect of duty and indifference by this department over a period of years had resulted in the deterioration of old barracks and faulty construction of new ones. The squalor and overcrowding of many barracks seriously weakened both the health and the morale of the army in Ireland.

The office of Muster Master General (or "Clerk of the Cheque") dated back to the early sixteenth century, and little but its antiquity justified its existence, for its sole duty was to record the strength of units stationed in Ireland. The fortunate holder of this sinecure received a fee for entering on his records the commission of each officer transferred from the British to the Irish Establishment. The actual management of the office was, of course, left to a deputy and a few clerks.

The existence of a headquarters staff, a "war office," and four civil departments, each representing vested interests and usually working at cross purposes to the others, led to endless delay, duplication, and waste, compounded by periodic interference from a parallel set of officials in England. It had long been the desire of Pitt's government to eliminate the "accidental differences" between the British and Irish Establishments, and it was "an important political principle to assimilate them as much as possible." [43] But it was only in the last years of the century that variations from British army clothing regulations and other anomalies began to disappear, despite London's complaints and queries. Nor was it until February 1799, when the office of examinator and comptroller of army accounts was created, that any "regular system" was introduced into the management of military finances. Prior to that date, payment of troops, the purchase, sale and exchange, and "sundry other military business" was carried on by the Dublin Castle "war office" through civilian "agents" whose fees and "expenses" were another drain on the army budget.[44]

Few of the civilian personnel who had a place in the administrative jumble of Irish military affairs were more than drones or timeservers; some of them were positively dangerous in their incompetence and rapacity. This is hardly surprising, considering the contemporary view that public office was nothing more than an institution for rewarding political stalwarts, no matter how idle or incapable they might be. Far more striking is the evidence of petty jealousy, weakness of character, and professional ineptitude in the high command, among those officers who were expected to lead the defense of Ireland.

Political conspiracy and terrorism had increased markedly in Ireland since the removal of the "liberal" Lord Fitzwilliam in 1795 and his replacement as viceroy by the inept Lord Camden, who allowed himself to be dominated by the ultra-conservative "Castle Clique." The efforts of

---

[43] Kilmainham Papers, MS 1011 (Memorandum, Feb. 13, 1792).
[44] McDowell, *Irish Administration*, 17.

this faction to extend its control over the army, and to employ the troops as a counterrevolutionary police force caused frequent changes at Kilmainham, as the Irish administration sought a manageable commander-in-chief. General Sir Robert Cunningham proved insufficiently "zealous" in the work of "pacification," and was supplanted in 1796 by General Lord Carhampton, who had already "crushed sedition" in Connaught. But Carhampton was too proud, ill-tempered, and violent a man to work well with Dublin Castle, and in December 1797 he was transferred to the ordnance. The new Commander-in-Chief, General Sir Ralph Abercromby, was a distinguished veteran officer, just back from campaigning in the West Indies. This blunt-spoken Scot insisted on applying professional standards to the distinctly unprofessional Irish army, which, after a brief, dismaying inspection, he declared to be "in a state of licentiousness which must render . . . [it] formidable to everyone but the enemy." [45] His plans for reform, which included consolidation of scattered units, intensive retraining, imposition of proper discipline upon the militia, and the weeding-out of idle, incompetent officers, met a prompt rejection from the viceroy and his cabinet, who found the "Scotch beast" [46] insulting in his manner and excessively independent in his way of doing business. Camden procured his recall to Britain in April 1798, and he was replaced on an "acting" basis, by Lieutenant–General Gerard Lake, the blustering, bullying commander of the Ulster district, whose brutal methods of rooting out United Irish suspects and fervid professions of loyalty had made him the favorite of

---

[45] Lecky, IV, 199. On Sir Ralph's acute criticism of the state of the Irish forces, and the "Abercromby incident" in general, see Lecky, IV, 198–210. Lord Dunfermline's *Life of Lieutenant General Sir Ralph Abercromby* (London, 1861), is also valuable for the commander-in-chief's personal reactions to Irish political and military affairs.

[46] Lord Clare to Lord Auckland, Mar. 26, 1798, *Auckland Correspondence*, III, 395.

the Castle Clique.⁴⁷ It was during Lake's tenure that the long-feared, long-expected rebellion broke out. Uncoordinated, leaderless, and desperate as it was, the rising almost proved too much for the disorganized forces of the crown, and on June 20, 1798, Lord Cornwallis arrived in Dublin to supersede Lake.

In sending Charles, first Marquess Cornwallis, to deal with the Irish rebellion, the London government felt that it was sending the best of its generals. The memory of his surrender at Yorktown—which, in any case, had been preceded by a series of notable victories—had been effaced by his achievements as Governor–General and Commander-in-Chief in Bengal. Since his return from India, he had been Pitt's principal military adviser and had superintended the organization of Britain's defenses against invasion. To assure his complete control over Irish affairs and Irish factions, he was named Lord Lieutenant as well as Commander-in-Chief, thus giving him an unprecedented combination of civil and military power.

But Cornwallis was in his sixtieth year, tired and in poor health. He had accepted the Irish appointment reluctantly and out of a sense of duty, rather than from enthusiasm or ambition.⁴⁸ Within a few weeks, he was complaining of his "wretched situation," and avowing that "the life of a Lord Lieutenant of Ireland comes up to my idea of perfect misery." The main rebel "armies" had been dispersed by the time he arrived, and Cornwallis' chief tasks were the supervision of "mopping-up operations" and the meting out of punishment. These responsibilities he found wearying and uncongenial. He was depressed by the "dirty business" of Irish politics, and disgusted by the jobbery and corrup-

---

⁴⁷ For evidence of Lake's character and opinions, the Lake Papers in the National Library of Ireland are far more revealing than H. Pearse's biographical sketch.

⁴⁸ Cornwallis to Maj. Gen. Ross, Mar. 31, 1798, *Cornwallis Correspondence,* II, 328.

tion involved in securing the legislative union which Pitt now desired.[49]

The landing of General Humbert's tiny expeditionary force in Mayo in August revealed how little of Cornwallis' old dash and energy remained to him. In America, and even in India, he had been noted for his "drive," his eagerness to pursue, to harass, to strike at the enemy. He had preferred boldness to caution; he would "sooner attack than entrench." But in 1798 he moved deliberately, almost ponderously, demanding overwhelming superiority in numbers before he would approach a mere thousand French troops. To be sure, he may have doubted the quality of his army (even though fresh British battalions had reached Ireland by this time), and lacked precise information on the number of the invaders; but the hesitancy and anxiety which he exhibited in this crisis suggest not merely a general who is worried about the military situation, but one who lacks confidence in himself. Cornwallis in his prime might have offered a serious challenge to Bonaparte. But Cornwallis was no longer in his prime.

With a very few exceptions, the other general officers commanding in Ireland were men of mediocre, or less than mediocre, ability, whose leadership would have contributed little to the defense of the country during an invasion. On the eve of the French War, the staff included a dozen generals; by 1798, without any proportionate increase in troops, their number had doubled. Obviously it was felt that a higher level of leadership was required, that officers of a more senior rank ought to undertake the responsibilities involved in pacifying the disturbed area. There is no reason to believe that Ireland was in any sense a safe "dumping ground" for officers of inferior quality. The senior commanders in Ireland, therefore, present a fairly rep-

[49] Cornwallis to Maj. Gen. Ross, July 1, 1798, *Cornwallis Correspondence*, II, 355–56.

resentative cross-section of British general officers of the period.[50]

In age, the generals ranged from the venerable Eyre Massey, born in 1719, down to men scarcely over thirty. The majority were neither septuagenarians nor striplings, being a few years younger than the commander-in-chief (i.e., born in the 1740s). They were about equally divided between Englishmen and Scots; although some others had Irish "connections," only two—Henry Johnson and John Hely–Hutchinson—might properly, by birth and residence, be called Irishmen. The latter, brother of the Earl of Donoughmore, was one of the half-dozen who belonged to titled families; the remainder, in so far as their backgrounds can be determined, were all of gentry or middle-class professional stock. Following the custom of the time, which permitted serving officers to hold seats in the House of Commons, five of them "represented" Irish boroughs, and two were Westminster M.P.s. Although a few veteran campaigners had experience going back to the Seven Years' War (the seventy-seven-year-old Charles Vallency had been Chief Engineer since 1762), or even the War of the Austrian Succession (both Massey and William Fawcett had fought Bonnie Prince Charlie in 1745), most of the generals on the Irish Staff had seen virtually all of their combat in the War for American Independence, as field-grade or subaltern officers. Of these, Henry Johnson, Charles Eustace, Eyre Coote, Sir Charles Asgill, and Gerard Lake shared Cornwallis' humiliation at Yorktown. A period of doldrums and slow promotions between 1783 and 1793 had been followed by new opportunities and advancement. Almost all of the British commanders in Ireland had acquired their rank within the previous three or four years,

---

[50] Biographical and other data on the generals described in the following paragraphs have been obtained from the Kilmainham, Melville, and Lake Papers, *passim*, supplemented by the *Dictionary of National Biography*.

and several of them only in the first months of 1798. But, to the extent that their rank was not based upon claims of seniority, it was rather a compensation for disappointment than a reward for victory, as the principal campaigns of the French War so far—in the Low Countries and the West Indies—had been inglorious for British arms. Thus, except for Cornwallis himself, with his Indian triumphs, none of the generals in Ireland had recent experience of anything but defeat.

The generals of the army in Ireland were, then, men of no particular distinction, unaccustomed to commanding large bodies of troops in combat, and with a disappointing record of being on the losing side. Even without the intervention of Bonaparte, the events of 1798 overwhelmed many of them. The elderly General Fawcett, after his first sortie against the rebels was repulsed, refused to move out of Duncannon Fort, and resigned himself to defeat. Sir James Stewart, the high-strung hypochondriac commanding in Munster, broke down completely, and threw his province into confusion with conflicting orders. Sir James Duff, though he was able to keep the peace in his own district, around Limerick, lost his head when ordered to advance into Kildare, massacred several hundred surrendering rebels, and had to be sent home on "sick leave." General Eustace, too, panicked by the rising, burned and ravaged indiscriminately, and had to be "retired" by his old comrade-in-arms, Cornwallis.

The commander-in-chief had, indeed, a poor opinion of most of his subordinates. General Johnson, despite his successful defense of New Ross against the rebels, was characterized by Cornwallis as a "wrongheaded blockhead," while Hely–Hutchinson, who was routed at Castlebar by a handful of Frenchmen, was scorned by the viceroy as "no soldier" at all. Lake, who shared responsibility for the Castlebar fiasco, resented Cornwallis' being placed over him, and this defeat, which exposed the weakness of his generalship, worsened relations between the senior commanders.[51]

Only two general officers displayed consistent coolness, skill, and initiative during the emergency of 1798. Major-General George Nugent, who had succeeded to Lake's Ulster command in April, crushed the insurrectionists promptly and vigorously and secured the province against invasion or further rebellion. His performance was gratefully applauded by Cornwallis, who was also impressed by the alert, common-sense attitude of John Moore. Junior in rank to most of the other generals (he had come to Ireland with Abercromby as a brigadier, and was promoted to major general in August 1798), the future hero of the Peninsular War had nevertheless gained attention by transforming the slack troops under his command at Cork into an effective force in only a few months, and by his innovations in the use of light infantry. His success against the rebels, and his share in the final defeat of Humbert's corps at Ballinamuck contributed to his growing reputation. But two real leaders out of twenty generals would scarcely have been enough to provide a margin of victory over a major French invasion army.

Such was the state of Ireland's defenses in the spring of 1798. In numbers, training, morale, experience, and equipment, the troops were inferior to those of Revolutionary France. Careless dispersal of forces, a disorganized supply system, non-existent transport—scarcely one of the cardinal military sins was lacking. With overlapping and conflicting administration of army affairs, political interference with headquarters, and constant shuffling of generals, not even a modest level of efficiency, let alone reform, was possible. The weak, timid, uninspired commanders of the army, instead of providing leadership, merely formed themselves in the army's image.

---

[51] Cornwallis to Maj. Gen. Ross, July 15, 1799; *Cornwallis Correspondence*, III, 116. See also II, 391, 395.

It is evident that Britain could not have defended Ireland had Bonaparte landed there in 1798. Her military strength in that island was illusory, nor was she capable of countering an invasion with adequate reinforcements.[52] The great mass of Irishmen would have joined immediately with the French and made the country untenable. Ireland could, indeed, have been conquered in 1798 had Napoleon chosen to do so. And with Ireland in the hands of the enemy, Britain would have been forced to sue for peace, leaving the way clear for French mastery of the Continent. Instead, Britain remained undefeated, and dedicated to the destruction of Revolutionary France and, ultimately, of Napoleon. Bonaparte's decision in the crisis of 1798 decided his own fate, and the fate of all Europe.

[52] On June 9, 1798, the Duke of York (Commander-in-Chief, England) informed the Duke of Portland (Home Secretary, charged with the supervision of Irish affairs) that not more than 950 cavalry and 8,000 infantry could possibly be sent from England to Ireland, and of these no more than half would be regular troops, the rest being fencibles. It would be useless, he said, to send to Ireland any of the "stricken" regular battalions which had lately returned from tropical stations (quoted in D. A. Chart, 508).

# 8

# "Young England" and Its Political Debut: 1843

## NICHOLAS VARGA

BETWEEN 1830 AND 1848, life in the "Great Republic" was once again stirred by what one historian has described as "hope and generous optimism." This bracing climate roused the enthusiasm of many, but among none was the response so evident as in the younger generation. The map of Europe erupted with such nationalist and revolutionary movements as "Young Italy" and "Young Germany." Nearly a decade after these had appeared, England also discovered within its body politic a group known as "Young England"; but where the Continental movements were dazzled by visions of the future, "Young England" sought part of its inspiration from a different source.

Nevertheless, the first public appearance of "Young England" was something of a shock to "Old England." In July 1843, the Conservatives in Commons were startled when, during the debate on an Irish Arms Bill, their positions were subjected to a rattle of political musketry from within their own ranks. More than one M.P. must have craned 'round to learn the identity of these "presumptuous upstarts." It did not take long for some Tory politicians to decide that the "upstarts" were merely Benjamin Disraeli's instrument for revenge. He was then nearly forty and, though he had worked diligently for a Conservative election victory, he had not been included in the Peel government of 1841. "Young England" was, therefore, viewed by some as little more than the tool by which Disraeli sought to relieve his disappointment. Others dismissed "Young England" as a coterie of immature gentlemen "who wore white waistcoats and wrote spooney poetry."[1] Such attention and confusion pleased the spirit of the romantic "dandy" that was imbedded in the character of each of the members; from the vantage of more than a century latter, however, it is possible to describe more realistically the origins and political debut of "Young England."

"Young England" had its birth in the discussions of Benjamin Disraeli and three young Tory M.P.s during the latter half of 1842. In July of that year, Disraeli broached the proposal to Lord John Manners, the charming and idealistic son of the Duke of Rutland, and the brilliant though erratic George Smythe, heir to the sixth Viscount Strangford. Manners and Smythe were close friends, and, as befitted their social position, they had entered Parliament after completing gentlemanly encounters with Eton and Cambridge. Disraeli's overture resulted in nothing definite, so he decided to winter in Paris. He took the precaution of addressing his constituents before departing and vowed to continue his support of the Conservative government unless it wavered on the question of the "corn laws." Upon arriving in Paris, he met Smythe, acting for Manners, and Alexander Baillie Cochrane, a "fiery and generous" young Scottish laird. The conversations quickly turned to the question of organizing a new political group. After some haggling, these men agreed to sit together in Commons and to

---

[1] Frances Hitchman, *The Public Life of the Right Honourable The Earl of Beaconsfield* (London, 1881), 126.

vote together with "the majority deciding." Such a rule was probably designed to insure control by the young Tories. Disraeli and Cochrane also wanted a stipulation that none would accept office, but Smythe would agree only to communicate any offers to the whole group. Against Disraeli's dream of an expanding party of at least forty or fifty members, it was agreed that only the original four would participate in the management of "Young England." [2]

Why had so ambitious a man as Disraeli involved himself with a little clique, especially one which quite clearly he could not dominate? His plans may be gathered from a memorandum which he submitted to the French government shortly after the meetings with Smythe and Cochrane. The Conservative majority of ninety, as Disraeli analyzed the situation, included forty or fifty "agricultural malcontents." These men were not yet prepared to undertake an active opposition but were restive enough to hold themselves aloof on questions which did not directly affect the life of the Peel ministry. In such circumstances, a young, vigorous group within the Conservative Party could influence the "tone" of the prime minister. "Young England," in Disraeli's conception, would generally support Peel on domestic policy but bend the government into a renewal of the Anglo–French *entente*. He told the French government that he had just become the head of such a group and could organize press support as well.[3] What his young colleagues thought of Disraeli's scheme was not evident until "Young England" made its political debut some months later.

Disraeli's political analysis and his desire to renew the Anglo–French *entente* were shared by important members

[2] Charles Whibley, *Lord John Manners and His Friends* (2 vols., London, 1925), I, 140–142; Benjamin Disraeli to his sister, Oct. 16, 1842 in *Lord Beaconsfield's Correspondence with His Sister, 1832–1852*, ed. Ralph Disraeli (New York, 1886), 131.

[3] "Memorandum for the King of the French, 1842," in William Flavelle Monypenny and George Earle Buckle, *The Life of Benjamin Disraeli, Earl of Beaconsfield* (2 vols., London, 1929), I, 807–11.

of the Conservative Party. The prime minister was himself opining that the "times and party were out of joint." Sir Robert Peel ascribed his distressing situation to four years of bad harvests and five years of deficient revenues. John Wilson Croker, the Tory factotum, was similarly concerned about possible defections among the "landed gentry."[4] An effort at renewing the alliance would also come at a critical moment. Early in 1842, the Duke of Wellington was privately expressing great concern over the irritated state of Britain's relations with France. The only checkrein on France's ambitions and insulting behavior, believed the "Iron Duke," was Britain's naval superiority in all parts of the globe where British and French interests were competing.[5] Peel, on the other hand, was worried about what effect the recent rises in the French, Belgian, and German tariffs would have on the British economy, which was already strained by unemployment, a heavy national debt, and a formidable tax for poor relief.[6] Benjamin Disraeli thus had chosen a delicate situation into which he was introducing a new political force.

"Young England's" opening political sally, however, was not aimed at easing the strained relations between Britain and France, but dealt instead with what Britons, at least, would consider a "domestic" issue. This turn indicated the divided character of the party and reflected the preferences of Smythe, Manners, and Cochrane rather than Disraeli.

[4] John Wilson Croker to Lord Brougham, Feb. 19, 1843, in *The Correspondence and Diaries of the Late Right Honourable John Wilson Croker,* ed. Louis J. Jennings (2 vols., New York 1884), II, 222.

[5] Charles O. F. Greville, *A Journal of the Reign of Queen Victoria. 1837 to 1852* (3 vols., London, 1885), II, 80.

[6] Sir Robert Peel to Croker, July 27, 1842, *Croker's Diaries,* II, 175; Greville, *A Journal,* II, 146–47; Queen Victoria to the King of Belgium, Oct. 17, 1843 in *The Letters of Queen Victoria,* ed., Arthur Christopher Benson and Viscount Esher (3 vols., London, 1907), I, 621.

The division was so evident that Smythe facetiously described the new group as the "Diz-union." While Disraeli paid studious attention to Britain's foreign relations, the three young Tory M.P.s pondered the religious and social condition of England.

They proposed to rouse the nation from its slough of "infidelity." Early in 1843, Lord John Manners published *A Plea for National Holy–Days*. In this pamphlet, Manners asked whether the recent military victories would inspire "the poor, and the needy, and the friendless" to throng into the churches? Would the rest of the day find the people of England gamboling on the commons "where the lusty apprentice shall not fear to outleap his master's son, nor the pauper's heir to contend with the guardian's brother, while the alms of the faithful . . . are making the widows and orphans heart sing with joy?" Manners answered his own question with an "Alas! no. Utilitarian selfishness has well-nigh banished all such unproductive amusements from the land. . . ." [7]

The incongruity of calling for such a celebration to commemorate a punitive expedition against the Afghans and the opening of China to trade (albeit in opium) did not deter Lord John Manners and his colleagues. Their callowness lent itself to satire. *Punch* published "Lines to a Judge" in which a "Young Englander" asked to be tied to a cart-tail and flogged in order to revive this salutary old English punishment.

There was, however, another side to "Young England's" attack on the then-prevailing spirit. They were dedicated to achieving a religiously integrated society, and thus may be viewed as the political expression of the contemporaneous "Oxford Movement." Smythe and Manners were acquainted with F. W. Faber and John Henry Newman, two of the leaders in the effort to revitalize the Anglican

[7] Lord John Manners, *A Plea for National Holy–Days* (London, 1843), 4–5.

Church by returning to traditional theology. For their part, the young Tories saw such a revivified Church as a link between the aristocracy and the laboring people. The Church to them was not an adjunct-policeman to maintain order but was rather a successful countervailing power to "excessive parsimony." [8] They hoped to convert or set down the prototypes for Ebenezer Scrooge by more conventional means than those employed by Charles Dickens.

If "Young England" was engaged in a different arena from that occupied by the "Oxford Movement," the impulse for both sprang from a similar source. Newman viewed his enemy as "Liberalism," which he defined as a "false liberty of thought, or the exercise of thought upon matters in which . . . thought can not be brought to a successful issue." Lord John Manners, too, would

> . . . journey with St. Paul down to Damascus on his way,
> And speechless fall with him to earth, and trembling adore
> The boundless love that bade him rise, and gave him sight
>   once more.[9]

Such a picture and posture was only moderately appealing to Benjamin Disraeli. During the Paris negotiations, Smythe and Cochrane sought to include "Oxfordism" among the principles of the new party. Disraeli avoided such a commitment and also the disruption of the negotiation by expressing a willingness to adhere to a "moderate Oxfordism." Smythe cynically judged "Dizzy's attachment to moderate Oxfordism . . . [to be] something like Bonaparte's to moderate Mohamedanism." [10] Nevertheless, ambition vaulted over scruple, and the four confederated their new party.

With such evidences of division—even distrust—the

---

[8] *Ibid.,* 33.
[9] "The Feast of the Conversion of St. Paul A.D. 1842," Lord John Manners, *English Ballads and Other Poems* (London, 1852), 78–79.
[10] Whibley, *Manners and His Friends,* I, 153.

wonder was how "Young England" ever came to be. George Smythe was well aware of the shaky character of the party. Nevertheless, he urged Manners to accede to the Paris agreement since "to be of power, or fame, or even office, we cannot have our party swell too much or be too much *lies* with Disraeli." Baillie Cochrane was somewhat reluctant because he did not know Disraeli well, dreaded his jokes, and feared he might soon abandon his younger collaborators. Smythe also considered Disraeli's secession a possibility. "But even if he [Disraeli] did, it is always better *to be in a position* to be thrown over, than to be *nothing at all*." [11] For the three young Tories, Disraeli was a passport to "power, or fame, or even office"; they were in turn willing to serve as Disraeli's "makeweight."

Since the foreign affairs of no modern nation can be easily divided from its domestic concerns, Disraeli and the young Tories had other concerns. "The Irish question," which provided the occasion for "Young England's" political debut, also had an international dimension.

There were groups in both America and France ready to capitalize on Britain's embarrassments in Ireland. The United States was on the eve of a crucial election for which President John Tyler was abandoning his connection with the Whig Party and attempting to strengthen the Democratic Party. His eldest son, Robert, became head of an association favoring Ireland's demand for repeal of the legislative union with Britain. His son's activities thus served President Tyler both diplomatically and internally: American relations with Britain were then strained over the question of Texan independence, as well as over the attempt by an officer in the Royal Navy to annex Hawaii. Robert Tyler's identification with the repeal movement

[11] George Smythe to Lord John Manners, Oct. 19, 1842, *ibid.*, 143.

would encourage Irish demands and warn the British government of the need to settle with the United States before the difficulties with Ireland became too severe. Internally, Tyler could hope to strengthen the bond between the urban Irish and the Democratic Party. Meetings were held in Washington, Philadelphia, New York, and Boston where not only was money collected but also a call was issued for Frenchmen to aid the Irish as they once had aided Americans in their fight for independence.[12]

This appeal found a ready response among a group of French political leaders, who opposed any renewal of the *entente* with Britain. At a civic feast in Paris, where were gathered the men who would lead the revolt in '48, one speaker declared: "Let England understand . . . France is ready to lend an oppressed people . . . experienced heads, resolute hearts, and sturdy arms." Daniel O'Connell, Ireland's leader, wanted no taint of treason to weaken his Repeal Movement, and thus forestalled French emissaries from reaching Ireland. Despite O'Connell's rebuff, the "war-party" in France declared its strength still would remain available at Ireland's call. News of these activities in America and France caused a sharp decline on the British stock market which, in turn, increased Sir Robert Peel's economic problems.[13]

On yet another level, Britain's Irish difficulties affected her relations with Austria and the Holy See. The Catholic bishops in Ireland began to demonstrate their support of O'Connell and the Repeal Movement during the early months of 1843. On May 15, the Bishop of Ardagh told a meeting, "I have reason to believe, I may add, I know that

[12] John Tyler to Daniel Webster, July 8, 1843 in *The Letters and Times of the Tylers,* ed. Lyon G. Tyler (3 vols., Richmond, Va., 1884–96), II, 272; *The Diary of John Quincy Adams, 1794–1845,* ed. Allan Nevins (New York, 1951), 570; James C. H. Paul, *Rift in Democracy* (Philadelphia, 1951), 13; Martin Van Buren and Robert Tyler to the Friends of Ireland in Georgia, June 19, 1843, in *Niles National Register,* LXV, 87–90; LXIV, 273.

[13] Sir Charles Gavan Duffy, *Young Ireland: A Fragment of Irish History, 1840–1850* (New York, 1881), 320–24; *Niles National Register,* LXIV, 336.

every Catholic bishop in Ireland, without an exception, is an ardent Repealer." [14] Prince Metternich viewed these developments with such alarm that he began to press Rome to sever the growing connection between the Irish bishops and the Repealers. Rome, on the other hand, was seeking Metternich's help to suppress the distribution of revolutionary pamphlets printed in British Malta. Therefore, it was not surprising when Britain's minister to Vienna, Sir Robert Gordon, suggested a *quid pro quo*. Rome was to force the Irish bishops to withdraw their support of the Repeal Movement, and Britain would more rigidly regulate the pamphleteering.[15] Action on this proposal was delayed for more than a year but the intertwining interests of London, Rome, and Vienna formed the backdrop for the parliamentary debate on Ireland in 1843.

Before that clash began, the members of "Young England" were engaged in some preliminary skirmishing. The difference between Disraeli's interests and those of his three young colleagues was also made evident. During the early part of 1843, Disraeli attacked the ministry during the parliamentary debate on the Afghan war. He called the war as unjustified as a French attack across the Rhine from vague fears of "encirclement." Manners, it might be recalled, was simultaneously urging that these victories be used as occasions for prayer and sports on the commons. Some days later, Disraeli spoke in defense of the Webster–Ashburton treaty which had settled the Maine and other boundary difficulties with the United States. He defended

---

[14] John F. Broderick, *The Holy See & The Irish Movement for Repeal of the Union with England, 1829–1847* (Rome, 1951), 132.
[15] Sir Robert Gordon to Lord Aberdeen, June 13, 1843, *ibid.*, 169. More than a year later, Rome sent an ambiguous admonitory letter to the Irish bishops, but by that time the Repeal Movement had begun to lose its momentum and was being displaced by other organizations.

the treaty for easing Britain's relations with both America and France. The occasion also permitted Disraeli to slap the Liberals for having lost the friendship of France and for nearly losing the good will of the United States. This was obviously meant to be the first flourish in his campaign to renew the Anglo–French *entente*. In April 1843, he again rose to ask some searching questions about Balkan affairs, but Sir Robert Peel refused to give a full answer on the claim that what he said might endanger the delicate negotiations then in progress.[16] On none of these occasions did Smythe, Manners, or Cochrane demonstrate any public support for Disraeli.

He, in turn, remained silent when his young friends spoke on subjects that interested them. Baillie Cochrane was urging the ministry to forestall a secession from the Scottish Church by a judicious compromise with those who objected to government interference in Church appointments. Lord John Manners appealed to Parliament for a distribution of land to the poor as well as a relaxation of the Statute of Mortmain so that the Church could again become a refuge for paupers.[17] Such reform would hardly have appealed to the "agricultural malcontents" on whom Disraeli was relying for assistance in bending the Conservative government. Nevertheless, in mid-April, Manners recorded in his journal not only the fact that "Young England" was still intact but added that "Disraeli is a very easy man to get on with, and incomparably clever." [18]

This feinting and skirmishing had merely been the prelude to the full engagement on the "Irish question." The demand for repealing the legislative union had come at an

[16] *The Parliamentary Debates,* 3rd Series, LXVII, 68, 169, 859, 1028, 1299–1313.
[17] *Ibid.,* 67, 71, 99–118, 466, 872.
[18] Whibley, *Manners and His Friends,* I, 159.

alarming moment: unemployment was widespread; there were riots in Manchester, Yorkshire, Scotland, and Wales. Assassins twice aimed their pistols at Queen Victoria, while her minister, Sir Robert Peel, was the intended victim of another attempt. The Church of England was torn by the "Oxford Movement"; Scotland was also divided by a religious controversy. Daniel O'Connell, hoping to repeat his success of a decade and a half earlier, was counting heavily on these evidences of discontent to force Peel and Wellington to arrange the repeal.[19]

The Conservative government permitted affairs to roll on almost unchecked for a time because of its weakness. Wellington was quoted as doubting whether a Conservative government could long endure because he had no small talk and Sir Robert had no manners. To some preliminary inquiries on reports from Ireland, Peel and Wellington answered differently. Wellington was also not informed of Queen Victoria's proposed visit to the French king.[20]

The Government seemed to survive mainly because there was no acceptable alternative. On the basis of his own political ideas, Peel could make no stirring appeal to the people. He was attempting to travel the middle of the road while under attack by those who wanted a repeal of the "corn laws," and by the Chartists who were demanding a reformation of Britain's political and social fabric. There were signs that the forces pressing for consideration of the "condition of England" were coalescing with those that were active on the "Irish question." [21] This turn on the "left" was soon to be matched by "Young England's" use of the debate on Ireland to attack Peel from the other side.

[19] Peel to Victoria, Aug. 18, 1842, *Victoria's Letters,* I, 531; Viscount Melbourne to Victoria, June 23, 1843, *ibid.,* 604; Victoria to King of Belgium, May 31, 1842, *ibid.,* 500–2; Melbourne to Victoria, July 4, 1842, *ibid.,* 512; Greville, *Journal,* III, 136, 141–43, 206; Peel to Croker, Feb. 21, 1842, *Croker Diaries,* II, 147; Duffy, *Young Ireland,* 248.
[20] Duffy, *Young Ireland,* 212–17; Greville, *Journal,* II, 196.
[21] Peel to Victoria, July 23, 1842, *Victoria's Letters,* I, 521; S. MacCoby, *The English Radical Tradition, 1763–1914* (London, 1952), 135–37.

Weak though it might be, the Conservative government had to do something about the situation in Ireland. There had occurred, early in 1843, several brazen murders; O'Connell was openly boasting that '43 would be the "Repeal Year." The movement, which he headed, was receiving support from such diverse groups as the Catholic bishops and the upper-class Protestants; even the lower-class Protestants seemed to have forgotten their ancient antagonisms. Ominously, more violent forces seemed to be gestating within the "Repeal Movement." Englishmen were alarmed by the appearance of "Young Ireland" and its call for unity on the basis of Irish nationality.[22]

These alarming developments finally forced Peel to act. He and the cabinet decided to ask Parliament for stringent laws to "pacify" Ireland. In Commons, Sir Robert declared that he would use any means "which the prerogatives of the Crown and existing law give to the Government" for maintaining the union. When asked if the ministry would moderate this determination if all Ireland demanded the repeal, the prime minister answered that such an event would not affect the policy of the government since it viewed that question as a dismemberment of the British Empire. It was in pursuance of this attitude that Lord Eliot, the Irish Secretary, introduced a bill on April 27, 1843, to restrict the sale, use, and licensing of firearms in Ireland.[23] The result was a parliamentary debate which continued from May through August. Sentiment on the "Irish question" was, therefore, to be tested by the use of this rather

---

[22] Peel to Julia Peel, March, 1843, in *The Private Letters of Sir Robert Peel*, ed. George Peel (London, 1920), 222; J. Venedey, *Ireland and the Irish During the Repeal Year 1843* (Dublin, 1844), 102; Thomas Davis to Owen Maddyn, n.d., Duffy, *Young Ireland*, 300; [John Wilson Croker], "Policy of the Ministers," *Quarterly Review*, LXXII (1843), 586. See also Randall Clarke, "The Relations Between O'Connell and the Young Irelanders," *Irish Historical Studies*, III (1942), 18–30.

[23] Peel to Prince Albert, June 11, 1843, *Victoria's Letters*, I, 603; Duffy, *Young Ireland*, 217-18; *Journals of the House of Commons*, LXXXXVIII, 227.

unimportant bill. The debate also provided "Young England" with the occasion for its formal debut.

The initial stages of the debate were dominated by those favoring broader and more favorable action than merely a "pacification." Several efforts were made to obstruct the Arms Bill by amending it to investigate Irish grievances. When these amendments failed, the Irish members changed their tactics. They got one of their number, William Smith O'Brien, who was not associated with the repeal agitation, to introduce a motion independent of the Arms Bill. O'Brien's resolution called for a committee "for the purpose of taking into consideration the causes of the discontent at present prevailing in Ireland, with a view to the redress of grievances, and the establishment of a system of just and impartial government in that part of the United Kingdom."[24] The last phrase, in particular, was ambiguous enough to permit the possibility of repealing the legislative union; it might also be read as a declaration that Ireland did not then enjoy a "just and impartial government." O'Brien supported his motion with a moderate and factual speech which was followed by a general debate.

On July 7, "Young England" spoke up and loudly enough to be heard; Baillie Cochrane rose first. He doubted that the Established Church in Ireland was a major grievance but attacked the government for not attending to the other, very real complaints of the Irish. Cochrane reminded Commons that American "Repealers" were openly threatening the annexation of Canada if there were any serious trouble between England and its "other island." Smythe chose a more precise target, Sir Robert Peel, but attacked him on more fundamental grounds than merely the Irish troubles. The prime minister, said Smythe, was trammelled by the

[24] *Journals of the House of Commons,* LXXXXVIII, 236–451 (*passim*).

pledges he made while he was seeking to unseat the Liberals. The effect of these pledges was a weakness and temporizing which would not satisfy either the friends of the government in Commons or the people out of doors. The ministers had been seized, said Smythe, with a fatal lethargy at the very moment when decision was needed; they were now "without rudder or compass, showing themselves as weak in office as they were in opposition." [25] "Young England" wanted to grapple with "Liberalism" armed with principles at least as potent as the enemy possessed and not with Peel's prudential policy of slowing the advance of "Liberalism" without, at the same time, attempting to rechannel the flow of events.

Four more days of this sort of thing were enough for Sir Robert; on July 11, he attempted to close the debate with a summary of the government's position. The proponents of the O'Brien motion, he said, had failed to introduce anything new or anything which could be handled by legislation. Turning to deal even more directly with "Young England," Peel released the Conservatives from party discipline but warned that a vote for the O'Brien motion would be taken as implying a want of confidence in the government. Lord John Manners rose on the following day to reject Peel's view of the motion; it was not a question of confidence but rather a lack of sympathy "with those who would dare to palter with the convulsions of the Kingdom, as if it were the plaything of political intrigue." He, for one, intended to vote for the O'Brien motion. The bravado failed to inspire any substantial support, since the O'Brien motion was defeated decisively by a majority nearly a third larger than the proponents.[26] Peel's majority was untouched despite the defection of "Young England." Only Disraeli

---

[25] *The Parliamentary Debates,* 3rd Ser. LXX, 747–50, 932.
[26] *The Speeches of the Late Right Honourable Sir Robert Peel, Bart., Delivered in the House of Commons* (4 vols., London, 1853), IV, 269; *The Parliamentary Debates,* 3rd Ser., LXX, 1055, 1060, 1088.

had remained silent and did not vote in any important division.

Lest it appear that he had abandoned his young confederates, Benjamin Disraeli, on August 9, contributed a long speech to the debate on the Irish Arms Bill. He was willing to indicate a lack of confidence in at least one member of the government. The appointment of Lord Eliot as Irish Secretary, said Disraeli, had been an admission by Peel that his former attacks on the Liberals were mistaken. This resulted in a growing cynicism among the people. More and more people could be heard denying the existence of any difference in principle between the Conservatives and Liberals. Disraeli, however, urged the Conservatives to review their history, to see whether hostility to Ireland was a "Tory principle." He thought it strange to find "descendants of Cavaliers . . . governing Ireland on the principles of the Roundheads." Disraeli was clearly inviting the Conservative Party to offer Lord Eliot up as a scapegoat.

He then turned to register his sympathy with the more general attacks of Cochrane, Smythe, and Manners. While Irish land tenure was the crucial question, Disraeli also urged the ministry to review the poor laws, electoral rights, and religious grievances of the Irish. The hour had struck for a "great man, to have recourse to great remedial measures" which must begin with a reconstruction of the government and "even the social state of Ireland." Modesty forbade him from hinting that he might be such a "great man," but Disraeli's peroration made clear that he was willing to serve as the leader of a new party, or at least of a Conservative Party which had returned to its "old principles." Such a party, "framed on true principles could do justice to Ireland . . . [and] put an end to a state of things that was the bane of England and the opprobrium of

Europe." He would not, however, avert his gaze from this grand vision to lower himself to voting either for or against the Irish Arms Bill.[27]

George Smythe, taking his cue from Disraeli, broadened "Young England's" sally. Not Eliot but Peel was denounced for a "do-nothing" policy which was not "Conservative and not constitutional conservative." The house was reminded of Metternich's remark on the eve of the 1830 Revolution in France; Prince Metternich, referring to Polignac's complacency and inaction, had said: "I should be less anxious if Monsieur Polignac were more so." Smythe also recalled the fate of Lord North who lost America by a policy which started by doing nothing and ended at Yorktown.[28] Such comparisons were singularly effective, because they were made by persons sitting directly behind the Treasury Bench. The Irish Arms Bill passed with a very comfortable margin for the government but without a registered vote from "Young England."

This political debut provoked strong opinions. John Wilson Croker, the Tory "straw boss," could not understand "Young England's" desertion, even making allowances for youthful ambition; the O'Brien motion in particular "was the most offensive to *Old England* which had been made for many years." Charles Greville, clerk to the Privy Council and an indefatigable diarist, thought "Young England" an "abusive and impertinent" little squad which had forfeited the approval of Englishmen by their sympathy for the Irish.

[27] *The Parliamentary Debates,* 3rd Ser. LXXI, 430–38. For Disraeli's views on Irish land tenure see Sr. Mary of the Immaculate Conception, "Disraeli and the Irish Question, 1837–1852" (unpublished doctoral dissertation, Fordham University, 1953) and Benjamin Disraeli, *Lord George Bentinck, A Political Biography* (New York, 1905), 80.

[28] *The Parliamentary Debates,* 3rd Ser., LXXI, 442–43.

Sir James Graham, the Home Secretary, dismissed Smythe, Cochrane, and Manners as the puppets of the able though "unprincipled and disappointed" Disraeli. He thought a little pressure might reclaim the young lords and force their mentor into the outer darkness.[29] The Duke of Rutland and Lord Strangford did remonstrate with their sons—apparently to no avail. Sir Robert Peel, early in the following year, snubbed Disraeli by failing to send him the customary circular, distributed to the Conservative M.P.s. A cool, though gentlemanly, exchange of letters kept the estrangement from resulting in a deeper division.

Not all opinions were antagonistic to "Young England." An anonymous writer in the *Edinburgh Review* defended their idealism against the charge that the members were only disappointed office seekers. In a more fatherly tone, the writer went on to object mildly against the group's tendency to presumption and exaggeration. He thought it unfair of "Young England" not to distinguish between compromise based on low expediency and that arising from prudence.[30] This friendly critique failed, however, to describe the calculus by which such a distinction was to be applied. Nevertheless, "Young England" had the consolation of a defense—such as it was.

The attention paid "Young England" was most heartening to Benjamin Disraeli. He gleefully chortled about how "the journals daily descant on the 'new party' that has risen to give new color to modern politics, etc."[31] He was lionized; invitations to important social functions were pressed on him with greater urgency than those extended to the Tory ministers. He savored the irony of meeting the King of Hanover only six months after shaking hands with the

---

[29] [Croker], "Policy of the Ministers," 554; Greville, *Journal*, II, 195; Sir James Graham to Croker, Aug. 22, 1843, *Croker Diaries*, II, 219.

[30] "Young England," *Edinburgh Review*, LXXX (1844), 519–22.

[31] Benjamin Disraeli to his sister, Sept. 1843, *Beaconsfield Correspondence*, 144.

King of the French. Clearly, "Young England's" debut had attracted public attention; now it was necessary to flirt with and fire the public's imagination.

To this end, Disraeli moved to convert his little party into a broader movement. His tool was to be the pen and a new kind of novel, one which not only used politics merely to provide the backdrop for the plot but rather aimed "to show political life in *action*." This determination, formed early in 1844, was sustained in a trilogy on politics and religion. *Coningsby or The New Generation, Sybil or The Two Nations,* and *Tancred or The New Crusade,* the last appearing in 1847, might be described as "Young England's" manifesto calling on Britons to disperse the foggy utilitarianism which still clung to their countryside. Disraeli was offering a new "state of mind" wherein a warm faith was to be preferred to decorous doubt; where history was to be emphasized as the key to understanding; where no apologies would be made for relying on a powerful aristocracy, but one which was no longer aloof; where the poor were not to be left to the mercy of "progress." In these three books, Benjamin Disraeli succeeded in pouring new literary and political wine into old forms.[32] The novels dazzled some and bewildered others but also served to keep their author's name before the British public.

The years covered by the trilogy also marked the dissolution of "Young England" as a political party. To ease some of his political discomfiture, Peel reshuffled the ministry early in 1845. Lord Eliot yielded up the seals as Irish Secretary while George Smythe accepted the post of undersecretary for foreign affairs. Smythe was soon to complain about being "fettered by party and muzzled by office," but during the crisis induced by Sir Robert's conversion to "free trade" he remained faithful to his new mentor. Meanwhile,

---

[32] Morris Edmund Speare, *The Political Novel* (New York, 1924), 184; Muriel Masefield, *Peacocks and Primroses, A Survey of Disraeli's Novels* (London, 1953), 127-241.

Disraeli had formed an association with Lord George Bentinck, and together they led a "protectionist" majority of the Conservative Party in opposition to Peel. Ireland was beset by famine and had lost its leader, Daniel O'Connell; its political life was soon feverish with a "Young Ireland," led by William Smith O'Brien. In 1846 Disraeli refused to support Peel's efforts to "pacify" Ireland, and thus brought down the Conservative government. He had by then become the leader not of three young M.P.s nor of forty or fifty "agricultural malcontents" but of a corps numbering more than two hundred. There was still a long "greasy pole" to climb before Disraeli became prime minister, but "Young England," both as a party and as a movement, brought him to the foot of that slippery challenge.

# 9

# Napoleon III, Venetia, and the War of 1866

## JOHN W. BUSH, S.J.

NAPOLEON III FELT PERSONALLY CHARGED, doubtless, with the commission to be architect and pacifier of the "Great Republic" as it was taking form in the nineteenth century. Yet because of sentimental, vaguely ideological, and geopolitical reasons he was excessively preoccupied with Italy. And in that area he failed, largely because the arc he began to construct from the Alps to the Adriatic was not completed on its scheduled date, 1859. Venetia remained in Austrian hands to be a major preoccupation in his foreign policy throughout the crucial '60s, and did not fall into place until another master builder, Otto von Bismarck, had replaced the nephew of Bonaparte.

How Napoleon III attempted on the occasion of virtually every international question that arose from 1859 to 1866 to find bargaining power enough to disengage Venetia from Austria has been expertly studied by French and American scholars. They have traced the "golden thread" of Venetia through the Mexican expedition,[1] the Polish crisis,[2] the

[1] Nancy Nichols Barker, "France, Austria, and the Mexican Venture, 1861–1864," *French Historical Studies,* III, No. 2 (Fall 1963), 224–45.
[2] Lynn M. Case, *Franco–Italian Relations, 1860–1865* (Philadelphia, 1932), 257–58; Charles W. Hallberg, *Franz–Josef and Napoleon III, 1852–1864* (New York, 1955), 314–35; Henry Solomon, *L'ambassade de Richard de Metternich à Paris* (Paris, 1933), 515–17.

Roman and Danish questions,[3] the problem of Moldavia and Wallachia.[4] As the conflict between the Austrian Empire and Prussia loomed on the horizon, Napoleon III's desire to complete his work in Italy lost none of its intensity. Moreover, his actions and decisions made before and during the short but intense duration of the "seven-weeks' war" were crucial for his whole career. It is important then to know how much these actions and decisions were influenced by his interests in Venetia. Also, since the war was the means by which Italy finally obtained Venetia, and since Venetia was itself a minor theater of the war, this essay may also contribute to the understanding of the Austro–Prussian conflict in 1866.

It is highly probable that there was an understanding concerning Venetia which helped induce the Italian government to accept from Napoleon III the agreement on the evacuation of Rome as presented in the Convention of September 15, 1864. In this agreement Italy accepted some rather heavy obligations: the guarantee of the pope's remaining territory, the provision that a corps of French "volunteers" might replace the regular garrison, the transfer of the capital from Turin, the transfer to Italy of the papal debt adhering to former papal territory. Public opinion noted immediately that the evacuation of Rome was inadequate recompense for such sacrifices as were made by the Italian

[3] Case, 267; Chester W. Clark, *Franz–Joseph and Bismarck. The Diplomacy of Austria before the War of 1866* (Cambridge, Mass., 1934), 40–44.
[4] Roul Bossy, "Napoleon III et l'Autriche de Villafranca à Sadowa (1859–1866)," *Revue d'histoire diplomatique,* 73rd year (July–September 1959), 220–30. The Venetian question in Austro–French relations is seen over a wider scope in Nancy Nichols Barker, "Austria, France, and the Venetian Question, 1861–1866," *Journal of Modern History,* XXXVI, No. 2 (June 1964), 145–54. See also John W. Bush, *Venetia Redeemed, Franco–Italian Relations 1864–1866* (Syracuse, 1967) drawn from the same material as the present article.

government,[5] and just as immediately observers supplied Venetia as possible compensation.[6] Of secret clauses there is no compelling evidence, but conversations held with General Alfonso La Marmora and Prince Richard Metternich reveal that the Emperor of the French in connection with the September Convention did arrange with Italian officials a program on Venetia.[7]

Shortly after the signing of the September Convention, General La Marmora, friend of the French emperor since the days of Magenta and Solferino and one who had enjoyed the confidence of the emperor as a special intermediary during the negotiation of the September Convention, became President of the Italian cabinet. During the next year it was evident that Napoleon and La Marmora were seeking some diplomatic means to entice Austria to yield Venetia. On his part, Louis Napoleon continually reassured Austria of his peaceful intentions, and tried strenuously to build up good relations between France and Austria. Yet General La Marmora was hard put to find a price equal to Francis Joseph's prized possession. Immediately after the signing of the September Convention, La Marmora resuscitated the "dream of Lord Russell," that oft attempted project of exchanging the Danubian Principalities for Venetia.[8] Later, in September 1865, La Marmora with unbelievable optimism sent Count Alessandro Malaguzzi, a private Italian citizen, to Francis Joseph offering a billion

---

[5] Pilet to Drouyn de Lhuys, Venice, Sep. 25, 1864, France, Archives du ministère des affaires étrangères, Quai d'Orsay, Paris, Venise, Vol. XXV, No. 44. This source will be referred to subsequently as FAE.

[6] Mulinen to Rechberg, Paris, Sept. 26, 1864, Vienna, Haus-, Hof- und Staatsarchiv, Karton 78, No. 36C. This source will be referred to subsequently as HHS; *Constitutionnel,* Oct. 12, 1864; Bloomfield to Russell, Vienna (circa) Oct. 1, 1864, Bloomfield Papers, Great Britain, Public Record Office, Foreign Office, London, 356, Vol. XX, No. 58.

[7] See Bush, 15–30.

[8] Nigra to La Marmora, Paris, Dec. 13, 1864, Archivio Storico, Vol. DCCCXXXVI.

lire as an outright purchase of Venetia.⁹ None of these offers was even seriously considered.

It was only when Venetia was brought out into the context of broader international issues that it finally became a negotiable item. While Malaguzzi was trying to "purchase" Venetia, Louis Napoleon was pacing the October sands with Otto von Bismarck at Biarritz. This famous interview, although shrouded in great mystery, did reveal an intimate connection between Venetia and the antagonism that was arising between Austria and Prussia over Schleswig–Holstein.¹⁰ The Biarritz meeting had in fact been preceded by a special mission dispatched to Florence by Bismarck to sound out the Italian government on a possible alliance.¹¹ As for General La Marmora, the chief of the Italian cabinet was as yet unwilling to accept the expedient of a military involvement with Prussia,¹² even if all he had to hope for was the exchange of the Danubian Principalities for Venetia.

Chimerical though it was, the "dream of Lord Russell" was actually the project that brought all the various strands of the problem together and determined that Venetia would after all be won, as was Lombardy, on the field of battle. In response to an opportunity presented in February 1866 by the deposition of Prince Cuza in Bucharest, La Marmora

⁹ Clark, 307–8.
¹⁰ Pierre Renouvin, *Historie des relations internationales,* Tome V, *Le XIX siècle* (Paris, 1954), 336; Ernest Lavisse, *Histoire de France contemporaine depuis la révolution jusqu'à la paix de 1919* (Paris, 1920–22), VII, 147; R. Fester, "Biarritz, eine Bismarck-Studie," *Deutsche Rundschau,* CXIII (Nov. 1902), 212–36; Émile Ollivier, "L'entrevue de Biarritz, 1865," *Revue des deux mondes,* Period 5, Vol. IX (June 1902), 502; Alfonso La Marmora, *Un peu plus de lumière sur les événements politiques et militaires de 1866* (Paris, 1874), 71. This source will subsequently be referred to as *Événements.*
¹¹ Drouyn de Lhuys to Malaret, Paris, Apr. 13, 1865, FAE, Italie, XII, No. 9.
¹² La Marmora to Nigra, Florence, Aug. 4, 1865; La Marmora, *Événements,* 53–54; Malaret to Drouyn de Lhuys, Turin, Apr. 20, 1865, FAE, Italie, XII, No. 32.

appealed to the Emperor of the French for direct support, mentioning the unceasingly urgent overtures of Prussia.[13]

In response to La Marmora's appeal, Napoleon III and Constantino Nigra, Italy's ambassador in Paris, devised a diplomatic offensive calculated to force Austria into a trade of Venetia for the Danubian Principalities. The plan was to offer the trade to Austria under the combined pressures of the French court and 10 Downing Street, just when Italy was threatening to join Prussia in an alliance.[14]

General La Marmora accepted the strategy, hoping that it would be effective before he had to involve himself militarily with Bismarck. La Marmora therefore sent General William Govone as special envoy to Berlin with instructions to explore the possibilities in a general way.[15] It became immediately evident, however, that the strategy as a whole would fail. Lord Clarendon, British Foreign Secretary, would not even hazard an approach to Austria.[16] Empress Eugénie, entrusted with the task on the part of the French court, received a chilly refusal from Prince Richard Metternich, the Austrian envoy.[17]

The exchange project indeed suffered a quick death, but a certain momentum carried the talks in Berlin to the point of no return. Within two weeks Bismarck offered to the Italians an attractive short-term alliance in exchange for the eventual cession of Venetia after a successful war against Austria.[18] Officially, the French Foreign Ministry did not

[13] Nigra to La Marmora, Paris, Mar. 1, 1866, E. Passamonti, "Constantino Nigra ed Alfonso La Marmora dal 1862–1866," *Risorgimento italiano*, XXII (1929), 446–50.
[14] *Ibid.*
[15] Bush, 48–49.
[16] Nigra to La Marmora, Paris, Mar. 17, 1866, La Marmora, *Événements*, 133.
[17] Metternich to Mensdorff, Paris, Mar. 27, 1866; Hermann Oncken, *Die Rheinpolitik Kaiser Napoleons III. von 1863 bis 1870 und der Ursprung des Krieges von 1870/71* (Stuttgart, 1926), I, 115–17.
[18] Nigra to Prince Eugene, June 23, 1866, Bettino Ricasoli, *Lettere e documenti*, ed. Tabarrini and Gotti (Florence, 1893), VIII, 8–18.

support this alliance.[19] But Constantino Nigra, in constant personal touch with the emperor, gave the impression in his dispatches that Napoleon favored the alliance all along the line.[20] Although the emperor's advice was ambiguous throughout the month of March, when the negotiations in Berlin were going on, he made it clear to La Marmora toward the end of the month through other mediaries that he could not any longer support the alliance and that his counsel was only "that of a friend."[21] In effect he had finally withdrawn all support from the treaty, leaving La Marmora in an embarrassing position.[22] Napoleon had obviously seen the alliance as too deep a commitment to Bismarck before the French could formulate a policy on the German question. More important, the emperor began to have visions of the German conflict beginning with an attack on Italy by Austria and the consequent undoing of his previous policy in Italy.

When General La Marmora finally realized that he did not have France's support he, too, became apprehensive about facing Austria. He made a last, futile effort to purchase Venetia through the Austrian House of Rothschild.[23] That failing, he felt that the pressure now built up in favor of military action within the Kingdom of Italy prevented him from retracing his steps. On April 5 La Marmora gave

[19] Drouyn de Lhuys to Benedetti, Paris, Mar. 31, 1866, France, Ministère des affaires étrangères, *Les origines diplomatiques de la guerre, 1870–1871* (Paris, 1910–32), VIII, 120–21. This source will subsequently be referred to as *OD*; Drouyn de Lhuys to Malaret, Paris, Apr. 3, 1866, FAE, Italie, XIV, 277–78.
[20] Nigra to Prince Eugène, June 23, 1866, Ricasoli, VIII, 8–18. See discussion of Nigra's role in Bush, 46–57.
[21] Arese to La Marmora, Paris, Mar. 30, 1866, Joseph Grabinski, *Arese, un ami de Napoleon III* (Paris, 1897), 225–26.
[22] Bush, 53–54.
[23] A complete report on these negotiations is found in the private papers of de Gramont but not in the official correspondence preserved at the Quai d'Orsay, Gramont to Drouyn de Lhuys, Vienna, Apr. 1, 1866 particulier et confidentielle, preserved on microfilm at Archives Nationales, Paris, Correspondance privée, Bobine No. 61.

consent to the treaty which was signed on April 8, 1866, binding Italy to take her stand beside Prussia if within three months the latter became involved in a war with Austria.[24]

The Prussian–Italian treaty began immediately to have its effect. When she heard of it, Austria rushed troops to the Italian border in Venetia, and tried to neutralize the diplomatic power of Italy by a bold offer of Venetia, not to Italy but to the Emperor of the French. On May 4, Prince Metternich, who had so often brushed off attempts to barter Venetia, was at Quai d'Orsay offering the territory to France for eventual retrocession to Italy. The conditions were that both France and Italy would pledge neutrality in the coming conflict.[25]

It would seem that Austria's new attitude evinced by this offer began to change the emperor's view of the war in Germany. He appeared thereafter more and more inclined to accept a diplomatic solution to the question of Venetia, and to forego the advantages of a timely intervention in the war. As for La Marmora, he was too honorable, or perhaps too helpless before the actionist forces in Italy, now to pledge neutrality. But, undaunted, the emperor began to pursue the peaceful solution by means of an international congress with not only Venetia but Schleswig–Holstein and the reform of the German Constitution on the agenda.[26] Here he found common sentiment with La Marmora. Both had hopes throughout the month of May that a congress might succeed. All powers responded favorably to the French invitation, if without great enthusiasm, but Austria's

[24] Benedetti to Drouyn de Lhuys, Berlin, Apr. 9, 1866, *OD,* VIII, 200.
[25] Drouyn de Lhuys to Gramont, Paris, May 11, 1866, *OD,* IX, 95–97; Nigra to La Marmora, Paris, May 5, 1866, La Marmora, *Événements,* 319–21.
[26] Nigra to La Marmora, Paris, May 11, 1866, Archivio Storico, Vol. DCCCXXXVIII.

answer was ambiguous. She ultimately felt that her position would be too weak at such a congress. Her refusal to put Venetia on the block[27] caused France and Italy to lose interest, and the emperor turned his ear to the earlier Austrian proposals.

When, by the end of May, Italian neutrality had been despaired of, the Austrian government began to work for the more active participation of France. Around May 25, the Austrians sought some "attitude" on the part of France that would guarantee them victory in the war.[28] On May 29, Napoleon III was asked to "restrain" his Italian protégé.[29] Always there were vague conditions that betrayed the Austrian desire for "restorations" in Italy anywhere from Modena to Naples.[30]

At the beginning of June, the French emperor was expecting Metternich to set a definite price for Venetia. Meanwhile he called an extraordinary meeting of the counsellors and ministers in order to define policy in respect to the Prussian conflict. It was decided to preserve neutrality and to be content with Bismarck's promise that "new arrangements" in Europe would not be made without agreement with the French emperor.[31] Then, in preparation for a visit from Metternich, Napoleon III prepared a formula by which the same promise could be wrung from Austria. Added to the conditions to be presented to Austria was the cession of Venetia whatever the results of the war.[32]

On June 3 Metternich sought an audience with the French emperor in the later's office in the Tuileries—the

[27] Mensdorff to Metternich, May 31, 1866 (tel), HHS, Karton 84.
[28] Mensdorff to von Hübner, Vienna, May 25, 1866, Karton 208, No. 3; Metternich to Mensdorff, May 23, 1866, Paris, Oncken, I, 227-30; Mensdorff to Metternich, Vienna, May 25, 1866, No. 3, Karton 84 (reservée).
[29] Metternich to Mensdorff, Paris, May 29, 1866, Oncken, I, 237-38.
[30] Metternich to Mensdorff, Paris, May 29, 1866, Oncken, I, 237-38; von Hübner to Mensdorff, Rome, Apr. 3, 1866, HHS, Karton 208, No. 13B.
[31] Émile Ollivier, *L'Empire Libéral* (Paris, 1903), VIII, 180; Drouyn de Lhuys to Gramont, Paris, June 19, 1866, *OD*, X, 216. Drouyn to Benedetti, Paris, July 2, 1860, *OD*, X, 303-4.
[32] Metternich to Mensdorff, Paris, June 6, 1866, HHS, Karton 83, No. 30B.

awaited visit. Metternich produced a note which, he said, contained the "maximum of our concessions." [33] France, the note stated, since the neutrality of Italy could not be guaranteed, should exert such restraint upon her protégé—obviously by force if necessary—as would allow Austria's military strength to be employed fully against Prussia. Austria, on the other hand, if given free hand in Italy would work along those same lines that French policy was thought to favor: namely, the independence of Italy; not necessarily her complete unification. Previously the Austrian government had noted that unity endangered not only Rome but Austria's Tyrol and her Dalmatian outlet to the sea.[34]

The emperor's answer to Metternich was to open the drawer of his desk and produce the note he had prepared, referring to it as "a little project short and simple." [35] The note requested the Austrian government to cede Venetia, not to Italy directly, but to France, at the conclusion of the peace whatever the results of the war. As for Germany, if an Austrian victory would lead to post-war adjustments which might disturb European equilibrium, they should not be made without consulting France. Besides her neutrality, France could offer only a promise "to make all efforts" to obtain the same attitude of neutrality in Italy.[36] Prince Metternich took the paper and, after a few melancholy moments, remarked dramatically that this was ". . . putting the knife to our throat." [37] After assuring Metternich that they were at one in their desire to prevent Italian unity and that his only concern was that Austria not try to retake Lombardy or occupy an insurrectionary Naples,[38] Napoleon III ended the interview with a note of

[33] Metternich to Mensdorff, June 6, 1866, HHS, Karton 83, No. 30B; von Hübner to Mensdorff, Rome, June 2, 1866, HHS, Karton 208, No. 22B.
[34] Metternich to Mensdorff, Paris, June 6, 1866, HHS, Karton 83, No. 30B.
[35] *Ibid.*
[36] Annex Drouyn to Gramont, June 4, 1866, FAE, Autriche, Vol. 71, Négotiation Secret No. 1.
[37] Metternich to Mensdorff, Paris, June 6, 1866, HHS, Karton 83, No. 30B.
[38] Von Hübner to Mensdorff, Rome, Apr. 3, 1866, HHS, Karton 308, No.

surprising bravado. "If you think," he said, "that you must refuse, I am going to have to arm and intervene before long." [39]

The "little project" with its accompanying discussion was then put into negotiation through the offices of Antoine de Gramont, ambassador at Vienna. The French emperor enjoyed such a position of strength at that juncture that Francis Joseph finally acquiesced in the project as presented by de Gramont, and the treaty was initialed on June 12, 1866. Besides the above conditions an additional clause guaranteed the "maintenance of the temporal power of the Pope" and the transfer to Italy of the public debt adhering to Venetia.[40]

Thus on the eve of the Austro–Prussian war Napoleon III had sold his neutrality at what was to him the highest possible price. It is all the more remarkable considering that neutrality was all he had to offer. Military commitment to any one side was, in spite of his threat to Metternich, unthinkable in view of the strong public opinion that prevailed in France from the time of the Polish crisis through the spring of 1866.[41] Moreover, since France held more than 40 percent of the debt of the Kingdom of Italy and virtually all of the papal debt,[42] the *rentiers* were a formidable lobby for noncommitment. The Bourse in April 1866, represented by Baron Rothschild, made a special appeal to the emperor to throw his influence on the side of peace.[43] Finally a wave of anti-Prussian feeling swept over all of France in May 1866, set off by a masterful speech in the

---

13B; von Hübner to Mensdorff, Rome, June 2, 1866, HHS, Karton 208, No. 22A.

[39] Metternich to Mensdorff, Paris, June 6, 1866, HHS, Karton 83, No. 30B.

[40] As ratified on June 23, 1866; from *OD*, X, 258–60.

[41] Lynn M. Case, *French Opinion in War and Diplomacy during the Second Empire* (Philadelphia, 1954), 178–95; 197, 198.

[42] Rondo Cameron, "French Foreign Investment, 1850–1880" (unpublished Ph.D. dissertation, University of Chicago, 1953), 45, 134.

[43] Case, *French Opinion*, 198.

*Corps législatif* by Adolph Thiers.[44] After the Convention with Austria was signed, the emperor found from the reports of the *procureurs généraux* reaffirmation that the French people wanted no involvement at that time in Germany.[45]

It is clear that Venetia was of primary importance in Napoleon III's assuming of a stance before the Austro-Prussian conflict. His actions render credible a summary of his policy that he confided to Prince Metternich on May 21, 1866:

> I have but one interest in all this; it is to be finished with the Italian question by means of the cession of Venice. If this cession can be achieved by peace, I will do all I can to contribute to it; if not, I shall profit from the chances that war between Austria and Prussia will offer me on this.[46]

In other conversations on May 22 and May 23, he assured Metternich that he had totally abandoned interests in Germany for the pursuit of Venetia, even though it meant the defeat of Italy or the settlement of the German question short of war. And Benedetti—to whom the emperor communicated more intimately than with his own Minister of Foreign Affairs—assured Barral, the Italian Ambassador in Berlin, that the only interest the emperor had in the German hostilities was that of Venetia.[47]

It might be appropriate to speculate as to why Napoleon III did not have more confidence in the treaty between Prussia and Italy to bring about the annexation of Venetia. Certainly his miscalculation of the relative strength of Austria and Prussia is one element. But the treaty itself, causing as it did the mobilization of both Italian and Austrian

---

[44] Metternich to Mensdorff, Paris, May 16, 1866, HHS, Karton 82, No. 25; *ibid.,* May 18, 1866, Oncken, I, 106–7; excerpts reproduced in Oncken, 153–59; Gustave Rothan, *La politique française en 1866* (Paris, 1883), 158.
[45] Case, *French Opinion,* 200–1.
[46] Metternich to Mensdorff, Paris, May 21, 1866, Oncken, I, 218–21.
[47] Barral to La Marmora, Berlin, May 23, 1866, *Événements,* 260.

troops on the Venetian border, presented a danger from another quarter. The war could have begun in Italy,[48] and the possibility of a quick Austrian victory there raised the whole question of an Austrian sweep down the peninsula, beginning with the nullification of the emperor's efforts in Lombardy in 1859. It was indeed this fear that best explains the attempts at the congress in May: it would at least give delay to the onrush of events in Italy. The emperor was at this point willing to give up his hopes of war in Germany for a peaceful solution of the Venetian question. The Convention with Austria assured Louis Napoleon, whatever the outcome of the war, not only of Venetia but of what he thought to be control of the balance of power in both Italy and Germany.

Once hostilities had begun, Venetia continued to exert its influence on the policy of the French emperor and even on the strategy and military outcome of the war. Venetia was an Austrian flank exposed to an aroused Italy, a situation threatening to drain off the energy and concentration necessary in Germany and constantly requiring the cooperation of France. On June 12, the very day that the French Convention with Austria was signed, Austria, sure of French neutrality and the cooperation of the secondary German states, broke off diplomatic relations with Prussia for having sent General Manteufel into Holstein.[49] On June 14 the Frankfurt Diet voted federal execution upon Prussia. After the subsequent entry of the Prussians into Hesse, Hanover, and Saxony, Victor Emmanuel II declared war on Austria on June 20, alleging the arming of Austria on the Venetian

[48] Drouyn de Lhuys to Malaret, Paris, Apr. 28, 1866, FAE, Italie, XIV, No. 29; Nigra to Prince Eugène, Paris, June 23, 1866, Ricasoli, VIII, 8–18; Nigra to La Marmora, Paris, April 25, 1866, La Marmora, *Événements*, 185–86.
[49] Gramont to Drouyn de Lhuys, June 12, 1866, *OD*, X, 133.

border as cause.⁵⁰ General La Marmora crossed the Mincio River with 120,000 men and entered Venetia on June 23rd.⁵¹

Decisions now left to the field of battle were unusually swift in coming. Within twenty-four hours after crossing the border the Italian troops were defeated at Custozza (June 24, 1866), and the Austrian thrust up through Bohemia to Silesia met with severe losses by July 1. So serious was the Austrian plight that Metternich appeared at the Tuileries on July 2 asking for vigorous French intervention against Italy. He wanted the emperor to obtain a military armistice in Italy, and then, upon the immediate cession of Venetia to France, the latter was to occupy the quadrilateral fortresses and all military positions in Venetia in order to relieve Austrian forces for the struggle in Bohemia. In addition, Metternich passed on to Napoleon III urgent entreaties from his government for outright military aid in Germany as the only way to avert the otherwise inevitable Prussian domination of Europe.⁵²

Over the next twenty-four hours the emperor pondered and doubtless consulted on the Austrian proposals. The result was that upon Metternich's return on July 3 he simply offered his offices as mediator to stop the war. Peaceful intervention was to be the answer to Austria's offer of Venetia: "The Emperor accepts the cession of Venetia and proposes at Berlin and Florence mediation on bases indicated by an armistice." ⁵³ The Ballplatz, faced with a possible attack on Vienna, accepted this offer of mediation—

⁵⁰ Annex to Malaret to Drouyn, June 20, 1866, FAE, Italie, XII, No. 72.
⁵¹ Victor Emmanuel II to Napoleon III, June 20, 1866, Ollivier, *L'Empire libéral,* VIII, 206–7.
⁵² Mensdorff to Metternich, Vienna, July 2, 1866 (tel), HHS, Karton 84; Metternich to Mensdorff, Paris, July 7, 1866, Oncken, I, 315–19. Gramont to Drouyn de Lhuys, Vienna, July 5, 1866, *OD,* X, 326.
⁵³ Metternich to Mensdorff, Paris, July 3, 1866; Oncken, I, 298–99. See also summary of negotiations by Drouyn de Lhuys in which the impression is given that France is accepting an offer of Venetia made by Austria, Drouyn de Lhuys to Malaret, Paris, July 23, 1866, FAE, Italie, XV, No. 51.

which, it was doubtless thought, might at least be successful in Italy.

Since the Italian people were expecting a new and successful onslaught on the quadrilateral to erase the infamy of Custozza,[54] this notice of the cession of Venetia and the offer of mediation caused only anger and frustration within the circles of the Italian government now headed by the francophobic Bettino Ricasoli. On July 5, when the hopes of mediation in Germany were fading fast, Napoleon III again faced the alternative of armed intervention. The decision to maintain neutrality was again largely determined by the pacifistic temper of public opinion which the Battle of Sadowa had not altered,[55] and by the determination of the bourgeoisie not to allow a war to endanger commerce on the Italian loans.[56] The fact that Venetia was guaranteed whatever the results of the war must have helped the emperor to rationalize this decision.

Meanwhile, expecting Venetia to be neutralized by its being in French possession, and anticipating an armistice in Italy, Austria began to deploy her troops from that sector to assist in the defense of Vienna. Ignoring the formality that Venetia was now French, the Italian advance began on July 9, General Cialdini crossing the Po on the southern border.[57] Eventually, between July 10 and July 24 the bulk of the Austrian army was withdrawn from all sectors in Venetia—amounting finally to about 70,000 troops and 15,000 horses to support Benedek in defense of Vienna.[58]

---

[54] Ricasoli to Buoncompagni, Florence, Sept. 5, 1866, Ricasoli, VIII, 160–64.
[55] Eugénie to Metternich, Aug. 13, 1866, copy annexed to Metternich to Mensdorff, Aug. 13, 1866, HHS, Karton 83, No. 173.
[56] André Armengaud, "Opinion français au moment de Sadowa et la crise nationale allemande" (unpublished Ph.D. dissertation, Faculté des Belles Lettres, Sorbonne, University of Paris, 1958), 58–60, 75–80, 103, 202.
[57] Malaret to Drouyn de Lhuys, Florence, July 9, 1866, *OD*, X, 347.
[58] Col. Merlin to Minister of War, Vienna, Aug. 25, 1866, France, Archives du ministère de la guerre, Archives historiques. Mission du Col. Merlin en 1866.

Cialdini, unopposed, not only swept through Venetia proper, but made northward for Trentino while a band of volunteers under Garibaldi was already hammering fiercely at the outposts of that region.[59] Thus another question, within that of Venetia, arose to complicate further the emperor's task. Ricasoli very clearly meant to include Trentino in the Italian conquest, and made haste to occupy it before negotiation began.[60] Inclusion of the Trentino in the cession of Venetia was actually raised on July 4 when there was question of Austria's cession of Venetia,[61] and Ricasoli did everything to delay an armistice until the Italian Tyrol could be secured militarily.[62] He wanted Bismarck to assist in this by delaying as long as possible in making an armistice in Germany.

The invasion of Venetia, since July 3 officially French territory, and the inclusion of the Italian Tyrol made it ever more imperative for the French emperor to isolate Italy. It was to this effect that Napoleon III threw his weight behind Bismarck's preliminary project of peace in order to end the war in Germany. On July 14 both Vienna and Berlin received from the French Foreign Office a list of six conditions—preliminaries drawn up by Bismarck and modified by Napoleon III—which if accepted by both parties would signal the end of hostilities in that sector of the war. The provisions were: (1) integrity of the Austrian Empire, save Venetia; (2) dissolution of the Germanic confederation; (3) formation of a Northern Confederation under Prussia; (4) freedom for the South German states to form their own union; (5) annexation of the Elbe duchies by

[59] Pilet to Drouyn de Lhuys, Venice, July 8, 1866, FAE, Venise, XXVII, No. 49.
[60] Ricasoli to Visconti–Venosta, Florence, July 8, 1866, Ricasoli, VIII, 51–52.
[61] Nigra to Visconti–Venosta, Paris, July 5, 1866, Archivio Storico, Vol. DCCCXXXVIII, No. 351.
[62] Malaret to Drouyn de Lhuys, Florence, July 10, 1866, FAE, Italie, XV, No. 82.

Prussia.[63] On July 20 these terms were accepted by Bismarck and Francis Joseph, and a five-day truce was arranged preliminary to an armistice.[64]

The armistice on the Italian front was expected to follow. Yet, on July 24 a detachment of General Cialdini's army broke through the Tyrolean defenses and occupied the greater part of the Trentino region, whereupon Ricasoli refused an armistice unless Trentino were considered included in the territory of Venetia.[65] Jerome Napoleon, who had been detailed to manage the irascible president of the Italian cabinet, had to settle this annoying complication hastily, because the armistice in Germany awaited the adherence of Prussia's ally. Promising the Italians that they could remain in military possession of Trentino while peace talks went on (the clause known as *uti possidetis*), Jerome on July 28 secured the Italian agreement for an armistice.[66]

The impossibility of dealing satisfactorily with three parties in this state of emergency was soon apparent. The Austrians knew nothing of the *uti possidetis* provision, and, when they met the Italian military officials at Cormons and learned that the Italian army was to remain in Trentino, they refused the armistice.[67] Moreover, the Austrian general staff had, since the cease-fire with Prussia, begun to redeploy their troops to Italy, specifically to the Trentino region, there hopelessly outnumbering Cialdini's detachment.[68] The Austrians now demanded evacuation of the

[63] Drouyn de Lhuys to Benedetti and Gramont, Paris, July 14, 1866, *OD*, XI, 30.
[64] Mensdorff to Metternich, Vienna, July 20, 1866 (tel), HHS, Karton 84. Gramont to Drouyn de Lhuys, Vienna, July 21, 1866, *OD*, IX, 137.
[65] Malaret to Drouyn de Lhuys, Ferrara, July 26, 1866, *OD*, XI, 279–332.
[66] Napoleon III to Drouyn de Lhuys, Vichy, July 29, 1866, *OD*, XI, 283.
[67] Visconti–Venosta to Nigra, Florence, Aug. 5, 1866, *Documenti diplomatici e negotiati commerciali, presentati al Parlimento*, pp. 764–65; *ibid.*, Aug. 6, 1866, Ricasoli, VIII, 93; Nigra to Drouyn de Lhuys, Vichy, Aug. 6, 1866 (tel), FAE, Italie, XV, 284.
[68] La Marmora to Ricasoli, Padua, Aug. 6, 1866, Ricasoli, VIII, 336. Drouyn de Lhuys to Malaret, Paris, Aug. 7, 1866 (tel), FAE, Italie, XV, 292.

Trentino by August 10 or they would resume hostilities.[69] Unable to move the Austrians from this resolve, the French peacemakers were at a dead-end, and the solution was an embarrassing one for Italy. Ricasoli was forced to allow a "strategic withdrawal" requested by the military in face of superior Austrian forces, and ordered the armistice to be signed on August 11th.[70] To add insult to injury, the Austrians refused the Italians a place at the peace table at Prague, and Italy had to accept a separate peace treaty with Austria under French mediation.[71]

The armistice, called "una pace miserabile" by the Italians,[72] was the first in a series of events that ironically made the winning of Venetia disastrous for Franco–Italian relations. Not having the Trentino, the Italians at least wanted to have Venetia by conquest, but Napoleon III insisted on the formality of the transfer from his hands. The Italian government circumvented every effort of the French to have the transaction carried out until the formality was finally accomplished in an unpublicized ceremony in a room of a Venetian hotel.[73] Meanwhile, the French government did achieve a satisfactory settlement between Austria and Italy, and a peace—the Treaty of Vienna—was signed on October 3, 1866, a task that took no little skill on the part of the new French Minister, La Valette.[74]

---

[69] Gramont to Drouyn de Lhuys, Vienna, Aug. 5, 1866, *OD,* XI, 386–87; Mensdorff to Metternich, Vienna, Aug. 5, 1866 (tel), Karton 85.

[70] Verbale delle deliberatione del Concilio, etc., 133–35, Archivio centrale Roma, Archivio di stato, Sessions of Aug. 6 to Aug. 9, 1866. Italian forces had also penetrated into Istria as far as the territory of Gorizia just beyond the Venetian border.

[71] Barral to Visconti–Venosta, Berlin, Aug. 10, 1866, Ricasoli, VIII, 337. Malaret to Drouyn de Lhuys, Florence, Aug. 11, 1866, *OD,* XII, 69.

[72] Nigra to Visconti–Venosta, Paris, Aug. 18, 1866, Ricasoli, VIII, 110–15. Ricasoli to Carlo Buoncompagni, Florence, Sept. 5, 1866, Ricasoli, VIII, 160–64.

[73] Ollivier, *L'Empire libéral,* VIII, 618; see also di Revel to Ricasoli, Verona, Oct. 8, 1866, Ricasoli, VIII, 269–70.

[74] See Bush, 109–19.

The primacy of the Venetian question in the policy of Louis Napoleon would seem to be established from the above. It was in the background of the September Convention and kept emerging into sharper focus until it was a major factor in the decisions made with respect to the Austro–Prussian conflict. Napoleon III led the Italian government in February and March of 1866 into an alliance with Prussia in order to put pressure upon Austria to release Venetia. The treaty turned out to be more than a device, and Italy found herself committed to military action in concert with Prussia. The emperor was unable to participate in this alliance because of the pacifistic temper of France in the mid-1860s and because he could not come to a satisfactory agreement with Bismarck. Therefore, in order to secure Venetia in the event of an Austrian victory (which he thought probable), he drove a hard bargain with Francis Joseph whereby the latter guaranteed him Venetia as the price of French neutrality whatever the outcome of the impending war.

The Battle of Sadowa frightened both sovereigns into a premature execution of their agreement, so that Venetia was ceded to France before the war had ended. Austria withdrew her forces from Venetia to strengthen the defense of Vienna. Ignoring the transfer of Venetia to France, the Italian forces proceeded to invade and occupy most of Venetia including the Trentino region. Napoleon III, reluctant to exert force in any sector, turned his attention toward stopping the war and met with surprising success, first in Germany and ultimately in Italy. He secured a cease-fire in Germany but was at first stymied in Italy by the occupation of Trentino. The latter problem was solved not without embarrassment to the Italian government, for the Austrians, having signed with Bismarck at Nicholsburg, wheeled about to confront the outnumbered Italian contingent in Trentino. Italy signed the armistice and for the moment gave up claims to Trentino, but after the peace was signed she carried out with France a bitter quarrel over the ambiguity: was Venetia won by conquest or ceded to her by France?

When confronted with the question of why Venetia meant so much to the French emperor, one is admittedly faced with the mind of Louis Napoleon in its most enigmatic form. Yet, granted the zig-zagging, plodding, delayed decision-making and miscalculation inherent in any foreign policy, it is possible to observe a basic *rationale*. Louis Napoleon was in the tradition of the French sovereigns who saw a foothold in Italy as a major objective of foreign policy. Finishing the work of '59 and all that it meant appears amid the scanty traces he leaves of his own thoughts and motives and is in the very logic of circumstances. After 1864, however, Venetia had a way of transcending the Mediterranean objectives and became related to other problems. In 1864 Venetia became linked with the Roman question by facilitating the evacuation of Rome. Then, when the Austro–Prussian conflict loomed, Venetia appeared in some way to contain the balance of power between the two forces. The Prussian–Italian alliance evened the odds in Germany to the extent that the conflict could be prolonged until the hated system of 1815 would be entirely destroyed. Venetia would strengthen Italy but keep her grateful and dependent. Moreover, the emperor had from both Bismarck and Francis Joseph promises of a voice in any readjustment of Germany. Compensations on the Rhine, Saarbrücken, and Saarlouis (Saarlautern) especially, at that time were not beyond expectation. Thus, while it can be said that the Italian question had primacy over that of Germany, it is probably more precise to say that it was the Venetian question that had primacy because it served French interests and French ideas in both areas. A German newspaper on the eve of the war noted epigrammatically that "For Bismarck, Venetia is a fortress on the Rhine." If this was true of Bismarck, how much more so of Napoleon III?

A further conclusion, one within the framework of the emperor's Italian policy, is possible from this study, in that it serves to draw the distinction in the French policy ever more clearly between "unification" and "liberation" of Italy. Obtaining Venetia is clearly directed at the exclusion of Austria from Italy. On the other hand, Napoleon's indifference to the possibility of reactionary revolts in Naples and central Italy suggests the lingering hope of redress against Cavour's machinations of 1860. At the high point of his exasperation with Italy there seemed to return to the emperor the hope of a Confederation of Central Italy. Such considerations bring into consistency his attitude on Rome. Reserving Rome to the pope not only helped him assuage the growing opposition of French Catholics, liberal and conservative alike, but served to prevent "unification" while not preventing "liberation."

Finally, Napoleon III's preoccupation with Venetia had its effects on the origins, course, and settlement of the "seven-weeks' war" itself. The Prussian–Italian alliance of April 8, 1866 which delivered La Marmora into Prussian hands gave Bismarck the means of precipitating the crisis with Austria in June. Once begun, the war was certainly limited in scope by the French concern for Venetia. First of all, the brief period of French sovereignty over the territory allowed Austria to transfer troops from the Italian theater to the German one. Secondly, it was Napoleon III who achieved the cease-fire in both the German and Italian sectors. In a final gesture, the French Foreign Ministry supplied the necessary mediation to bring the peace negotiations between Austria and Italy to a successful conclusion in the Treaty of Vienna, October 3, 1866.

# 10

# Crisis in East-central Europe: The Teschen Dispute

## EUGENE KUSIELEWICZ

ONE OF THE MOST REMARKABLE CHAPTERS in twentieth-century diplomatic history was the creation of the Czechoslovak state. A vindication of the principle of self-determination, it nonetheless succeeded in subjecting a greater number of irredentist nationalities under its sway than fell under the domination of any other state created, resurrected, or altered by the peacemakers who met in Paris. It acquired large areas inhabited by Germans, Hungarians, Ukrainians, and Poles, not so much through a resort to arms as through victories at the conference table—victories, some of which followed upon sure defeats from which the Czechs apparently had no hope of escape. When defeat appeared inevitable, as happened in the settlement of the Teschen crisis, the Czechs would seek some pretext to postpone a decision, hoping to gain an advantage at a more fortuitous time. These victories belonged to the Czechs, not to the Slovaks, for though Czechoslovakia was supposed to be a federated state, a Czecho–Slovakia—an East-European Switzerland which would enable Czechs, Slovaks, and Germans to live in peace and harmony—the Slovak junior partners felt themselves so deceived and oppressed that many looked upon the Munich Conference as a deliverance from their woes. The principal architect of these triumphs was Eduard Beneš, the Czech Minister of Foreign Affairs, one of the greatest diplomats of our times. Armed with only an ancient tradition, the Crown of St. Wenceslaus, an intuitive knowledge of men, and a keen appreciation of the value of public relations and the press, his diplomatic victories helped create one of the most successful of the East-European "successor states."

The acquisition of the Sudetenland from Austria and those parts of ethnic Hungary incorporated into Slovakia were among his most obvious achievements. Yet the addition of the greater part of the Duchy of Teschen into the newly formed Czechoslovak state was perhaps his greatest triumph—and, ultimately, his greatest mistake. Historic, economic, and military arguments were much more favorable to the Czechs in their disputes with the Germans and Hungarians than they were in those with the Poles. In the former instances, too, the Czechs could count upon the generally favorable attitude of the Allied and associated powers, and especially upon that of the French, who sought to create a strong and viable state able to play a significant part in resisting any revival of German expansionist ambitions. No such advantage accrued to the Czechs in their dispute over Teschen, because the Poles, who also claimed the region, were not one of the vanquished, but another of the East-European "successor states" which the victorious powers wished to strengthen.

The crisis over the Duchy of Teschen was one of the earliest and one of the most prolonged to come before the attention of the peacemakers at Paris. It first came to their attention in January 1919. At times its fate appeared to be settled through an agreement of its inhabitants, by a decision of the peacemakers, by direct negotiations between the Poles and Czechs, and by a plebiscite. Yet when the peacemakers left Paris, the dispute was still not settled. When an unfavorable decision appeared certain, the Czechs proposed an alternative method of solution which would prove more palatable to the major powers who wished to avoid offending the Poles or Czechs. But the acquisition of the duchy, at least of its valuable coal resources, railroads, and industries, was only one aspect of the problems the Czechs faced, because their victory had to be such as to avoid the alienation of the Poles, whose cooperation was necessary in face of a common threat from Germany, and whose access to the sea was a necessary ingredient for a truly independent Czech economy. During the critical phases of the Russo–Polish War, Beneš secured all the concessions the Czechs had sought, but under such conditions as transformed the Teschen dispute into a Polish Alsace–Lorraine, a stumbling block to that cooperation between Poles and Czechs which alone could promise any hope for an independent eastern Europe capable of maintaining itself against larger neighbors to the east and west.

The Duchy of Teschen nestled along the slopes of the Beskid Mountains on the northern frontiers of the Austro–Hungarian Empire. Originally a part of the medieval Polish kingdom, it was lost to the Czechs in 1335, along with the rest of Silesia of which it was a part. When Frederick the Great acquired Silesia in 1742, the duchies of Teschen and Troppau remained with the Hapsburgs until their dynasty was finally overthrown. Though separated from Poland for nearly six hundred years, the region maintained its Polish character to such an extent that, according to figures obtained by the Austrian government, Poles formed 54.8% of the population in 1910, as compared with 27.1% for the Czechs and 18.1% for the Germans.[1] Despite these statistics, the testimony of their own leading ethnographers[2] and of the various inter-allied commissions sent to the

---

[1] B. Koszusnik, *The Problem of Cieszyn Silesia: Facts and Documents* (London, 1943), 60–64.

[2] Witold Sworakowski, *Polacy Na Śląsku za Olza* (Warsaw, 1937), 30–31.

duchy,[3] the Czech statesmen at the Paris Peace Conference persistently maintained that Czechs and not Poles were the dominant group within the duchy.

The lengths to which the Czechs were willing to go to secure this region are understandable in terms of the precedent its disposition would set in determining its remaining frontiers, and in terms of its great economic wealth. If Teschen were lost to Poland on the basis of self-determination, then the Sudetenland might be lost on similar grounds as well. It was therefore important to the Czechs to maintain the indivisibility of the crownland. But of even greater concern, for the Czechs were well aware that France would not permit the growth of Germany through the incorporation of the Sudetenland, was the vast industrial and mineral wealth of the region, the economic importance of which stems from its fortuitous possession of rich supplies of coal and coke and its location along the principal route between north-central and south-central Europe. As a result, industries were attracted to the region in such numbers that by the end of the nineteenth century it became one of the most highly industrialized and most densely populated regions in the Austro–Hungarian Empire. Of particular interest to the Czechs was the fact that the principal railroad link between the Bohemian and Slovakian parts of the newly created state ran through the duchy's passes.[4]

Though the Teschen dispute primarily concerned Poles and Czechs, German expansionist claims precipitated the crisis when, in 1916, extreme German nationalists demanded that Prussia annex the regions immediately adjacent to it.

---

[3] See, for example, the "Report Presented Jointly to the Supreme Allied Council by the Commission on Polish Affairs and the Commission on Czecho–Slovak Affairs on the Question of Teschen and Orava," State Dept. MSS, 180.03501/46, Sept. 3, 1919.

[4] Robert F. Young, "The Czecho–Slovak Plebiscite Areas; A. The Teschen Question," *A History of the Peace Conference of Paris*, ed. H. W. V. Temperley (London, 1921), IV, 348–63.

The Polish population of these regions protested vehemently against these claims and against an accelerated program of Germanization begun by the Germans within the duchy. Early in 1917, the Poles petitioned the Austrian Minister for Galicia for the immediate annexation of the Duchy of Teschen to Galicia,[5] the only action they felt sufficient to counteract that program of Germanization and to safeguard their future interests. As the Czechs considered this region an integral part of the Crown of St. Wenceslaus, a dispute immediately arose.

The settlement of the question was not expected to be an easy one—or so, at least, one could conclude from the results of some meetings held in 1917, between Roman Dmowski, President of the Polish National Committee, in Paris, and Thomas Masaryk and Edward Beneš, the elder statesmen of the Czech national movement. At a time when a solid front between Czechs and Poles was considered a vital necessity for achieving the independence of their respective states, neither side was able to agree upon a plan for settling the difficulties over Teschen. According to the testimony of Masaryk and Beneš,[6] Dmowski absolutely refused to accept a plan for partitioning the duchy along the line of the Vistula. This proposition would have safeguarded for the Czechs the important Karvin coal fields and the Oderberg–Jablunka railroad, the principal link between Bohemia and Slovakia, but it would have sacrificed almost 200,000 Poles to the Czechs.

Sometime later, in May 1918, discussions were held in Prague, between Polish and Czech members of the Austrian Parliament. According to the Polish version of these proceedings, it was decided that the duchy should be divided on an ethnic basis, the actual division to be performed by a

---

[5] *Ibid.*, 355.
[6] Edward Beneš, *Světová valká a naše revoluce* (Prague, 1927–28), II, 97–98 and 386; and Tomas Masaryk, *Světová Revoluce za války u ve válce 1914–1918* (Prague, 1925), 295.

mixed commission of five Poles and five Czechs, none of whom was to be a resident of the region.[7] According to the Czech version, a vague oral agreement was reached to maintain the status quo until a permanent settlement was concluded, either by direct agreement between the two or by a decision of an anticipated peace conference.[8] While these negotiations were taking place in Prague, Masaryk and Ignacy Paderewski, the representative of the Polish National Committee in the United States, were reviewing the question in Washington, D.C., where they agreed that the matter should be settled by friendly discussions after the expected defeat of the Central Powers.[9]

The general tenor of these meetings seems to have been that a settlement of the dispute should be left to direct negotiations between the interested parties, after the conclusion of the war. However, immediately after securing the recognition of their state as a belligerent power,[10] the Czechs began a campaign to secure such a preponderant diplomatic backing for their claims that the Poles would be faced by a virtual *fait accompli*. In this way they sought to secure the duchy for themselves free from the hostility of the Poles, which they hoped would be directed against the major powers. And to cement their relations with the Poles, they would then voluntarily cede the non-essential parts of the duchy to them. These attempts were crowned with success when Beneš won the agreement of the French (September 28, 1918) to support the reconstruction of Bohemia within historic frontiers that would include the Duchy of Teschen. This recognition was a shrewd diplomatic triumph which, as Beneš himself admitted, caught the French offguard. According to his testimony, "France did not realize that there would have been a dispute over

---

[7] Koszusnik, 9.
[8] Ferdinand Peroutka, *Budování státu* (Prague, 1934), I, *Rok 1918,* 230.
[9] Young, 355.
[10] The first such recognition was that from Great Britain, on Aug. 9, 1918.

Teschen. She was concerned mainly with the German frontier." He noted that if he "had mentioned the problem of the Polish frontier during these negotiations, the agreement would never have been concluded." [11] To the Poles, these and similar negotiations were a violation of the Prague agreements. Nonetheless, at the time, they were not aware of them.

While these events were taking place, the Central Powers were collapsing. The residents of the duchy, almost completely unaware of the arrangements being made for their future, were faced by the pressing problems resulting from the collapse of the Austrian Government. Local officials, both Polish and Czech, joined hands in the spirit of cooperation which characterized their relations for centuries past, and staged a military coup against the few vestiges of Austrian authority that remained. Two local organizations, the Czech National Council in Ostrava and the Polish National Council in the city of Teschen, provisionally assumed power in the name of their respective states. On November 5, 1918, they concluded an agreement for dividing the duchy and for exploiting its economic wealth. The division, based upon the results of the elections to the borough councils, was temporary in nature, to last until a final settlement would be reached between Warsaw and Prague. Its purpose was to provide a basis for maintaining law and order in the transitional period and to avoid a dissipation of forces in petty local quarrels. It should be noted that, at the time the agreement was reached, no recognized government existed in either Warsaw or Prague. As a result, the agreement reached was completely free from the pressures of either state and from the extreme nationalistic claims soon to be raised in both. According to the provisions of the agreement, the duchy was divided on an ethnographic basis. A multinational central body of

---

[11] Edward Beneš, *Problémy nové Evropy a zahraniční politika československá* (Prague, 1924), 62.

Czechs, Poles, and Germans was established to organize and control the distribution of food supplies. The rights of national minorities were to be guaranteed, especially with respect to their educational and political freedom. Any minority problems were to be settled only after mutual consultations.

Statistically, the Poles received 1,762 square kilometers of territory with a population of 293,661, according to the census of 1910. These included 207,092 Poles (70%), 16,433 Czechs (5.6%), and 63,418 Germans (21.6%). The territory awarded to the Czechs had an area of 519 square kilometers with a population of 141,160, including 99,171 Czechs (70.2%), 26,758 Poles (18.9%), and 13,498 Germans (9.5%). In light of subsequent claims and counterclaims, it should be noted that there were more Poles in the territory allotted to the Czechs than there were Czechs in the territory allotted to the Poles. By the agreement, the Poles gained control of the coveted railway line, but the Czechs acquired control of the greater part of the coal basin, gaining twenty-six pits against the ten awarded to the Poles. On the whole, the agreement was one which the local inhabitants considered just and reasonable. In the troubled months to come, it was to remain the model toward which the majority of the peacemakers strove.

The provisional government in Warsaw immediately confirmed the proceedings of the Polish National Council in Teschen and unreservedly accepted the agreement of November 5. The provisional government in Prague was somewhat embarrassed by the proceedings as they seemed to conflict with the policy Beneš had embarked upon. According to the Polish version, the Narodni Vybor Česko–Sloventky of Prague (the provisional Czech government) at first accepted the agreement. Apparently, all it protested was the recognition of the National Council of Silesia as the executive authority of the Czechs within the duchy.[12]

[12] Koszusnik, 15.

On November 12, however, the *Narodni Listy,* the official organ of the provisional Czech government, issued a blistering attack upon the agreement, which it claimed was made without its knowledge or consent, "by individuals who do not have any title to decide such matters." The government demanded the whole of the duchy, denying the Poles any claims whatsoever until the problem would be settled "definitely and legally by the Peace Conference." It laid the initiative for the agreement to "chauvinists from Silesia who before the World War had served the Germans." [13] The Polish Government claimed that this attitude was changed several days later, when, on November 15, the Provisional Government in Prague informed the Polish National Council in Teschen that

> ... the report in the *Narodni Listy,* alleging that the Narodni Vybor of Prague annulled the agreement between the Czechs and Poles in Silesia, is untrue. The agreement remains valid as it was concluded between the contracting parties.[14]

No confirmation of this Polish claim has been found in any Czech sources. At any rate, the Prague authorities tolerated the agreement. Rather than strain relations with Poland at this critical juncture, the Czechs preferred to concentrate upon Beneš' original plan: to secure international recognition for their claims to the duchy in the same way that their claims to Slovakia were secured. Beneš still sought, as did Masaryk, to strengthen the bonds between Czechoslovakia, Poland, Yugoslavia, Rumania, and Greece so that they could act as a bloc at the Peace Conference and improve their bargaining position with the great powers. He hoped, too, that this cooperative spirit would be the foundation upon which the stability of east-central Europe would rest in the postwar period. To challenge the Poles to an armed

---

[13] *Narodni Listy,* Nov. 12, 1918, in the Hoover Library on War, Revolution and Peace, Stanford, California.

[14] Koszusnik, 15.

conflict for the possession of the Polish-occupied sections of the duchy would not merely jeopardize the possibility of a successful result in this regard, but would destroy the impression of moderation and responsibility which the Czechs were trying to establish for themselves. Beneš therefore hoped to win the duchy through a decision of the Allied Powers, and then, having gained it, to cede the nonessential districts to the Poles in a magnanimous gesture designed to win their lasting friendship.[15]

At first Beneš seemed to have succeeded in his plans. In December he secured the wholehearted support of the French and a reaffirmation of their guarantee that, "at least until the decision of the Peace Conference is reached," the Czechs should have "the boundaries of the historic provinces of Bohemia, Moravia and Austrian Silesia." [16] Karel Kramar, the Prime Minister of the newly formed Czech Government, substantiated Beneš' achievements in France, claiming that on his visit to Paris, in January 1919, he found Clemenceau and Pichon favorable to the Czech designs on Teschen.[17] Beneš was equally successful with the English, even though the British experts considered the Czech claim to the duchy "a flagrant violation of the ethnic principle." [18] Nonetheless, he was able to convince them that the best solution of the question was to award the greater part of the duchy to Bohemia, with only a small correction in the east in favor of the Poles.[19] As a result, he won the authorization of the British Foreign Office for a Czech occupation of the duchy pending a decision of the

---

[15] Dagmar Horna, "The Diplomatic Struggle for the Boundaries of Czechoslovakia, 1914–1920" (unpublished Ph.D. dissertation, University of California, Los Angeles, 1954), 217–18.

[16] U.S. Department of State, *Papers Relating to the Foreign Relations of the United States, Paris Peace Conference* (hereafter cited as *For. Rels.*) (Washington, D.C., 1942–47), II, 382–83.

[17] Karel Kramar, *Kramaruv soud nad Benesem* (Prague, 1938), 74.

[18] David Lloyd George, *The Truth About the Treaties* (New Haven, 1939), II, 604.

[19] *Ibid.*

Peace Conference. Having reached this point, Beneš now sought to maneuver the French into occupying the duchy for him, in order to avoid alienating the Poles by an outright Czech occupation. Alleging that the whole of Eastern Europe was in jeopardy because of the inability of the Poles to exploit the mines in the areas they had occupied, and that the Bolshevism supposedly rampant in Galicia would soon spread to the duchy, Beneš insisted on an Allied or at least a French occupation of the region as the only means of restoring law and order there. Again his efforts were crowned with success, for the French agreed to send their troops to occupy the region. Unfortunately for the Czechs, the French occupation did not materialize as quickly as they had hoped. The Czechs considered it vital to complete the proposed occupation prior to January 26, the date scheduled by the Poles for elections to their National Assembly. The election day was fast approaching and still no French troops arrived. Despairing, the Czechs decided to oust the Poles themselves. However, just before the scheduled invasion, the French Minister in Prague informed the Czechs that French occupation troops were on their way. Accordingly, the Czechs decided to wait; but when, four days before the scheduled election, still no French troops had arrived, the militant nationalists in Prague decided that they could wait no longer.[20]

While the Czechs were thus preparing to wrest the duchy through military means, Marshal Jozef Pilsudski, Poland's Chief of State, attempted to settle the dispute through direct negotiations, in accordance with the understandings reached earlier at Prague and Washington. Toward this end, Pilsudski sent a personal appeal to President Masaryk for the convocation of a mixed commission to examine and regulate the Teschen question and all matters which affected Poland and Czechoslovakia as a result of the collapse of

[20] Report of Lieutenant R. C. Foster to Professor A. C. Coolidge, Jan. 27, 1919, *For. Rels.,* XII, 320–21.

the Austro–Hungarian Empire.[21] While awaiting Masaryk's arrival in Prague, scheduled for December 21, 1918, Stanislaw Gutowski, Chairman of the three-man delegation to whom the delivery of Pilsudski's personal appeal was entrusted, met with Prime Minister Kramar and discussed the general condition of Polish–Czech relations. According to Damian S. Wandycz, a second member of the delegation and author of the only account dealing with the events of this mission, Gutowski left the meeting with Kramar convinced that Kramar, at least, looked upon Poland as an enemy and upon Pilsudski's initiative as an unwanted interference in other plans already undertaken for the settlement of the question.[22] Several days after Masaryk's arrival in Prague, the delegates were finally able to secure an interview with him. Masaryk received them warmly. He noted that the marshal's suggestion was the best method for settling the disputes between the two states, but claimed that under the Czechoslovak Constitution he could not act upon this matter. He then referred the entire question to his prime minister, who, he expected, would give the matter full consideration. When the delegates formally met with Kramar, however, the latter claimed that, interested as he was in the proposition, he could not act upon it without first consulting his Minister of Foreign Affairs, Beneš, who was then in Paris. He said he would pass on the proposal to him, but that he would not expect a reply for at least ten days. Near the end of this period, Wandycz, who remained in Prague to receive Kramar's reply, met with the prime minister. At this meeting he learned that Kramar still had not heard from Beneš and that he did not expect to hear from him for at least one week more. In light of continuing reports of Czech troop-movements in the direction of the duchy, and what Wandycz interpreted as deliberate

[21] Damian S. Wandycz, *Zapomniany List Pilsudskiego do Masaryka* (London, n.d.), 15.
[22] *Ibid.*, 24.

delaying tactics on the part of the Czech Government, he returned to Poland and reported that military action was imminent. He held that further attempts at negotiations in Prague were worthless and that if military action was to be averted it could only be accomplished at Paris.[23] Before Wandycz's observations could be acted upon, the Czechs invaded the duchy, thus precipitating the crisis.

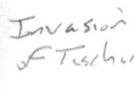

At 11:00 A.M. on January 23, 1919, four Allied officers appeared in the city of Teschen, presenting themselves as representatives of the Peace Conference. They delivered an ultimatum to the Polish commander there, ordering him to evacuate the Polish army from the duchy by ten o'clock that evening. According to the results of an investigation made shortly thereafter by Lt. Col. Rawlings of the British Peace Mission, the "Allied Officers" insisted on the evacuation in the name of the Principal Allied and Associated Powers. Colonel Latinik, the Polish commander, requested time to communicate with his superiors, attempting in the meanwhile to treat the "Allied Officers" with the dignity that belonged to the representatives of the powers that were responsible for the restoration of the Polish state. The authorities in Warsaw knew nothing of the "Allied" mission and ordered Colonel Latinik to defend the regions of the duchy assigned to Poland with the forces at his disposal.[24] Even before the ultimatum had expired, Czech troops entered Czech Teschen. As each town was entered proclamations were posted, stating that the occupation was ordered by the Entente because of the "threatening economic breakdown of Silesia."[25]

[23] *Ibid.*, 20.

[24] Coolidge Mission to Austria to the American Commission to Negotiate Peace, State Dept. MSS, 186/3114/33, Jan. 27, 1919. See also the Report of Lieutenant Foster to Professor A. C. Coolidge, *For. Rels.*, XII, 320–21.

[25] Lt. Arthur Voska, Report of the Neutral Commission sent by the Czecho–Slovak Government to the Polish Commander of Teschen, State Dept. MSS, 186.3114/29, Jan. 23, 1919. The Czechs continually raised the argument of economic unrest and Communist infiltration in the duchy as the cause for their movement; however, Allied investigation proved these

On first hearing of the participation of an "Allied Commission" in these events, Rawlings and Foster communicated with General Barthélemy, head of the French Military Mission to Poland, and learned from him that he knew nothing of this "Allied Commission," nor of any authority from the Entente for the occupation of Silesia by Czechoslovak troops. A similar query of Colonel Wade, Chief of the British Mission to Poland, proved that he too was not informed of the matter.

Deciding to meet this "Commission" in person Rawlings and Foster set off for Mährisch–Ostrau, the headquarters of the commission. Here they inquired of the officers involved concerning the authority for their actions. Each of the officers indicated that he had acted under the orders of the Czechoslovak Government, to which each of their respective Allied Governments had assigned them. They were next asked if these orders of the Czechoslovak Government had been authorized by the Entente. Each of the officers stated that he did not know. When questioned later, however, they indicated an awareness of what the Czech Government was attempting, but added that they "took this action in the hope that bloodshed might be avoided and that the matter might be settled by peaceful negotiations." [26] Commenting upon this reply, Foster noted that "there could have been very little idea of negotiation when troops were already massed on the Polish frontiers and plans laid for occupation at 2 o'clock that afternoon." [27] The attempt at a peaceful settlement is further challenged by Professor Kerner, of the American Peace Mission, who happened to be present at the interview between the "Allied Commission" and Colonel Latinik. Professor Kerner reported that Major Crossfield, a British

---

charges groundless. See Major Ernest H. Schelling to the American Commission to Negotiate Peace, State Dept. MSS, 186/3114/40, Jan. 31, 1919. This document is also to be found in the House MSS.

[26] Lt. R. C. Foster to Professor A. C. Coolidge, *For. Rels.*, XII, 320–21.
[27] *Ibid.*

member of the "Allied Commission," said to him: "We are going to order them out"—a statement Kerner interpreted as not manifesting an attitude suited to negotiation.²⁸ Foster further notes that

> It was very clear that this "Allied Commission" had hoped to force the Poles to accept the evacuation of the territory by the appearance of acting in the name of the Entente. Posters signed by them, which must have been previously printed, showed that every effort was made to bring out the fact that the maneuvers were favored by the Entente Powers.²⁹

So intensely did the Czechs try to create this impression that, in the announcements of their Press Bureau, they stated not only that a "Commission of Entente Officers" went to Colonel Latinik, but that resistance to the invading Czechs was resistance to the "representatives of the whole Entente." ³⁰ These "Entente Officers" were truly officers of the Entente Powers, but in the service and under the direct orders of the Czechoslovak Government. When questioned later, Masaryk stated that his government acted "with his entire accord and approval." ³¹ Against this background, Czech armies moved, shattering all hopes of Polish–Czech cooperation.

During the course of the subsequent discussions at Paris, the Czechs attempted to mitigate the reaction of the powers toward their actions by claiming to have sent a courier to Poland, prior to the invasion, with an appeal from President Masaryk for the withdrawal of Polish troops from the duchy. The Czechs claimed that it was only after the failure of the Poles to reply to these requests that their troops were forced to move; adding that it was only the unforeseen arrest of the courier by some over-zealous Polish

---

²⁸ *Ibid.*
²⁹ *Ibid.*
³⁰ A. C. Coolidge to the American Commission to Negotiate Peace, Feb. 5, 1919, *For. Rels.*, XII, 328–29.
³¹ Lt. R. C. Foster to Professor A. C. Coolidge, *For. Rels.*, XII, 320–21.

officers in Cracow that was responsible for the miscarriage. The Czechs failed to note that the arrest took place at 7:30 P.M. on the day of the invasion, just two-and-one-half hours before their armies crossed into the Polish-held sections of the duchy.[32] The fact that the courier was still in Cracow eight hours after the delivery of the ultimatum is difficult enough to comprehend; but how the Czechs expected him to travel to Warsaw, present his note and receive a reply in two-and-a-half hours, the time that remained before the movement of their troops, is impossible to understand, unless these maneuvers are looked upon as an invention designed to create an aura of respectability for an otherwise unpalatable act. Equally unconvincing is Kramar's protest to the Peace Conference that armed force was used only after negotiations with the Poles had failed.[33]

The invasion of the duchy reflected a division existing within the Czech Government. One party, headed by Beneš and Masaryk, contained moderates who sought to achieve Czech national aspirations through subtle diplomatic means; the other, headed by Kramar, contained extreme Czech nationalists who sought to achieve their aspirations regardless of the methods used.[34] The invasion of the duchy marked the triumph of the latter, though the extent to which the former contributed to the decision will probably never be known. At any rate, both Beneš and Masaryk expressed their regret at the incident. Shortly thereafter, Beneš stated his conviction that the problems existing between the Czechs and Poles should have been settled through direct negotiations.[35] Masaryk, in a letter to Paderewski, denied the Czech National Council in Silesia any

[32] The details of the arrest are in Lorcher to Kramar, Jan. 23, 1919, a copy of which is in the Paderewski MSS, in the Archiwum Akt Nowych, Warsaw, Folder 345. Dr. Lorcher was the courier involved.
[33] Minutes of the Council of Ten, Jan. 29, 1919, *For. Rels.*, III, 783–84.
[34] Henry Wickham Steed, *Through Thirty Years* (Garden City, N.Y., 1925), II, 247–48; and Harold Nicolson, *Peacemaking, 1919* (Boston, 1933), 240.
[35] Beneš to Paderewski, Paderewski MSS, Feb. 23, 1919, Folder 345.

authority to sign the agreement of November 5, but asked Paderewski if he thought it still possible for the two of them to discuss their outstanding differences. He assured him of his own feelings toward Poland, and pointed to the common dangers and interests which they both continued to share.[36]

Apparently the decision for the invasion came from the extreme nationalists in Prague who then occupied the most important offices in the first Czech cabinet. Commenting upon the general temper of the times, Horna implies that this view better reflected the attitude of the masses of Czechoslovaks than did that of the more conservative Beneš and Masaryk. She noted that "Czech public opinion generally was under the sway of exuberant national optimism."[37] As the basis for this, she pointed to the ease with which the revolt against the Austrians was staged, the news of the successes which Czech diplomacy was achieving in securing international recognition for its frontiers, and the exploits of Czechoslovak armies abroad. All these, she held, contributed to a "climate of opinion in which the realities of the international position of the new state were obscured."[38]

Indeed, the Czechs had much to be optimistic about. They had come through the war without any significant destruction inflicted upon their cities or farms. Not a single major battle was fought upon their lands, and, when the war was done, they emerged with their frontiers generally defined and guaranteed. Even before the conclusion of the war, the leaders of their independence movement agreed on the formation of a provisional government. Only three days after the Armistice was proclaimed, they adopted a provisional constitution for the government of their realms. On that very day, the first units of their legions formed

---

[36] Masaryk to Paderewski, Paderewski MSS, Feb. 23, 1919, Folder 345.
[37] Horna, 228.
[38] *Ibid.*

abroad began to arrive in Prague, and shortly thereafter to drive the Germans and Hungarians from the lands assigned to them. By the end of December they were masters of all the land they claimed, with the sole exception of the Polish-occupied areas of Teschen.[39]

The position of Poland was the reverse. With few exceptions, her lands were almost completely ravaged by the ebb and flow of Russian and German troops. Her frontiers were never clearly defined, and, even after the Peace Conference was over, no solution for her eastern frontiers had been effected. Her leaders at home and abroad could not agree on the establishment of a provisional government, being split among themselves almost as badly as were their people among the powers that partitioned them. After the failure of a coup d'état earlier in the month, a government headed by Paderewski was formed, and this only on January 16, just seven days before the Czech invasion of the duchy. To make matters worse, Bolshevik armies were penetrating into the heart of Poland and the Poles of Lwow were surrounded by Ukrainian armies awaiting its expected fall. With starvation and epidemics raging throughout Poland,[40] the Czechs could feel somewhat confident that the Poles would not contest their occupation of the duchy. But in this, as in the expectation that the occupation would be met with the approval of the Allies, they seriously miscalculated.

The repercussions of the Teschen crisis were immediately felt in Paris where already overworked delegates of the Allied and Associated Powers were confronted with a novel situation: a war between two Allied states over a region which the delegates scarcely knew existed. Lloyd George's reaction might be looked upon as typical of the conference.

---

[39] F. J. Vondrachek, *The Foreign Policy of Czechoslovakia, 1918–1935* (New York, 1937), 13–23.
[40] Paderewski to House, House MSS, Jan. 1, 1919, Jan. 4, 1919, and Jan. 12, 1919.

Addressing his House of Commons (April 16, 1919), he noted:

> I do not mind saying that I had never heard of it, but Teschen very nearly produced an angry conflict between two Allied states, and we had to interrupt the proceedings to try and settle the affair at Teschen.[41]

Sometime after news of the conflict reached Paris, Clemenceau summoned the disputants to appear before the supreme council. There, on January 29, both the Polish and Czech delegates to the conference presented the positions of their respective governments.

The Polish representative, Roman Dmowski, was apparently caught unaware of the recent developments in the duchy, as were the members of the council themselves. His reference to Teschen consequently was brief, lacking both the detail and breadth which the council expected; it was scarcely more than a reference to the Czech invasion as a violation of the November 5 agreement and a demand that the Czechs withdraw their troops pending a decision of the conference.

The Czechs, on the other hand, "proceeded to deal with the question at length on statistical, ethnographical, historical, and economic grounds." [42] They stressed their government's attempts to settle the dispute through peaceful means, pointing to the unanswered Czech note as a case in point. To their surprise, "the Poles invaded this territory, mobilized its population, and even went so far as to fix an election day." When the local Czech population complained, the Czech Government replied that "the Peace Conference must decide the question of the disputed territory," even though it knew that "if present conditions continued Bolshevik activity would follow." As a result of their failure

---

[41] Young, 357.
[42] Minutes of the Council of Ten, Jan. 29, 1919, *For. Rels.*, III, 783.

to arrive at a private agreement with Poland, the Czechs now stated their desire to place themselves entirely in the hands of the conference, "in full confidence that the Great Powers would not forget the great sacrifices which they had made in their cause during the war." [43] Arguments completed, the Council of Ten referred the situation to the newly formed Inter-Allied Mission to Poland.[44]

After meeting with the Czechs and Poles, the Mission to Poland proposed a temporary compromise, according to which the Czechs would occupy the mining regions and that part of the railroad north of Teschen, while the Poles would occupy the southern and eastern parts of the duchy adjoining Galicia. In other particulars, until the final decision of the Peace Conference was reached, the status quo would be maintained in accordance with the agreement of November 5, 1918. To insure the execution of this compromise and to prevent any further disputes from arising in the Teschen region, it was also agreed that a special Inter-Allied Commission would be sent to the duchy. After a number of delaying tactics in which the Czechs showed that they were not quite ready "to place themselves entirely in the hands of the Conference"—at least not if they did not get what they expected—they accepted the recommendations of the Mission to Poland, as outlined in an agreement signed on February 3. Signing the agreement did not mean that the Czechs intended to adhere to its provisions. As

---

[43] *Ibid.*
[44] The Inter-Allied Mission to Poland was authorized by the supreme council on Jan. 29, 1919. It was the first of the territorial commissions established by the conference. It was to go to Poland to accumulate information necessary for the conference's deliberations and to see to the effective execution of its decisions. This commission is not to be confused with the Inter-Allied Polish Commission, authorized by the supreme council on Feb. 12, 1919. This latter commission remained in Paris; its purpose was to process information received from the Inter-Allied Mission to Poland, from the Teschen Commission, and from the other commissions established to treat with the various phases of the Polish question.

events were soon to prove, it merely required the Czechs to find another means for achieving their objectives.⁴⁵

When the Inter-Allied Teschen Commission provided for in the agreement of February 3 arrived in Teschen, it found that the Czechs had not withdrawn their forces to the line outlined in their agreement. Rather they found the natives of the duchy unalterably opposed to the Poles and demanding the retention of the Czech troops. In his first dispatch to the conference, Marcus A. Coolidge, the American representative on the Teschen Commission, noted how impressed the commission was with the "earnest protest they received against the occupation of the town of Teschen and the southern part of the railroads at this place," ⁴⁶ the latter being one of the principal points the Czechs wished to secure. He noted that a group of "indigenous Polish inhabitants who call themselves Slezaki manifest especial dread of the arrival of Polish troops . . . and fear that their existence and even more their lives will be endangered." The attitude of the Polish nationalists was found to be "violent and provoking" and in bad contrast with that of the Czechs and Germans who were "calm and orderly." In fact "there is no doubt that the Czechs maintain the public peace and order in a most satisfactory manner." ⁴⁷

Because of these conditions brought to the attention of the Teschen Commission, the Czechs prevailed upon the commission not to enforce the agreement of February 3, but to permit the Czech occupation of the entire duchy until it would be able to propose a final solution to the problem.

Though it was subsequently to change, this hostile first

---

⁴⁵ Beneš and Kramar to Clemenceau, State Dept. MSS, 186/3114/43, Feb. 1, 1919; Beneš to Clemenceau, State Dept. MSS, 186/3114/44, Feb. 2, 1919; and Henry Wickham Steed, II, 278–79.

⁴⁶ Coolidge to the American Commission to Negotiate Peace, State Dept. MSS, 181.213102/1, Feb. 16, 1919.

⁴⁷ Ibid.

TESCHEN DISPUTE 241

impression of the Poles was manifest in all the early correspondence of the Teschen Commission. However, as their investigations continued and their conclusions began to be based on personal observations rather than on the reports of volunteer informants, the impressions of the commissioners began to change radically.[48] In time they came to realize that the only territory they had visited was that which the Czechs arranged for them to see and that the Czechs prevented the Poles from securing access to them.[49]

While the Teschen Commission was gradually learning that it had been duped, its decision to set aside the agreement of February 3 created a new crisis in Warsaw, Prague, and Paris. When the Teschen Commission finally ordered the local Czech authorities to comply with the terms of the agreement, the Czechs refused, claiming that such orders would have to come from Prague. As a result, a special Inter-Allied Commission had to be sent to Prague to force the Czechs to agree to permit the evacuation of those sections of Teschen as the Agreement of February 3 required.[50] When the Teschen Commission began to insist upon Czech compliance with the remaining provisions of the agreement, the local Czech authorities refused on the grounds that they had received no specific instructions from Prague. When the supreme council in Paris ordered that the decisions of the Teschen Commission made within the framework of the February agreement be binding at the moment of their promulgation, without reference either to Warsaw or Prague, the Czechs again refused, claiming that it "would be dangerous to grant such rights which would seemingly infringe upon the historical sovereign

---

[48] Coolidge to the American Mission to Negotiate the Peace, State Dept. MSS, 181.213102/2, Feb. 22, 1919.

[49] Minutes of the Inter-Allied Mission to Poland, State Dept. MSS, 181.21301/16, Feb. 22, 1919.

[50] Report of the Inter-Allied Mission to Poland, State Dept. MSS, 181.213102/40, Feb. 28, 1919.

rights of the Czecho–Slovak State over the Duchy of Teschen." [51] As a result, the commission was left helpless. The commission itself noted that, as Warsaw had agreed to accept its decisions, "this attitude of the Prague Government is making our work impossible . . . ; the position of the mission will become ridiculous unless the same recognition can be exacted from Prague." [52] Nevertheless, as late as April 28, the Czechs kept excusing their failure to submit to the Teschen Commission. They did not, in fact, adhere to the Big Ten's request at any time during the history of the dispute.

One of the principal tasks before the Teschen Commission was the submission of recommendations for a final settlement of the crisis. Unfortunately, with all the other problems to come before it, not until the end of March could it submit a report on the division of the region.

The chief difficulty facing the Teschen Commission and the various commissions in Paris to study the problem was how to reconcile the ethnographic and economic claims of the two contesting parties. The Poles, supporting the wishes of the inhabitants of the duchy as expressed in the agreement of November 5, 1918, insisted on an ethnographic division. They held that the economic interests of the Czechs were not vital and could be provided for without subjecting 170,000 people to a government to which they had shown their military hostility. They agreed to award the predominantly Czech district of Frydek to Czechoslovakia. They asked only for the predominantly Polish districts of Freistadt, Teschen, and Bielitz. The Czechs, on the other hand, insisted on a division of the duchy on economic grounds. They claimed that the duchy's coal and coke were indispensable to the industries of Bohemia and Moravia, and that the railway through the Jablunka Pass

---

[51] Inter–Allied Teschen Commission Reports, State Dept. MSS, 181.213102/32, Apr. 12, 1919.
[52] *Ibid.*

# TESCHEN DISPUTE

was the arterial connection between Bohemia and Moravia on the one hand and Slovakia on the other.

Though they were to dispute many aspects of the Czech presentation, the Poles generally recognized the validity of their economic arguments and were therefore willing to enter into international undertakings to guarantee the Czechs that part of their coal requirements not satisfied by the production of the mines left to them. They likewise were willing to pay for the construction of any segments of railroad that would be necessary to give the Czechs effective communication with Slovakia other than that along the Jablunka–Oderberg line which cut across densely populated areas inhabited by Poles. The Czechs, however, refused to accept these concessions, claiming that "a State in their geographic position must be in complete control of the mines and lines of communication which were of vital importance to their economic existence." [53] They therefore insisted on receiving the districts of Frydek, Freistadt, and Teschen, and were eventually willing to permit the Poles to retain possession of Bielitz.

On March 26, the Teschen Commission finally sent its recommendations for the division of the duchy to Paris. The majority report called for the creation of an independent duchy under the guidance and guarantee of the Allied Powers; failing this, it called for the division of the duchy along the watershed of the Vistula and Olsa Rivers, the latter of which would have met all the Czech demands. However, it soon became apparent that neither the Teschen Commission nor those commissions in Paris that were to act upon its recommendations were in possession of some of the most salient facts. At the time they drew up their report, they were unaware of other railway links between Bohemia and Slovakia and of the actual amount of coal available to both Czechs and Poles from other areas under

[53] Young, 354.

their control.⁵⁴ Nonetheless, on the basis of the recommendations of the Teschen Commission, a series of joint meetings between the Commission on Polish Affairs and the Commission on Czecho–Slovak Affairs in Paris divided the duchy according to the recommendations of the Teschen Commission.⁵⁵ Before the supreme council could act on these proposals, however, Secretary of State Lansing suggested that "Poland and Bohemia should attempt to reach a friendly settlement between themselves if possible as it would leave a much better feeling than if it were settled by others." ⁵⁶ As a result, action upon the recommendations of the Teschen Commission report was postponed, pending direct negotiations between Poles and Czechs.

While these events were taking place, the Teschen Commission continued its manifold activities, especially its investigation into the ethnic composition of the duchy. On the basis of their own investigations, as opposed to the reports the Czechs had supplied them, they came to alter many of their original views, and on April 28 they submitted a new report in which they unanimously recommended a division of the duchy along a line almost identical to that embodied in the agreement of November 5, 1918. In explaining the unanimity reached in the new report, they referred to the nature of the information on which their earlier report was based. "At the beginning . . . the Czechs were better prepared than the Poles and presented in support of their thesis a large number of very well written documents." On the other hand, "the Poles began only three weeks later, and in this struggle for influence, this circumstance placed them in an unfavorable situation." ⁵⁷

⁵⁴ *Conference de la Paix 1919–1920, Recueil des Actes de la Conference,* Partie IV, *Commissions de la Conference C, Questions Territoriales (3), Commissions Relative Aux Affaires de Teschen, Spisz et Orawa* (hereafter cited as *Recueil*) (Paris, 1929), 136–40.
⁵⁵ The Minutes and Reports of these Joint Meetings are to be found in the *Recueil,* 1–134.
⁵⁶ Lansing to Wilson, Apr. 13, 1919, Lansing MSS, Library of Congress.
⁵⁷ *Recueil,* 264–65.

This report, based on a realization of "the true state of affairs," was the first unanimous recommendation made for the division of the duchy. It was radically different from the Majority Report of the Inter–Allied Polish and Czecho–Slovak Commissions, presented to the Council of Foreign Ministers shortly before. Had it been presented one month earlier, it might indeed have been accepted. When it did arrive, however, a settlement of the dispute through direct Polish–Czech negotiations was already agreed upon.

During the three months that had passed since the outbreak of the Teschen crisis, several conflicting solutions had been advanced. Though the Allied Powers could not agree on any of these, they were unanimous in their insistence upon a speedy solution, whatever it might be. Not merely did the Supreme Economic Council and the American Relief Administration share this view, but every report of the Inter–Allied Teschen Commission pointed to the tragic consequences of the lengthening delay. Despite the urgency of the task, neither the Czech nor Polish Government took the initiative in entering upon the negotiations proposed by the Council of Foreign Ministers; nor did the conference seem interested in hurrying them along. As a result, it was not until some three months later that the long-awaited talks got under way.

The consequences of this delay were becoming more and more intolerable as time went on. A rash of strikes crippled the economic output of the duchy and its dependent regions. During this time the position of the Teschen Commission degenerated, and with it the prestige of the Allied Powers. Had the decisions of the conference and its commissions been binding upon the contending parties, a different state of affairs might have come to pass. But the Allied Powers had been unable to bring the Czechs to accept the resolutions of the Teschen Commission. As a result they now found it impossible to count upon the further good will of the Poles. By May, the Inter–Allied Commission was little more than a third party contending for control of the duchy.

As the proposed negotiations between the Czechs and Poles still had not taken place by July, some three months after the supreme council had endorsed this method of solution, the Council of Foreign Ministers notified both governments that it would grant them only until July 22 to reach an understanding. Under this pressure, both governments agreed to appoint nine commissioners each to meet in Cracow on July 21. After seven meetings, this Mixed Czecho–Polish Commission realized that it was impossible to break the deadlock which appeared as early as their second meeting. Accordingly, on July 29, they adjourned without arriving at any positive result.[58]

Now that the direct negotiations between Poland and Czechoslovakia had proved a failure, the question was taken up once again by the Peace Conference. On the basis of the Second Report submitted by the Teschen Commission, the Joint Meetings of the Commission on Polish Affairs and the Commission on Czecho–Slovak Affairs recommended a division of the duchy on an ethnographic line that was somewhat close to that contained in the agreement of November 5, 1918.[59] After seven months in which a score of conflicting solutions were advanced, a unanimous decision was finally suggested.

It only remained for the supreme council to ratify the recommendation of the Joint Meetings of the Commissions on Polish and Czecho–Slovak Affairs for the Teschen dispute to be settled. Unfortunately, before the supreme council acted upon the report, word of it leaked out, and tremendous pressures were brought upon the conference to confuse and delay a solution

---

[58] The Minutes of the Mixed Czecho–Polish Commission are to be found in the *Recueil*, 188–220.
[59] Minutes of the Eighth Meeting of the Joint Meetings of the Commissions on Polish and Czecho–Slovak Affairs, Aug. 20, 1919, *ibid.*, 50–58.

The final, supposedly secret, draft of the Joint Meetings was completed on August 22. On that very day, Beneš complained to Clemenceau of the far-reaching consequences that would develop if the Czech claims were not granted.[60] And, parallel with Beneš' new appeal, the Czechs sponsored a series of mass meetings to protest "the favorable Polish tendency reported prevailing" in Paris.[61] Reports coming from Prague indicated that the acceptance of any proposal which did not grant the Czechs what they wished would bring about the fall of the pro-French Masaryk–Beneš government, which it was believed was the only hope of preventing the Socialist Party, which favored a rapprochement with Berlin and Vienna, from gaining power.[62] When the Teschen question was again brought before the conference, the French now radically reversed themselves and refused to go along with the unanimous report of the Joint Meetings. They insisted on a line that would grant the Czechs all their demands, in complete opposition to the determined insistence of the remaining delegates for accepting the unanimous report.[63] As it proved impossible to secure the adherence of the French, it was agreed upon that a plebiscite would be the only way of avoiding the new impasse, especially as the Czechs now agreed to one. In commenting upon the new turn of events, Arthur Balfour, the British Delegate, expressed his fear that the result of the new solution would be to deprive Czechoslovakia not of forty percent of the coal but of one-hundred percent of it. He held that "the territory was Polish" and that the Teschen Commission attributed part of it to Czechoslovakia because of the railway running through it. He added that a

---

[60] Beneš to Clemenceau, State Dept. MSS, 180.03501/46, Aug. 22, 1919.
[61] Crane to the American Mission to Negotiate the Peace, State Dept. MSS, 186.3114/239, Aug. 31, 1919 and General Pelle to the Peace Conference, State Dept. MSS, 186.3114/232, Aug. 28, 1919.
[62] Ibid.
[63] Dulles to Polk, State Dept. MSS, 186.3114/253.

plebiscite was contrary to the interests of the Czechs; but, as Beneš appeared to accept it, he would go along.[64] Accordingly, the supreme council agreed that a plebiscite should be held in the duchy, leaving the details of the plebiscite to the Commissions on Polish and Czecho–Slovak Affairs.

Though everyone agreed that haste was all-important in arriving at a final settlement of the Teschen question, it was not until two months after the decision to hold a plebiscite that the supreme council agreed on the plebiscite terms. During the discussions in the Commissions on Polish and Czecho–Slovak Affairs which drew up the conditions, the French sided completely with every suggestion made by the Czechs. Apparently, they would do nothing which would jeopardize the position of Masaryk and Beneš. On one point the Czechs were particularly insistent: that no member of the Teschen Commission serve on the Plebiscite Commission. Having experienced Czech tactics, the Teschen Commission was extremely suspicious of their moves. The Czechs, therefore, preferred to start with a clean slate.

The plebiscite was originally to have taken place by December 31. Unfortunately, the Allied military occupation of the region, which was to precede the actual vote, had not yet taken place, nor had the Plebiscite Commission arrived in the duchy. As a result, it was again necessary to postpone the date of the plebiscite to a time three months after the arrival of the commission in the duchy. This eventually was put off until May 3, 1920, as the Plebiscite Commission was not ready to begin the tasks assigned to it until February 3rd.[65]

From its arrival in the duchy, the activities of the Plebiscite Commission were seriously handicapped by an absence of any recognized authority within the region. And it soon

[64] Minutes of the Heads of Delegations, Sep. 11, 1919, *For. Rels.*, VIII, 184–85 and 194–98.
[65] Minutes of a Meeting of the Heads of Delegations, Nov. 14, 1919, *For. Rels.*, IX, 167, and 169–72.

proved that the provisions made by the powers to avoid the weaknesses of the earlier Teschen Commission were inadequate: the executive authority granted the new commission was seriously compromised by the uncertainty of America's participation, for the chairmanship of the commission was assigned to the American member; and the police powers granted it were gravely weakened by the lack of sufficient troops. Had the three battalions scheduled to serve in Teschen arrived with the Plebiscite Commission, conditions might have been different. As it was, only the French battalion arrived on time. The delay in the arrival of the Italian troops jeopardized the security of the French troops who had arrived before them, and the American contingent never showed up at all. As a result, the Plebiscite Commission found itself in the same condition as its predecessor: without sufficient authority to enforce its decisions. Under these conditions, the commission had to devote so much of its time to re-establishing law and order that it was not until the beginning of April that it was able to complete its plans for the administration of the plebiscite. As it expected that the lists of eligible voters would be challenged and that an indeterminable delay would take place before all the claims and counterclaims could be examined, it requested the Council of Ambassadors, who now continued the work of the conference, to postpone the plebiscite another two months.[66]

During this period the Czechs attempted to secure concessions from the commission that would exclude various categories of Polish residents from participating in the election. When the commission refused to agree to the Czech demands, the Czechs began to attack it and to condemn the Poles for their bad faith. In a meeting with the American representative in Prague, shortly thereafter, Beneš attempted to undermine the foundations of the commission by claiming that it was so unable to control the

[66] Plebiscite Commission to the Conference of Ambassadors, State Dept. MSS, 184.612/63, Apr. 12, 1920.

violence within the duchy that neither party would accept the plebiscitary result. He further elaborated upon this theme in a letter written soon thereafter to the Council of Ambassadors. Here he described the Poles as "determined to prevent the execution of the plebiscite at any cost" because it would "not produce the result which they had hoped for." [67]

The Poles had little time to counter Beneš' charges. At this time they were far too busy fighting the Russo–Polish War of 1919–21. At the time of Beneš' letter, quoted above, Polish armies were threatened by Russian forces in the vicinity of Smolensk. By June 11, they were retreating from Kiev, which they had occupied just a few short weeks before, and ten days later they were evacuating Wilno and then Grodno as well. By then, Russian armies had entered the Congress Kingdom and had begun to concentrate for their final drive on Warsaw. By mid-August, when Warsaw was about to fall, Pilsudski struck out and saved the day for Poland. By then, however, the fate of Teschen was already sealed. In these circumstances, the Polish Government was unable to devote to the duchy the attention that it deserved.

Before the Council of Ambassadors had an opportunity to act upon the request of the Plebiscite Commission for an additional extension of time, Beneš began an active campaign to settle the dispute through other means. In a series of meetings with representatives of the major powers, he indicated the disadvantages of a plebiscite and claimed that, regardless of its outcome, neither of the contesting parties would accept the result as final. He therefore suggested that the Council of Ambassadors encourage direct negotiations between the Czechs and Poles, or, failing this, that it

---

[67] Crane to the Secretary of State, State Dept. MSS, 760c.60F/2, May 17, 1920, and Beneš to the Council of Ambassadors, State Dept. MSS, 184.612/524, May 20, 1920.

settle the dispute through its own decision.[68] So well did Beneš succeed in undermining faith in the plebiscite that, when the Council of Ambassadors met on June 5, everyone seemed to have taken it for granted that neither side would accept the results of a plebiscite.[69] Actually the Poles still wished the plebiscite and nowhere did they indicate the contrary. They did claim that they would not agree to continue the preparations for the plebiscite until the Czechs released all those held as political prisoners, and until all Poles driven from their homes were permitted to return.[70] Instead of attempting to strengthen the authority of the Plebiscite Commission, the council decided that a "plebiscite would be without value." They then decided to sound out the Czech and Polish governments on the possibility of arbitration, and to enquire of the King of Belgium as to his availability as an arbitrator.[71]

The council was assisted in arriving at this decision by a series of "spontaneous" mass meetings that were reported to have taken place throughout the length and breadth of Czechoslovakia. These meetings condemned Polish atrocities and ill will. They denounced the Plebiscite Commission for being unable to deal with its duties and held that all confidence in the plebiscite was completely lost.[72] At the same time, Beneš openly came out against a plebiscite under any condition. He now frankly declared before the Council of Ambassadors that he never had any faith in a plebiscite and that he agreed to one only to avoid having to reject the

[68] Minutes of the Council of Ambassadors, State Dept. MSS, 180.03301/46, May 29, 1920.
[69] Minutes of the Council of Ambassadors, State Dept. MSS, 180.03301/48, June 5, 1920.
[70] Speech of Patek before the Polish Diet, State Dept. MSS, 760c60F/17, June 9, 1920.
[71] Minutes of the Council of Ambassadors, State Dept. MSS, 180.03301/48, June 5, 1920.
[72] Crane to the Secretary of State, State Dept. MSS, 760c60F/7, June 5, 1920.

unanimous report of the Joint Meetings. "I accepted the Plebiscite knowing I would have to convince the Peace Conference of the impossibility of it." [73] Beneš thus succeeded in removing the question from an arena in which its settlement would have been unfavorable. He could not, however, permit the question to be settled by a neutral arbitrator, who would probably arrive at the same conclusion reached by the unanimous reports of the Teschen Commission and of the Joint Meetings of the Commissions on Polish and Czecho–Slovak Affairs. His government therefore rejected the proposed arbitration. Beneš then set off for Spa, to seek another solution from the supreme council.

Because of their consequences, the negotiations at Spa on July 10, 1920 were the most significant of all those affecting the settlement of the Teschen crisis. Unfortunately, we possess no firsthand accounts of what then took place. We know that Beneš left for Spa following the refusal of his government to submit the dispute to arbitration. This was shortly after the Polish Parliament demanded the suspension of diplomatic relations with Prague over the latter's refusal to permit the transit of arms destined for Poland during the critical phases of the Russo–Polish War.[74] We know too that Grabski, the Polish Minister of Foreign Affairs, followed Beneš to Spa, to secure Allied aid for his country at that most desperate hour in her existence. Then we learn that Grabski and Beneš signed an agreement in which they asked the Allied Powers to suspend the plebiscite and to take any measures necessary for definitively settling the dispute, pledging to execute loyally whatever

---

[73] Minutes of the Council of Ambassadors, State Dept. MSS, 180.03301/6, July 19, 1920.

[74] Crane to the Secretary of State, appended to Davis to the American Legation in Prague, State Dept. MSS, 760.60F/28, July 9, 1920. While the Czechs were preventing the shipment of arms to Poland, the reaction of which on Polish public opinion is rather obvious, Beneš was protesting to the Plebiscite Commission that he was doing everything possible to conciliate the Poles.

decisions the powers would formulate.⁷⁵ When or how this agreement came about, we do not know. It appears certain, however, that Grabski was told that, as a primary condition for Allied aid against the Russians, he would first have to submit all Poland's outstanding disputes to the powers and to accept any decisions which they might make.⁷⁶ As Poland's collapse was expected within a matter of days, the Poles had no alternative but to agree.

As a result of the agreement signed by Beneš and Grabski, the supreme council divided the duchy along the line suggested by the Czechs, leaving it to the Council of Ambassadors to draw up the details for putting this decision into effect.⁷⁷

The details drawn up by the Council of Ambassadors were supposed to be secret. Yet during the deliberations, the Czechs made a number of suggestions on specific points, all of which were conceded. So one-sided were the deliberations that Count Bonin Longare, the Italian representative, observed that "the fact remains that at the request of one of parties we are imposing on the other an obligation without consulting it." Later when he protested that the Poles were forced to concede every advantage they possessed, Jules Laroche, the French delegate, noted that the "Poles will also gain an advantage, an end to Czech enmity." ⁷⁸ In the course of this debate, Laroche provides us with a clue as to the reason for the preferential treatment given to the Czechs:

. . . it must not be forgotten that we were much more concerned in this question in supporting Mr. Beneš, who personally represents in Czecho–Slovakia the element most favorable to the Allies, and whose

⁷⁵ Grabski and Beneš to the Spa Conferences, State Dept. MSS, 184.612/738, July 10, 1920.
⁷⁶ Titus Komarnicki, *Rebirth of the Polish Republic: A Study in the Diplomatic History of Europe, 1914–1920* (London, 1957), 605–19.
⁷⁷ Young, 362.
⁷⁸ Minutes of the Council of Ambassadors, State Dept. MSS, 180.03301/63, July 21, 1920.

departure at the present moment would be disastrous. [In fact,] Mr. Beneš is guiding his country toward us, and is attacked by the Kramasch party, which is quite opposed to the Allies and looks eastwards instead of to the west.[79]

When the draft was completed, the two contesting parties were invited to sign. The Poles signed on the following day but protested vehemently. Paderewski doubted "whether the noble aim of the Supreme Council, which was to liquidate the conflict and promote normal, friendly relations between the Polish and Czecho–Slovak Republics is likely to be attained." He held, rather, that "the decision of the Council of Ambassadors has formed a chasm between the two nations which nothing will be able to reduce." [80]

According to the award, Czechoslovakia secured the coal fields and the railway line she demanded. She received 287,592 inhabitants, including 139,898 Poles, 113,309 Czechs, and 34,265 Germans, and was granted every concession she requested.

Beneš won. He secured all the concessions the Czechs had sought, but under such conditions as transformed the Teschen dispute into a Polish Alsace–Lorraine, a stumbling-block to that cooperation between Poles and Czechs that alone could promise any hope for an independent eastern Europe capable of maintaining itself against larger neighbors to the east and west. Though Polish–Czech relations were generally correct in the interwar period, a tremendous gulf separated the two.

Beneš came to regret his triumph when, on the eve of the signature of the Munich Pact, he proposed the re-establishment of "friendly relations and a new collaboration between Poland and Czechoslovakia" on the basis of a frontier rectification.[81] The Poles accepted this offer on September 27,

[79] Minutes of the Council of Ambassadors, State Dept. MSS, 180.03301/69, July 27, 1920.
[80] Paderewski to the Council of Ambassadors, State Dept. MSS, 184.612/817, July 30, 1920.
[81] Koszusnik, 45–49.

1938. But when, after the signature of the Munich Agreement on September 29, it appeared that the Czechs would not be permitted to cede the Teschen area to Poland (the Germans intended taking it for themselves), the Poles determined to save their minority from what they feared would be a permanent loss. Accordingly, they presented an ultimatum to the Czechs on September 30, demanding the restoration of the predominantly Polish communes of that region. By protocols signed on November 23 and December 4, Czechoslovakia officially recognized the line of November 5, 1918 as the frontier in the Teschen area. Actually six boroughs more were ceded to Poland, five largely Polish, one a Czech enclave.[82] Without knowing the background to the dispute or the events which brought about the Polish ultimatum, Winston Churchill described the Poles as "vultures upon the carcass" and then proceeded to use the incident for expressing his invective against them.[83] His views of the incident are the basis for the attitude generally held by those who comment on the subject, and were in large part responsible for the return of the region to the Czechs at the end of World War II.

Polish–Czech relations could not improve in any lasting way in the period from 1920 to 1938, but a rapprochement developed rapidly after that. But for the opposition of the Kremlin, a Polish–Czecho–Slovak Federation might even have come to pass.[84] At the end of World War II, the Soviet Union restored the duchy's pre-Munich division. In so doing, it opened old wounds, old hostilities that are reflected in the subsequent crises in east-central Europe. Despite the protestation of friendship between the Polish and Czech Communist parties, the bitterness of Teschen still remains.

[82] *Ibid.*
[83] Winston Churchill, *The Gathering Storm* (New York, 1948), 322–23.
[84] Piotr S. Wandycz, *Czecho–Slovak–Polish Confederation and the Great Powers, 1940–1943* (Bloomington, Indiana, 1956).

11

# Alcide De Gasperi: The View from the Vatican, 1929–1943

## ELISA A. CARRILLO

PROFOUND DISILLUSIONMENT AND DISAPPOINTMENT were characteristic of the European mentality in the era following the First World War. A sane and just international order had not been established, and a spirit of malaise, moreover, pervaded the ranks of victor and vanquished alike. But it would be erroneous to consider the postwar doldrums as emanating exclusively from the conflagration that ravaged Europe and other parts of the world between 1914 and 1918; the prevalent cynicism and despair were rather a reflection and continuation of a crisis in Western civilization. This crisis had matured during the three decades preceding the First World War, and the war and its aftermath merely intensified and communicated to the masses the nihilism, irrationalism, or propensity for violent solutions that had previously been embraced only by small minorities.[1]

In the interwar period, as faith in the institutions and thought patterns of Western civilization declined precipitously, Germany became a fountainhead of the forces of

---

[1] On the crisis in Western Civilization, see the brief but brilliant analysis in C. Grove Haines and Ross J. S. Hoffman, *The Origins and Background of the Second World War* (New York, 1947), 202–48.

irrationalism, while the Soviet Union provided, albeit sporadically, the impetus and inspiration for disrupting the international order. In Italy a new regime emerged which called itself "Lo Stato Totalitario Corporativo," and while Mussolini denied that Italian Fascism was for export, this totalitarian ideology, or a variant of it, appeared to be the wave of the future.

An acute observer and victim of the seedtime of the Second World War was Alcide De Gasperi, member of Don Luigi Sturzo's Popular Party (1919–26), founder of its successor the Christian Democratic Party, and Premier of Italy (1945–53). Though born an Austrian subject (this foreign birth was to be a source of reproach throughout his entire Italian political career), De Gasperi had become a subject of Victor Emmanuel III when the Treaty of St. Germain transferred his native Trentino from the Hapsburg Empire to the kingdom of Italy.[2] Entering the newly founded Popular Party, whose appeal was interclass, and which sought to combine social Catholicism with political democracy, De Gasperi rapidly established a commanding position, and in 1924, following the forced retirement and exile of Don Sturzo, he became the party's secretary. An able opponent of Fascism, De Gasperi soon aroused the ire of Mussolini and his henchmen. Surveillance by Public Security agents became rigorous after 1926, and in 1927 he was arrested and charged with attempted clandestine expatriation. On the basis of circumstantial evidence he was convicted and sentenced to four years of imprisonment in the infamous Regina Coeli Prison. Mercifully, illness and then a royal pardon effected his release after a little more than a year's imprisonment.[3]

[2] For De Gasperi's life from his birth to 1929, see my book *De Gasperi: The Long Apprenticeship* (Notre Dame, 1965), Chaps. I–V.

[3] On his surveillance, arrest, and conviction: Archivio Centrale dello Stato (Rome), Ministero dell'Interno, Direzione Generale di Pubblica Sicurezza, Casellario Politico Centrale, Busta 55, Fascicolo 2, No. 6775. For Letters written to his wife and reflecting his political and social philosophy: *Lettere dalla prigione,* ed. Francesca De Gasperi (Milan, 1955).

In April 1929, after months of leading a wretched existence in Rome—without work, ostracized by former associates, and dependent upon the charity of the few friends who remained loyal—De Gasperi succeeded in obtaining a position in the Vatican Library, which already sheltered some anti-Fascist "refugees." De Gasperi's entry into the employ of Pope Pius XI coincided with the settlement of the Roman Question, and in fact was facilitated by the signing of the Lateran Accords.[4]

The enforced political inactivity of the years from 1929 to 1940 were to afford the former parliamentarian and party chieftain an opportunity to reflect upon his own career and also to view with some detachment the crucial developments of the period. Such meditation and observation were to provide by 1943, when De Gasperi permanently left the Vatican, the materials for the ideological foundations of the Christian Democratic Party.

The presence of De Gasperi in the Vatican was, of course, displeasing to Mussolini, and in 1931 during the crisis over Italian Catholic Action the Duce sought to have him discharged on the ground that his continued presence "could only augment suspicions and misunderstandings." Pius XI, whose employment of De Gasperi was an act of charity rather than an expression of anti-Fascist feeling, replied that he did not regret and would not regret having given "an honest man and an honest father of a family a little of the bread" of which he had been deprived by Mussolini.[5]

The controversy over Italian Catholic Action was ended by a compromise which De Gasperi considered humiliating for the Church. In a meditative mood he wrote:

For too long the precepts of dignity have been neglected. To get on one's knees is all very well, but religious instruction should also teach

[4] For a more detailed analysis of De Gasperi's views on the Lateran Pacts, based upon confidential letters, see my article "Alcide De Gasperi and the Lateran Pacts," *The Catholic Historical Review,* XLIX (1964), 532–39.

[5] Angelo Martini, *Studi sulla questione romana e la conciliazione* (Rome, 1963), 139, 145.

one how to stand on one's feet. The attacks of the outlaws are violent, but whoever acts according to his own conscience has nothing to fear. The evil becomes greater when through insincere condescendence one loses one's self-respect.[6]

The subservient attitude of many Italian prelates toward Fascism and their characterization of Mussolini as a "man of Providence" was distressing and incomprehensible to De Gasperi. The testimonials on behalf of the regime increased during the tenth anniversary of the March on Rome, and to his old friend and journalistic collaborator, Don Giulio Delugan of Trent, De Gasperi exhorted, "Work, for it is the only way to alleviate the bitterness of certain inexplicable spectacles."[7] In his scrapbook De Gasperi pasted an article from *L'Osservatore Romano* under which he wrote, "I cried and suffered and wished I could still be in prison rather than witness such a lack of conscience and such cowardice."[8]

Meanwhile, as a cataloguer in the Vatican Library, De Gasperi was learning the art of classification according to the Library of Congress system. Whether he ever mastered the system is debatable; in later years, after he had once again achieved fame in public life, his former colleagues in the catalogue room maintained that his cards were models of how they should *not* be prepared. Nevertheless, the overall performance of his duties must have been satisfactory to his superiors, for he was given tasks of increasing responsibility. Thus from 1934 to 1937 he was entrusted with the organization of an international exposition of the Catholic press. In the course of the work he dealt with forty-five national committees, composed of the best-known representatives of the Catholic press of Europe and America. It

---

[6] Quoted in Maria Romana Catti De Gasperi, *De Gasperi uomo solo* (Milan, 1964), 152.
[7] Letter of De Gasperi to Don Giulio Delugan, Apr. 23, 1932. Private Archives of De Gasperi family, Rome.
[8] Scrapbook is in Private Archives of De Gasperi family, Rome.

was an enterprise which enabled him to expand his external contacts and widen his intellectual horizons.[9]

In 1939, at the request of Anselmo Albareda, the Spanish Benedictine who was Prefect of the Vatican Library, Pope Pius XI appointed De Gasperi as Secretary of the Library. Father Albareda had been unaware of De Gasperi's political past, having become prefect only in 1936. When he went to the pope to suggest the appointment, the pontiff was startled. He said, "We have taken him out of Regina Coeli," adding, "What will the people on the other side say about this?"[10] But in spite of what the other side might say, Pius XI acceded to Albareda's request. De Gasperi was profoundly moved by the appointment, coming as it did after so many years of frustration and loneliness.

De Gasperi's reactions to the crises and problems of the 'thirties can best be discerned through a column which he wrote in the Vatican bi-monthly, *L'Illustrazione Vaticana*, from 1933 to 1938. Entitled "La Quindicina Internazionale," it was written under the pen name of "Spectator," and, though the language was sometimes ambiguous, the perceptive reader could conclude that the author was unreconciled to Fascism, devoted to the principles of Christian democracy, and open to change and experimentation.

In surveying international politics and diplomacy at the outset of the year 1933, De Gasperi noted the increasing complexity of modern diplomacy. At one time a diplomat or statesman was considered a success if he mastered European politics; now he had to be an expert on world politics, for "the war and the dynamism of our epoch have multiplied, complicated, and universalized problems."[11]

Developments in Germany following the appointment of Hitler as Chancellor caused De Gasperi deep concern; par-

---

[9] The exposition was described by De Gasperi in *La Stampa cattolica nel mondo. Risultati ed insegnamenti della stampa cattolica nella Città del Vaticano* (Milan, 1939).

[10] Testimony of Cardinal Albareda in *Concretezza,* Aug. 16, 1964, 10.

[11] *L'Illustrazione Vaticana,* Jan. 1–15, 1933, 9.

ticularly distressing to him was the disappearance of the Center Party, the party he had long admired for its non-confessionalism, its advanced social-welfare program, and its devotion to constitutional government. On the occasion of its dissolution in the summer of 1933, De Gasperi wrote at length on its origins, development, and services on behalf of the German people. He predicted correctly, "The Center Party leaves a patrimony of experience and of thought that will survive the dissolution of its organizational form not only in the memory but also in the culture of German Catholics." [12]

De Gasperi reprobated the cooperation of the Catholic politician Franz von Papen in undermining the Weimar Republic, and he characterized the Nazi regime as dictatorial and totalitarian. The ideology of Nazism was a denial of Christian personalism; Nazism could be described as personalist only in the sense that it deprived citizens of their personalities in order to concentrate them in a single person, Adolf Hitler. After the June purge, De Gasperi was convinced that Germany had lost all sense of human dignity and personality.[13]

As De Gasperi saw the picture, German Catholicism faced a far more formidable enemy in Hitler's neopaganism than it had in Bismarck's *Kulturkampf*. Taking cognizance of episcopal protests against Nazi policies, De Gasperi was heartened by the German Catholic resistance in the face of social pressure and outright persecution. In view of Nazism's postulation of a religion that was essentially pre-Christian, he did not foresee a more promising future for the Protestant churches of Germany.[14]

[12] *Ibid.*, July 16–31, 1933, 555–56.
[13] *Ibid.*, Jan. 16–31, 1933, 55; July 1–15, 1933, 494; July 16–31, 1934, 626; Aug. 1–15, 1934, 666; Aug. 16–31, 1934, 716.
[14] *Ibid.*, Aug. 1–15, 1933, 597; Nov. 16–30, 1933, 905; Dec. 16–31, 1933, 987; Apr. 16–30, 1934, 360; Aug. 1–15, 1934, 666; Nov. 1–15, 1934, 941; Mar. 16–31, 1935, 293–94; Apr. 16–30, 1935, 414; Aug. 1–15, 1935, 819–20; Sept. 1–15, 1935, 953; Nov. 16–30, 1936, 1039; Apr. 16–30, 1937, 343; June 1–15, 1937, 527.

As a former Austrian, De Gasperi took a special interest in the country that constituted one of Hitler's prime objectives. Looking at the small Danubian republic in 1933–34, De Gasperi observed that it was in a state of suspension as far as parliamentary government was concerned. The Christian Socialists were forced to abandon the parliamentary system, at least temporarily, in order to strengthen the state against the inroads of Nazism. At the same time, they sought a solution of the center—that is, a government that was neither statist nor individualist, a government based on "the force of laws and not on the law of force." Austria's regime of the center was headed by a "clever and energetic man," Engelbert Dollfuss, and De Gasperi regarded his tragic death in July 1934 as a great calamity. Toward Austrian socialism, with which he had a familiarity dating back to the turn of the century, De Gasperi was totally lacking in sympathy. He accused Austrian Socialists of always having one foot in Parliament and another on the barricades, and of utilizing political power to "destroy the family and stifle the faith." Nevertheless, he found praiseworthy the efforts of Ernst Karl Winter, the Catholic deputy mayor of Vienna, to win over the forces of the left.[15]

In 1938 De Gasperi watched with dismay the German annexation of Austria, and when the Austrian episcopacy called upon Catholics to ratify the *Anschluss* with Germany, De Gasperi hastened to point out to the readers of *L'Illustrazione Vaticana* that the bishops had acted without the knowledge or approval of the Holy See. It was not long before he was recording Nazi attacks upon the Catholic Church in Austria and noting the bitter disillusionment of those who had previously accepted Hitler's assurances of respect for the rights of the Church.[16]

[15] *Ibid.*, May 1–15, 1933, 329; July 1–15, 1933, 494; Oct. 1–15, 1933, 765; Mar. 1–15, 1934, 217; May 16–31, 1934, 447; June 1–15, 493; Aug. 16–31, 1934, 716–17.
[16] *Ibid.*, Mar. 1–15, 1938, 187; Mar. 16–31, 1938, 232; Apr. 1–15, 1938, 276; Sept. 16–30, 1938, 755; Oct. 1–15, 1938, 800; Oct. 16–31, 1938, 843.

French Catholicism was another subject to engage the detailed attention of De Gasperi. Surveying the French nation as a whole, he divided it into the "fils de Voltaire" and the "fils des Croisés." He considered it unfortunate that French Catholics should be divided among themselves, even though most of them were careful to avoid the old errors of Boulangism, anti-Dreyfusism, and monarchical conservatism. He admired the *Parti démocrate populaire,* the Catholic party which stood for a republican democracy, a planned economy (as opposed to state capitalism), and a parliamentary reform that would ensure greater political stability.[17]

De Gasperi was also pleased to observe that French Catholics were once again becoming integrated into the national fabric. Anticlericalism was on the decline, and Church–state relations were constantly ameliorating. In the Chamber of Deputies, a Socialist minister was quoting with approval Pius XI's *Quadragesimo Anno.* De Gasperi regretted, however, that while French Catholics were making themselves felt in political and intellectual circles an insufficient number of them were actively interested in social justice. French Catholicism had not yet succeeded in winning over the masses; to do so, it had to offer them a mystique as attractive as Communism.[18]

For the neoscholastic philosopher Jacques Maritain, De Gasperi had the most profound admiration. In his opinion, Maritain, together with Gilson, was endeavoring to "aggiornare" French Catholicism. He quoted Maritain to the effect that it was time wasted to admire medieval Christian forms and that the modern state should be pluralist and autonomous. These were concepts which De Gasperi could heartily second, for they constituted part of his own po-

[17] *Ibid.,* Aug. 1–15, 1934, 667.
[18] *Ibid.,* Apr. 16–30, 1936, 368; June 16–30, 1936, 559; July 1–15, 1936, 607; Sept. 1–15, 1936, 799; Feb. 1–15, 1937, 111; June 16–30, 1937, 528; Oct. 16–31, 1937, 877–78; Dec. 1–15, 1937, 1009; June 16–30, 1938, 492; July 1–15, 1938, 536.

litical philosophy, derived from his experience in both Austrian and Italian politics. Perhaps another reason why he was partial to Maritain is that he saw a similarity between the French philosopher's social thought and that of his preceptor in social Catholicism, Giuseppe Toniolo. Both Maritain and Toniolo called for a repudiation of regimes based upon bourgeois humanism, and both insisted on personal sanctity as a prerequisite for a new order.[19]

When he turned from a consideration of French Catholic thought to the day-to-day operations of the French government, De Gasperi displayed his usual pragmatism. The instability of French parliamentary life and crises such as the Stavisky Affair convinced him of the necessity of strengthening the executive branch of the government. In his opinion the deficiencies of the constitutional structure gave a handle to the rightist leagues, which he compared with the *fasci di combattimento*.[20] The squadrism of some of these leagues provoked in the French people the reaction which helped to bring the Popular Front to power.[21]

The Popular Front government of Léon Blum, which was supported by the Communists, was by no means anathema to De Gasperi. He pointed out that some of its policies, such as protection for unionization and collective bargaining, had long been supported by French social Catholicism. Insofar as the Front involved collaboration between men of differing ideologies, the experiment was also of interest to De Gasperi, who in the mid-twenties had considered a coalition with the Italian Socialists against the Fascists. However, in 1937–38 De Gasperi advised French Catholics to be wary in accepting the hand that was being extended to them by Maurice Thorez, the French Communist

---

[19] *Ibid.*, Feb. 16–28, 1935, 179–80.
[20] *Ibid.*, Feb. 16–28, 1934, 169–70; Apr. 1–15, 1934, 313; Sept. 1–15, 1934, 764; Mar. 1–15, 1935, 235.
[21] *Ibid.*, May 1–15, 1936, 414; May 16–31, 1936, 463; Nov. 16–30, 1937, 965.

leader.²² The papal encyclical against Communism, issued in 1937, may have influenced De Gasperi's thoughts on the subject. In 1924 the same pope had issued an admonition against an alliance between the *Popolari* and the Socialists.

The politico-religious life of Spain also occupied many lines in "La Quindicina Internazionale." De Gasperi saw no essential incompatibility between republicanism and Spanish Catholicism, but he urged the republic to abandon the anticlerical legislation that was so offensive to the majority of the Spanish people.²³ What Spain needed was a government of the center, and he believed that *Acción Popular*, the Catholic political organization headed by Gil Robles, could give Spain a centrist program, one that would be both reformist and legal. De Gasperi rejoiced over the defeat of the left in the 1934 elections, and he expressed confidence that the Catholics who came to office would be able to steer a middle course, combating both socialism and capitalism. He praised the Minister of Agriculture, Jiminez Fernandez, for supporting agrarian reform, and compared his ideas with those of Toniolo.²⁴

The results of the February 1936 Spanish elections came as a painful surprise to De Gasperi. Nevertheless, he did not regard the victory of the Popular Front as justification for the launching of civil war. "Better a constitutional mill that grinds as best it can, though making terrific noises and sometimes turning in vain, than a series of sanguinary and fratricidal conflicts." He hoped that the war could be brought to a speedy conclusion and that it would serve to bring about a more equitable socio-economic order. When the war continued, however, with the Church the apparent special target of Republican forces, De Gasperi gave his support to General Franco. At the same time, he was criti-

²² *Ibid.*, Jan. 1–15, 1938, 12; Jan. 16–31, 1939, 55–56.
²³ *Ibid.*, May. 16–31, 1933, 374; Nov. 1–15, 1933, 851; Jan. 1–15, 1934, 38.
²⁴ *Ibid.*, Dec. 16–30, 1933, 987–88; May 1–15, 1934, 406; Nov. 16–30, 1934, 982–83; Dec. 16–31, 1934, 1079; Jan. 1–15, 1935, 12; May 1–15, 1935, 487.

cal of the Falange, the Fascist organization which supported Franco.[25]

Of the constitutions of Catholic countries, the one which De Gasperi singled out for special praise was that of Ireland. He described its constitution of 1937 as a document which avoided offending against liberty and tolerance while simultaneously recognizing the rights of God and nourishing healthy traditions. Ireland was a state which openly acknowledged the primacy of natural law and applied the principles laid down by Pope Leo XIII in his encyclical on Christian constitutionalism.[26]

Another Catholic country that De Gasperi admired was Portugal, seeing in that nation's government a reconciliation between "liberty and authority." In a somewhat myopic fashion, he characterized Antonio Salazar as a follower of the "golden mean." With reference to the corporate constitution of Portugal, he quoted a Portuguese professor who maintained that Portuguese corporativism was based on the traditional practices of the nation rather than on a mere imitation of the Italian model.[27]

De Gasperi's references to the Soviet Union are comparatively sparse, but this is not surprising in view of the relative dearth of information on the USSR in Mussolini's Italy. De Gasperi attributed the Soviet adoption of the Popular Front technique in 1935 to two factors: Stalin's fear of Germany and Japan, and the Soviet failure to bring about a world revolution. To avoid losing their freedom to develop as a political party, native Communists were instructed to resort to the Popular Front. Nevertheless, commented De Gasperi, the mere employment of the technique indicated a certain evolution, perhaps still remote, toward recovery of the Russian body politic. The fact that Communist parties

[25] *Ibid.*, Feb. 16–29, 1936, 157; Mar. 1–15, 1936, 203; Aug. 1–15, 1936, 703; Aug. 16–31, 1936, 751–52; Sept. 1–15, 1936, 799–800; Sept. 16–30, 1936, 848; Sept. 1–15, 1937, 745–46; Aug. 1–15, 1938, 624.
[26] *Ibid.*, June 1–15, 1937, 483.
[27] *Ibid.*, Nov. 16–30, 1935, 1209–10; Nov. 1–15, 1937, 922.

were now defending the established social order and were even singing the praises of patriotism was significant insofar as it portended a reconsideration of doctrinal positions on these matters.[28]

The promulgation of the Soviet constitution of 1936 and the adoption of legislation to strengthen marriage and family ties gave encouragement, thought De Gasperi, to those who hoped that the Russian dictatorship would evolve eventually into a Western-type democracy. He noted, however, that the supremacy of the Communist Party had in no way been diminished by the new domestic developments, and there was no evidence that basic objectives had changed.[29]

Casting his eyes across the Atlantic, De Gasperi found the New Deal a newsworthy item for the readers of the Vatican journal. He characterized the New Deal as evolution rather than revolution, and he pictured Franklin D. Roosevelt as following in the footsteps of Wilson's "New Freedom." The American President was a "pragmatist," an experimenter, and De Gasperi obviously admired him for avoiding a doctrinaire approach to the problems of the day and for utilizing varied techniques in trying to bring the United States out of the throes of the depression. However, he criticized Roosevelt for refusing to allow the World Economic Conference, which convened in London in June 1933, to consider currency stabilization.[30] De Gasperi's analysis of the situation proved to be correct: American rejection of monetary stabilization paralyzed the conference and thereby retarded world economic recovery.

Fearful of embarrassing the Vatican, De Gasperi had few comments to make concerning the actions of the Italian government, except where the pope had already taken a stand. Thus he rejected Mussolini's contention that the Fascist corporate system was in the tradition of Italian

[28] *Ibid.*, Aug. 16–31, 1935, 876; Mar. 1–15, 1936, 203; June 1–15, 1936, 507.
[29] *Ibid.*, July 16–31, 1936, 655; Nov. 16–30, 1936, 1040; Jan. 1–15, 1937, 18.
[30] *Ibid.*, July 16–31, 1933, 556; Aug. 16–31, 1933, 641–42; May 16–31, 1934, 447; Oct. 16–31, 1934, 895–96.

social Catholicism and in accord with the principles of *Quadragesimo Anno*. On the contrary, asserted De Gasperi, Fascist corporativism was an "absolute novelty," embracing as it did the entire nation and linking itself inextricably with the Fascist totalitarian party. As for *Quadragesimo Anno*, this encyclical was concerned with the social, not the political, order, and its directives were not to be identified with any particular political structure or constitution.[31]

De Gasperi's comments on the Ethiopian War were for the most part quotations of foreign articles on the subject. Thus he quoted the *Reichspost* of Vienna, which stated that the blessing given by Italian clergymen to Italian soldiers was given to individuals and did not signify any judgment on the merits of the war. Another citation was from an article by the Belgian jurist, Charles de Vischer, in the *Bulletin de l'Union belge pour la Societé des Nations*, in which the author maintained that while aggression with the aim of expansion was not justifiable, Italy possessed the right to protest against the political and economic order of the postwar world. These were undoubtedly De Gasperi's sentiments as well.[32]

In discussing Italy's adoption of racist legislation in 1938, De Gasperi was openly critical. In mid-July of that year, a group of Italian professors, supported by the Ministry of Popular Culture, had published ten theses on race. In his commentary on the theses, De Gasperi noted that they diverged from Nazi concepts on race in that there was no exaltation of any super-race and in the admission that present races were made up of diverse proportions of different races. Nevertheless, continued De Gasperi, the theses embodied racism, and Thesis 9 excluded the Jews from the Italian race. He correctly attributed the promulgation of

[31] *Ibid.*, Dec. 16–31, 1933, 988; June 1–15, 1934, 493; May 1–15, 1935, 488; Aug. 16–31, 1935, 877; Apr. 1–15, 1936, 316.
[32] *Ibid.*, Oct. 1–15, 1935, 1043; Nov. 1–15, 1935, 1157; Dec. 16–31, 1935, 1334; Jan. 1–15, 1936, 14; Jan. 16–31, 1936, 61; Feb. 16–29, 1936, 158.

the racist program to the strengthening of cultural and ideological ties between Italy and Germany.[33] His abandonment of guarded language in discussing a policy of the Italian government probably stemmed from the fact that this was a period of extreme tension in Church–state relations, with Pius XI also denouncing racialism.

With Konrad Henlein and his demands for the Sudeten Germans of Czechoslovakia, De Gasperi manifested little sympathy. If the German community of Czechoslovakia was entitled to full administrative autonomy, then, queried De Gasperi, why not also the minorities of all countries, be they creeds, races, or nationalities. Henlein's demands could not be supported because they were postulated on the "right of race," an "egocentric concept" which had nothing to do with the essential equality of all men.[34]

Ever since his student days in the Trentino, De Gasperi had taken a deep interest in social movements, and his column in the Vatican journal reflected this continuing concern. To show that totalitarianism, insofar as it was a social movement, was incompatible with a Christian conscience, he suggested the following criteria in judging any social movement: does the movement harmonize with the supreme end of man; does it respect the free and responsible activity of the human personality; does it abide by the supreme evangelical laws of charity and justice; are the relations between individual, family, and state consonant with the natural law and the precepts of the social encyclicals?[35] Obviously, totalitarianism could not meet these criteria.

Analyzing the contemporary Catholic social movement throughout the world, and with particular reference to France and Belgium, De Gasperi saw it as possessing a positive character. Its exponents did not intend to solidify the existing social order but rather to achieve a substantial recti-

[33] *Ibid.*, Aug. 16–31, 1938, 667.
[34] *Ibid.*, May 1–15, 1938, 359.
[35] *Ibid.*, Sept. 16–30, 1933, 726.

fication of it. De Gasperi did not believe that the Church could or should identify itself with the forces of the right, and he urged Catholics to take the lead in bringing about the end of socio-economic injustices. Too often, he complained, Catholicism merely trailed behind other -isms.[36] To modern ears, De Gasperi's charge has a familiar ring.

Another subject of lifelong interest to De Gasperi was international peace and justice. He recognized the inequities in the Paris Peace Settlement, and he did not think that this settlement should be permitted to stand for all time. On the other hand, however, he insisted that the deficiencies of the Versailles order be corrected by peaceful methods. In 1933 De Gasperi was hopeful that the Geneva Disarmament Conference would be the first step toward the establishment of a more equitable and peaceful world, but the subsequent inability of the French and English to agree on a disarmament formula, in addition to Hitler's withdrawal from the conference and from the League of Nations, shattered this optimism.[37]

De Gasperi admired the League of Nations, but he feared that the international organ had been weakened from its very inception by the failure of the United States to become a part of it. The league policy of the Americans had had unfortunate repercussions on that of Britain,[38] and the weakness of the international body had enabled Japan to defy it with impunity in 1932–33.[39] While De Gasperi did not say so, he undoubtedly realized that Mussolini gave the league the *coup de grâce* when he invaded Ethiopia. By 1938, when war clouds were visibly hovering over Europe, De Gasperi warned: ". . . today, in view of the progress

---

[36] *Ibid.*, Mar. 16–31, 1936, 256; Apr. 1–15, 1936, 315; July 1–15, 1936, 607; Aug. 16–31, 1936, 751.
[37] *Ibid.*, Jan. 1–15, 1933, 10; April 16–30, 1933, 294–95; May 1–15, 1933, 329; May 16–31, 1933, 373; Nov. 16–30, 1933, 904; Feb. 1–15, 1938, 100.
[38] *Ibid.*, Jan. 1–15, 1933, 9; Nov. 1–15, 1933, 851; Jan. 16–31, 1934, 80.
[39] *Ibid.*, Jan. 16–31, 1933, 55–56; Feb. 1–15, 1933, 97–98; June 1–15, 1933, 413.

of technology, war is an evil far more terrible and universal than ever before. To resign oneself to its inevitability would be to entrust oneself to the demon of destruction." [40] A few months later, as Europe took the Munich road to war, *L'Illustrazione Vaticana* abruptly ceased publication.

It must be remembered that De Gasperi's writings during the crisis period of Western civilization were not intended for any clandestine press; they were published in a country where Fascism was at the height of its power. Palmiro Togliatti, the head of the Italian Communist Party from 1944 to his death in 1964, wrote a book in 1958 in which he took De Gasperi to task for not using stronger language against Fascism during the Mussolini era—but the fact is that De Gasperi, unlike Togliatti, had not found safety abroad.[41] It was necessary for De Gasperi to use cautious language in order to protect his family and at the same time to keep alive the message of Christian democracy. By continuing to write, though in muted tones, he was able to reaffirm Christian democratic principles concerning a just domestic and international order and to place on guard those who were accepting Fascism as a salvationist creed.

Viewed against the backdrop and vocabulary of the global revolution of the late 'sixties, the political and socio-economic thought of De Gasperi in the 'thirties may seem too traditionalist; but it should be noted that for his own day his philosophy, though rooted in the past, was advanced and progressive, particularly when compared with that of his contemporaries in public life. And unlike many of his contemporaries, both in public and private life, he did not believe that Fascism was the wave of the future, and he was willing to bide his time until the turn of events demonstrated the bankruptcy of that ideology.

For Italy the turning point came in June 1940, when Mussolini brought Italy into the Second World War. The

[40] *Ibid.*, Apr. 1–15, 1938, 275.
[41] *L'Opera di De Gasperi* (Florence, 1958), 61–74.

day after Italy became a belligerent, De Gasperi called to his home on Via Bonifacio VIII some former members of the Popular Party who were residing in Rome. He predicted that Italy would lose the war, because Britain would succeed in bringing the United States into it, and the American entry would be decisive. With Italy's defeat on the field of battle, the Fascist regime would crumble, and consequently it was necessary to plan for the future.[42] During the next two years De Gasperi met regularly but cautiously with his anti-Fascist friends, and discussed with them the organization and program of a revived Christian Democratic party.

The entry of students into such a party was of particular interest to De Gasperi, and the development of the *FUCI–movimento laureati* had encouraged belief that these groups would help provide leadership for the projected party. In 1925 the Federation of Italian Catholic University Students (*FUCI*) had been reorganized by Igino Righetti of Rimini and an ecclesiastical assistant, Monsignor Giovanni Battista Montini, the future Pope Paul VI. As president of *FUCI,* Righetti sought to guide an intellectual elite in its Christian social and intellectual responsibilities. In 1932 he organized, outside of Catholic Action, the *movimento laureati* for Catholic university graduates; a basic premise of the movement was that the culture of the Church must be brought into closer touch with contemporary society.

In 1942, as the Italian Army was enduring a succession of humiliating defeats, several of the *FUCI–movimento laureati* groups established ties with De Gasperi, who had always attached great importance to the role of students in ideological movements, and both came into contact with two anti-Fascist formations in the North, the La Pira circle of Catholic Action in Florence and the Guelf movement in Lombardy. Subsequently all of these varied groups and

---

[42] Interview with the Honorable Mario Scelba, who was present at the meeting called by De Gasperi.

movements were to fuse to form the Christian Democratic Party.[43]

Meanwhile, other anti-Fascist parties were beginning to form or to revive, such as the Party of Action, the Socialist Party, the Communist Party, the Liberal Party, and the Labor Democratic Party. By the end of 1942 the leaders of the anti-Fascist parties were known to each other, and all were frequenting the home of Ivanoe Bonomi, the pre-Fascist politician, in Piazza della Libertà in Rome. When the Christian Democrats met separately, it was in the study of Giuseppe Spataro, the former deputy of the Popular Party. By reason of his experience, temperament, and character, De Gasperi was recognized by all as the logical head of the Christian political party that was in the process of being revived. Interestingly enough, in June 1944 Mussolini told a journalist at Salò that of the veterans of the old democratic parties, De Gasperi was the man best suited to lead postwar Italy.[44]

The gatherings at the homes of Bonomi and Spataro laid the foundations for the formation of the multiparty anti-Fascist front and the Committee of National Liberation. On April 27, 1943 the Anti-Fascist United Freedom Front was formed, with Bonomi as its spokesman; the agreement was later put into writing and signed by De Gasperi for the Christian Democrats, and by the representatives of the Socialist, Liberal, Communist, and Labor Democratic parties.[45] The pact pledged the parties to a political truce during the war and period of reconstruction. Their common goal would be a democratic regime based upon the popular will.

In the period immediately before and after the fall of

---

[43] On *FUCI* and the *movimento laureati,* see Augusto Baroni, *Igino Righetti* (Rome, 1948); Francesco Magri, *L'Azione cattolica in Italia* (2 vols., Milan, 1953); Richard A. Webster, *The Cross and the Fasces* (Stanford, 1960), 137-43.

[44] Giulio Andreotti, *De Gasperi e il suo tempo* (Milan, 1956), 133.

[45] Ivanoe Bonomi, *Diario di un anno* (Milan, 1947), xxiv.

Mussolini, politically conscious Italian Catholics were much preoccupied with the role that they should play in the forthcoming new order. Some doubted that it was opportune for them to form a political party; they feared that such an attempt would result in a recrudescence of anticlericalism, and hence they preferred joining the existing parties. Others took the position that no collaboration was possible with parties that contained Marxists. One faction, however, held that it was possible to "baptize Communism" and they formed a party of Catholic Communists, headed by Franco Rodano and Adriano Ossicini. De Gasperi's attitude was that it was necessary for Catholics to form their own party; though independent of the Church, it would be of Christian inspiration and would seek to create a new order based upon the precepts of Christian Democracy.[46] It was this point of view which won out in the end, although the Christian Democratic Party, insofar as De Gasperi was its principal representative, never claimed that it was the only legitimate party for Italian Catholics. The Fascist experience undoubtedly had had the effect of clarifying and sharpening De Gasperi's views on the limited and autonomous character of political parties and on the distinction that must prevail between the sphere of state action and that of ecclesiastical action.

While the anti-Fascist bloc and the Christian Democratic Party were both still in the process of formation, De Gasperi continued working at his Vatican post, making preparations for the celebration of the quadricentennial of the Council of Trent. To judge from his correspondence with his longtime friend Don Giulio of Trent, the anniversary of the council was his primary concern. On July 16, 1943, when the annual summer vacation began for the staff of the Vatican Library, De Gasperi took a "leave of absence" which turned out to be a permanent leave. Three

[46] Giorgio Tupini, *I Democratici cristiani* (Milan, 1954), 48–49.

days later, he witnessed from the Museo Lapidario Vaticano the first aerial bombardment of Rome. He saw hundreds of Allied planes circle the city and then drop their bombs on its periphery. Among the edifices hit was the Church of San Lorenzo fuori le Mure, the church in which De Gasperi would be buried eleven years later. San Lorenzo also contains the tomb of Pope Pius IX, under whom Italian Catholics had been excluded from participation in the political life of the Kingdom of Italy. It was under De Gasperi, who was to serve as Premier of Italy from 1945 to 1953, that Italian Catholics were to achieve full insertion into the life of the nation.

By the summer of 1943 the Second World War was nearing a climax as far as Italy was concerned. At the beginning of June, Bonomi had been received by Victor Emmanuel III, whom he urged to overthrow the Fascist regime, detach Italy from the German alliance, and end the war. The king had listened with interest but had not allowed a word to betray his intentions. In July, after the invasion of Sicily by the Allies and the aerial bombardment of Rome, the king finally acted. On the night of July 24–25 the Fascist Grand Council met and called for a restoration of all powers to the king. On July 25 Mussolini was arrested as he left the royal residence. On this same day De Gasperi and his associates formally adopted the name of *Democrazia Cristiana* for their party. A new era had begun for the Italian nation.

12

# The New Nationalism and the Old: America and Europe

## C. RICHARD CLEARY

NATIONALISM HAS BEEN DESCRIBED by one contemporary scholar as "the organizing principle of human society";[1] by another as "a principle of disintegration and fragmentation. . . ."[2] One authority claims that nationalism is still "the strongest, most pervasive force of our day";[3] another asserts that "Nationalism has had its day," having been appropriate only to the "post-feudal and pre-atomic past."[4] It is no small question to determine which of these views has the greater cogency.

If we consider the fact that more than eighty new nation-states have come into existence during the past century, and that about two dozen of these have achieved independence during the past fifteen years, it seems clear that nationalism is not yet a waning force in the present age. Whether we consider the motives that led the leaders of the new states to seek independence, or the political slogans

---

[1] Barbara Ward, *Five Ideas that Changed the World* (New York, 1959), 33.
[2] Hans J. Morgenthau, "The Paradoxes of Nationalism," *The Yale Review* (June 1957), reprinted in Alvin Z. Rubinstein and Harold W. Thumm, *The Challenge of Politics: Ideas and Issues* (Englewood Cliffs, N. J., 1962), 269.
[3] Ward, 275.
[4] Morgenthau, 275.

by which they elicited and are seeking domestic support, or the policies which they pursue in the international arena, there can be little doubt that nationalism is the predominant force at work. The pugnacity of a new state like Indonesia in attacking the newer state of Malaysia, and the firmness of an old state like France, in opposing an American-inspired Atlantic multilateral force, indicates that the nation-state and nationalism in one form or another remain the stark political realities in our age.

Though not the only force at work, its manifestations are still sufficiently important to support the view that the "Age of Nationalism" that began in Europe with Rousseau and Herder had not passed; and that the idea of nationalism is now world-wide in its influence.[5] But nationalism has passed through many phases since the French Revolution. Neither its geographical base nor its ideological content remains what it was a generation ago.

Before considering the present state of nationalism in modern Europe, it is important to notice some of the distinct forms and phases of nationalism. Considered as an ideology, "old-fashioned" nationalism belongs exclusively to modern history. Viewed as an abstract idea, nationalism is considerably newer than the older of the nation-states, which are themselves much younger than the older dynastic and imperial states from which they evolved. Modern nationalism began with the fusion of the fact of nationality and the older fact of patriotism, welded together by the heat of convictions that one nation ought to equal one state, that each national group ought to determine both the sovereign state to which it would belong and the form of government by which it would be ruled. As an ideology, nationalism has always been linked with some form of democracy and is inseparable from the idea of sovereignty.

Most of the elements from which this force was compounded are neither ignoble nor historically inorganic. The

[5] Hans Kohn, *The Idea of Nationalism* (New York, 1948), vii.

facts of ethnography and the age-old process of nation-building cannot profitably be praised or blamed. Rational patriotism—a natural and ennobling attachment to the institutions and landscapes of one's own country—is not of itself a menace to humanity. Yet nationalism—both as ideology and as sentiment—has had enormous impact on the history of the world. It was necessarily fatal to the earlier political order based on multinational imperial states. This disruption, or reorganization, occurred first in Europe, then extended into all the areas over which European dominion or influence were exercised. Though the principle of nationality did not solve the problem of self-determination for small or scattered ethnic groups, or security for larger nations, the partition of empires under the impact of nationalism was certainly not an unmitigated evil.

At the same time, it was far from being an unqualified benefit for Europe or mankind. In the course of its development European nationalism at times tended to reject the most fundamental and constructive values of Western civilization; it was a potent force in provoking the most destructive wars in recorded history. It has "made the divisions of mankind more pronounced and . . . spread consciousness of antagonistic aspirations to wider multitudes of men than ever before." [6] Having disrupted international relations in the past, nationalism still seems likely to imperil peace in the future.

To explain the savagery unleashed by modern nationalism it is necessary to consider some of the other elements that went into the compound. The age of mass communications elaborated and intensified the phenomenon of collective ego on a national scale. Marshall McLuhan might call it a "return" to village consciousness. From self-consciousness to self-assertion is a short step. From self-assertion to self-righteousness is a still shorter one. In this connection Reinhold Niebuhr reminded us a generation ago

[6] Hans Kohn, *Prophets and Peoples* (New York, 1959), 4.

that political evangelism—the conviction that one's nation is acting to achieve moral goals—has often been one of the forms in which a national will-to-power could be rationalized and respectably asserted.[7]

The ideological side of modern nationalism owes much to the Rousseauist or Jacobin tradition. From Rousseau nationalism incorporated the notion of national omnipotence.[8] According to this brand of democratic doctrine, the common man taken *en masse* was infallible. Mood and emotion became the norm of national conduct; absolute power of life and death was conferred on the mass of people composing the nation, and the sole source of authority in any society was a nebulous but almighty General Will. The notion of right based upon reason was undermined; popular impulse and collective self-love became the sole source of morality, justice, and a power that was limitless.[9] This deification of sentimentalism had a devastating effect on man's concept of himself, and degrading consequences for his collective conduct.

Some historians have been able to discern these ideas in action in the world of nation-states. The Reign of Terror foreshadowed in a small way the shape of modern times. It was not a very long step from Rousseau to Hitler. Germans were among the most industrious pupils of the French pedagogue—as they were to be of other French masters of Arts and Letters. Many worked diligently to hasten the progression from Rousseau's elegant eighteenth-century *Essays* to Hitler's emphatic *Mein Kampf*. Georg Hegel, for example, propounded the theory that the nation-state was "a super-personality, whose essence is power." His less abstruse but more comprehensible disciples sedulously popularized this doctrine in Germany, where ultimately the

[7] *Children of Light and Children of Darkness* (New York, 1944), 11–22. St. Augustine discovered—and shed—this same delusion considerably earlier.
[8] Thomas Neill, *Makers of the Modern Mind* (Milwaukee, 1949), 190.
[9] *Ibid.*

worship of national purity came to be celebrated by the incineration of ethnic or racial "impurities."

While prophets of nationalism flourished elsewhere throughout Europe, not even America, with all her interoceanic "isolation," was immune from these impulses. In this country nationalist imperialism was called "Manifest Destiny" in the 1840s, when it achieved grandiose proportions. After pausing at the water's edge for some decades, distracted by internal disorders, exertions and growth, it reappeared at the turn of the century when America discovered the "Dawn of a New Destiny."[10] The ingredient of self-aggrandizement was never lacking from America's "missionary diplomacy,"[11] though there was also a conscious element of benevolence in our renewed national dedication to "dollars, duty and destiny."[12] It would be parochial and perhaps imprudent to forget that European nationalists have also had benevolent impulses.

Western European nationalisms from 1815 to 1880 were predominantly highminded, dedicated to individual and national liberty, associated with constitutionalism, championed by the growing middle class, and sometimes pacifistic in outlook. Liberal nationalists of this period seemed convinced that the goals of nationalism—one nation or people equals one state—could be achieved by education and persuasion. The most obvious accomplishments of the nationalistic spirit during this period were the creation of unified German and Italian national states and the emergence of Greece, Serbia, Rumania, and Bulgaria into independent statehood. Intense national feeling was further manifested by agitation and insurrections in Poland, Ireland, and Hungary.[13] In the early part of the century, nationalism struck

[10] Alexander De Conde, *A History of American Foreign Policy* (New York, 1963), 317.
[11] *Ibid.*, 422.
[12] Thomas A. Bailey, *A Diplomatic History of the American People* (New York, 1964), 471.
[13] Norman D. Palmer and Howard C. Perkins, *International Relations* (New York, 1953), 47.

roots in Latin America, whose peoples terminated Spanish and Portuguese control; a few decades later, the movement spread to Asia, where Chinese leaders—and, more emphatically, Japanese ones—took to nationalism as readily as a subsequent generation was to adopt chewing gum and cigarettes.

Yet, even during this early period of the development of nationalism in Europe and its implantation abroad, the hard facts of history brought disillusionment to nationalists of the liberal or irenic school. By the 1880s there were few nationalists who still believed that the goals of national independence, or liberation of an ethnic *irredenta*, could be achieved by peaceful methods. Thus pacifism was sacrificed to the assertion of national will, and individual liberty was compromised wherever it seemed to obstruct national liberation.

The last three decades of the nineteenth century—described by Carlton Hayes as "a generation of materialism" —witnessed a great intensification of national rivalries and revealed that nationalism was no less aggressive and imperialistic in spirit than any of the dynastic empires it was disrupting. The acquisition of prestige became increasingly important to nationalist sentiment. A massive confusion of national interests with merely nationalistic aspirations was evident in the foreign and colonial policies of the great European powers; the political map of Africa and Asia was revolutionized by their imperial contests.

In the generation preceding World War I, nationalism as an idea unfolded in its full totalitarian dimensions: it metamorphosed into "integral nationalism." [14] As expounded by Hippolyte Taine (1828–93), Maurice Auguste Barrès (1862–1923), and Charles Maurras (1868–1952), in-

---

[14] For an analysis of integral nationalism see Carlton J. H. Hayes, *The Historical Evolution of Modern Nationalism* (New York, 1948), 164–231; also his *Generation of Materialism* (New York, 1941), Chap. vii, "Seed-Time of Totalitarian Nationalism," 242–85; and Hans Kohn, *Nationalism* (Princeton, 1955), Chap. vii, "Racialism and Totalitarianism," 73–80.

tegral nationalism, with its fatalism, determinism, and deliberate irrationality, embodied the total negation of Christian ethics. The dethronement of Deity could scarcely be more complete than in the supreme exaltation by integral nationalists of the history, biology, and mores of their own tribes or nations. This school proclaimed power for its own sake a supreme national goal. Some supported "Catholicism," not because they believed in God, but because the Church was considered a useful tool for the attainment of power, or the symbolization of past national achievements.

The xenophobia inherent in integral nationalism was enlarged after 1860 to incorporate the newly developed "science" of race, which flowered in this period. There was a kind of logic in the fact that anti-Judaism and anti-Semitism were evident in this movement from the beginning,[15] and the relation between nineteenth-century nationalism and twentieth-century Nazism is nowhere more evident than in the racist characteristics of both movements. For the integral nationalist as well as for the Nazi, hatred for Jews had a theological as well as a pseudo-biological basis.

While this *fleur du mal* was germinating in the old Continent, America did what it could to remain competitive in neo-Darwinian social science. In the new Continent this science was called Anglo-Saxonism, and if its biological underpinning was inferior to that flourishing in the scholarly circles of Europe, its abundant messianic theology more than compensated for the defect. In prestige and mass appeal on both continents, this popular new science outclassed the old doctrines of the Christian Church, like those reiterated in the 1940s by Pius XII, who proclaimed that all

---

[15] It was again a Frenchman, Comte de Gobineau, who produced the pioneering work in the doctrine of racism, *Essai sur l'inegalité des races humaines* (1859); but it was the literarily inferior book of his Anglo-German disciple, Houston Stewart Chamberlain, *Die Grundlagen des neunzehnten Jahrhunderts* (1899), which fanaticized these doctrines and popularized them among the intellectual "middle-brows" of Europe. Chamberlain's fantastic opus was widely distributed in Germany by his friend Kaiser Wilhelm II and intensely admired by the young Adolf Hitler.

Catholics are spiritually Semites, or in the 1950s by John XXIII, who asserted that all races and sects were part of the mystical body of Christ.

To the integral nationalist, such views were not only anachronistic but subversive as well. How could a rational man reconcile a universal prescription to love God and man with the higher duty of loving one's own national myths, monuments, and *Macht* to the exclusion of all contrary values? Especially intolerable was the attack on Race, which, in combination with nation-worship and physical science, would one day enable men to achieve new summits of technology at Dachau, Buchenwald, Auschwitz, and Hiroshima. In the nineteenth century these accomplishments were glimpsed only mistily—and mainly by men of modest ambition or historical outlook, like Lord Acton.[16] Death denied Acton whatever satisfaction could be found in seeing his prophecies fulfilled.

The path to World War I was paved by exaggerated nationalism, and, in view of the nihilistic tendencies of integral nationalism, it was no accident that this degenerated into the biggest, bloodiest, and, on the whole, the most senseless war that great states had ever fought. With the advent of the man-eating machinery of mass conscription and the adoption of policies of unlimited military-manpower attrition by all principal belligerents, nationalism now seemed to menace biological existence itself. These techniques of war, plus the wholesale propaganda needed to sustain them, contributed to an enormous popular intensification of nationalism.

The world might easily have survived the territorial and other terms of the Paris peace settlement were it not for the

---

[16] Acton feared that the course of nationality "will be marked with material as well as moral ruin, in order that a new invention may prevail over the works of God and the interests of mankind." In his view, nationality did "not aim either at liberty or prosperity, both of which it sacrifices to the imperative necessity of making the nation the mould and measure of the State." "Nationality" (1862), *Essays on Freedom and Power,* ed. Gertrude Himmelfarb (New York, 1955), 169.

ruinous economic nationalism that followed it. A world-wide accentuation of nationalism was faithfully mirrored in the policies of both new and old nation-states.

From an economic viewpoint, the greatest damage resulting from World War I was not the vast physical destruction of facilities in Europe; it was the augmentation of the nationalistic spirit in economic policy. In some ways, international trade relations between the two World Wars resembled an institutionalized economic warfare of all against all. Every industrialized state (and some others) contributed to mutual economic enfeeblement by dedicated pursuit of protectionism and other forms of nationalism in postwar economic policy. The American example is one that should be mentioned, because the impact of its policy on the world economy was greater than that of any other country. In the period from the inauguration of President Harding to the collapse of American prosperity ten or twelve years later, our national policy was one of regressive —even tribalistic—tariff and immigration laws. These reflected a quasi-pathological brand of nationalism,[17] called isolationism—a kind historically new in North America. In Europe, nationalism openly admitted—even began to boast of—its totalitarian character. Nazi and Fascist versions of nationalism bellowed their belief in the destiny of the nation to assert its will over all other values. In the Soviet Union, where ambition wore a red-colored rather than a black ideological mask, it was possible to see that nationalism could not only co-exist with Marxism, but would probably prove itself the stronger of the two forces.[18] In Germany, the repudiation of constitutionalism and adoption of racism

---

[17] The intransigence of Senator Lodge, the xenophobic babblings of Senator Borah, the blatant racism of new national immigration policies, and the jingoistic babbitry depicted in the novels of Sinclair Lewis, were indicators of a new fever abroad in this incredible American era.

[18] Though this tendency was there to see as early as 1928, very few saw it, mainly because of two forms of myopia: Bolshevik ideology and anti-Bolshevik ideology.

as an official ideology completed the compounding of a new period of horror.

Hitler's murderous assault upon Poland inaugurated six years of destructive fury and bloodshed the world will never forget. For the first time since the West became civilized, the goal of national and racial mass-murder became the deliberate policy of a great nation eager and able to put it into execution.

More than two decades have passed since Germany was defeated and Hitler destroyed. But what of the seedbed in which he was bred? Was it also destroyed?; purged in the flames of defeats he inflicted on others and the destruction and disgrace he brought down on the German nation?; or only fertilized by the blood and frenzy of those six years that shook the world?

Since the early 1960s, these questions have been deeply disturbing to many Americans (and to some European Americanophiles). After more than two decades of American leadership in a Cold War that began in Europe with Europe as the main stake, a dismayed America is rediscovering the phenomenon of European nationalism. At the same time it is obvious that nationalism, viewed on a world scale, has vastly increased in extent and intensity since 1945. This force extends from Castroism in the Caribbean, throughout the continent of South America, across black, white, and tan Africa and the Middle East; it embraces India, China, and the island nations of the Pacific as well. Everywhere except Europe and parts of Latin America this force, which has catapulted more than fifty new nation-states onto the international stage, has been generally applauded and supported by Americans from official Washington down to the once insulated, now "internationalist," citizens of Zenith.

Many Europeans have noted the apparent contradiction in an American outlook on foreign nationalisms,[19] which

---

[19] On America's ambiguous attitude toward nationalisms, old and new, see: Maurice Duverger, Special Introduction to *De Gaulle: Implacable Ally,*

sees them as good in Africa and the Middle East, but bad in Europe. One key to the paradox can be found just beneath the surface. America has twice spent blood and treasure to resolve European wars that threatened her security. During or after both wars, America has also launched vast international enterprises designed to promote values higher than (but including) her own security and prosperity. President Wilson's postwar ambitions aborted; Roosevelt's gave birth to a mouse that has not yet roared. President Truman's doctrine fell on fertile soil and grew abundantly.

Building on costly and courageous commitments to the economic reconstruction and military defense of Europe in the late 1940s, by the early 1960s America had developed a fairly clear official doctrine regarding the question of European unity. The European Common Market would be the basis for closer economic integration. The community would be expanded; would develop a political superstructure which would move toward complete federation. This federation of (Western) Europe could then assist America in all the great projects of economic upbuilding and military defense of the extra-European parts of the free world. This is America's Grand Design. In its conception of two Atlantic partners equal (or almost equal) in wealth and perhaps eventually in military power, coordinating their strategies of trade, aid, and defense on a global scale, there is an undeniable grandeur.

As the decade neared completion, it became clear that the American-made Atlantic design was not prospering in Europe. America's dismay deepened, as Britain decided to abandon her last outposts east of Suez and moved closer to the Continent, while Germany adopted a coalition regime

---

by Roy C. Macridis (New York, 1966); David S. McLellan, "The Changing Nature of Soviet and American Relations with Western Europe," *Annals*, CCCLXXII (July 1967), 18–20; Stanley Hoffmann, "Obstinate or Obsolete? The Fate of the Nation-State and the Case of Western Europe," *Daedalus*, XCV (Summer 1966), 862–915.

which revived the Franco–German concert and looked more and more to Paris for guidance.

There seems much to praise and little to damn in the record of European nationalism since 1945. Thanks to the new nationalisms of the old world, much has been saved from the post-Hitler wreckage of the Continent—and perhaps something gained.

Western European sentiments of nationality were an insurmountable obstacle to the extension of Bolshevik dominion from Moscow. This sentiment has grown strong during the past two decades, and remains an obstacle to "instant" federation, but not to growing cooperation or further steps toward eventual organic unity and perhaps confederation.

Even in the dwindling and doctrinally diluted Communist parties of Western Europe there is no longer a serious question of Soviet control. When nationality collided with ideology, it was the "native" that prevailed over the "alien." The posthumous testament of Palmiro Togliatti, long-time leader of the Italian Communist Party, was a landmark in the disintegration of Communist "internationalism."[20] His polycentrist thesis, proposing national party independence of both Moscow and Peping, has long since become a fundamental premise of Communist party leaders in Western Europe.

In Eastern Europe, Soviet Party domination seemed to be dissolving as early as 1953. Poland has regained internal autonomy. Rumania has achieved a measure of independence in diplomacy as well as internal affairs. Yugoslavia had made its break in 1948. Stalin aimed to implant Communism in states that would be "national in form, socialist in content." Many Marxist states of today—from Poland to Cuba and many points between—could more accurately be described as "socialist in form, nationalist in content."

These wholesome and highly visible developments have been viewed with skepticism and even incredulity by some

[20] Philadelphia *Inquirer*, Sept. 5, 1964.

policy analysts and experts on Communism, especially in America. Yet, they should not come as a surprise to any observer equipped with historical sense; nor should it be a source of disappointment to anti-Communists to discover that there was more soft clay than granite in the construction of the Soviet monolith.

If Communism is weakened in the old world, what of the European nationalism that America rediscovered a few years ago? Admittedly a species of nationalism informed the political performance of Charles de Gaulle, just as (unadmittedly) it influences the policies of all other successful statesmen. If America's apprehensions are understandable, it is still possible that her perceptions of European realities have been dulled or distracted during the 1960s, if not earlier.

There is little if any chauvinism, imperialism, xenophobia, or isolationism in contemporary Europe. European nationalism is today "restrained, unideological, and on the whole rather tame." [21] If a kind of nationalistic politics flourishes in France and elsewhere in Europe, it is no longer concerned with a simple power-struggle among nations. The great issues of past struggles—including that of national self-determination—have been settled. It is difficult to imagine how a new world war could arise from a European issue (other than the German question).[22]

If the "old-fashioned" European nationalism was a curse, it has not been demonstrated that the new-fashioned nationalism of the old world is not a blessing. In any event, nationality is a fact that cannot be argued away. On this fact nationalism is based. Nationalism is not especially dangerous to men who do not believe that their "nation should enjoy special privileges as the result of special

[21] Harold Van B. Cleveland, *The Atlantic Idea and Its Rivals* (New York, 1966), 30.
[22] *Ibid.* See also Theodore Geiger, "The Ending of An Era in Atlantic Policy," *The Atlantic Community Quarterly,* V (Spring 1967), 93.

virtue."[23] It can be an incentive to real virtue in men who desire to prove by the rectitude of their actions that they are worthy citizens; and to men who demand a high standard of probity in the conduct of their own government and society. Such men can pursue the opportunities for self-realization offered by their own national cultures. They can even support reasonable projects of international organization or union, and yet remain convinced that life would be appalling in a "world without national differences, without variety of culture and temperament, without the possibility of counterpoint and harmony in international life."[24]

It would be reckless to ignore forces and tendencies hostile to variety, taste, counterpoint, and harmony among nations; but nations are among the most durable artifacts of history. Despite dangers, the future of nationalities and nations is not as dim as Marxist dialectic decrees, American computers calculate, or Arnold Toynbee prescribes. It should be added that no state—with or without nationalism, old or new—is finally secure from all dangers.

Among America's best friends and oldest allies there are many who see a danger in the fact that one nation now possesses more engineering ability, more energy, more weapons, and more visionary aptitude than any other people on the planet. Some fear that the North American superpower could succumb to its recurrent tendency to eliminate the menace of foreign or old-fashioned "-isms" with a streamlined nuclear solution for the problems of an "overpeopled" planet.

American energy and courage to fight impossible fights are a precious part of our national patrimony. Like other peoples, we are subject to illusions. American energy, vision, and courage are not unreal; but American policy assumptions about European nationalisms might well be unreal or

[23] Keyserling, 1.
[24] Ward, 30.

obsolescent. If America were damaged by another grand disillusion, the world would be a poorer place.

Our European Marxist adversaries are everywhere abandoning their earlier vision of an homogenized world. There is an appetite for variety in every civilized man, for without variety there can be no harmony, but merely unity—the monotonous unity of universal conformism. The dream of humanity all the same type—"all possibly wearing Chinese dungarees"—is a nightmare.[25] Civilized men in Europe and America hope that no force—Communist, capitalist or industrialist—will succeed in destroying the pluralism and counterpoint implicit in the spectrum of nationalities.

National differences are an organic reality that fosters variety, taste, and creativity in the midst of our march toward industrial uniformity.[26] This reality is not on the verge of extinction. If it has sometimes seemed that national leaders—in new states and old—are crazed with the fever of nationalism, it is still presumptuous to pontificate on "what appears probable in the light of what is actual," for "nothing is easier to mistake than the trend of the times." [27]

[25] *Ibid.*
[26] *Ibid.*
[27] Ross J. S. Hoffman, *The Spirit of Politics and the Future of Freedom* (Milwaukee, 1950), 1.

# 13

# Crisis and Progress in Postwar France

## JOSEPH N. MOODY

VISITORS RETURNING TO PARIS in recent years have been impressed by the sparkling appearance of much of the central city. A vigorous Ministry of State for Cultural Affairs —itself something of a novelty—has done remarkable work. The dingy façade of many public and private buildings has been scrubbed and one of the world's loveliest cities has recovered the smiling face of youth.

Could this be a symbol of what has happened to the French nation during the first few years of the Fifth Republic? Certainly, the current regime would have us so believe. Nearly any agency of the French government will supply a student with material that would preempt for the Fifth the title of "progress" while it would imply that its predecessor deserves the designation "crisis." The case has a certain appeal.

The present constitution, submitted to the referendum of September 28, 1958, was approved by 80% of those voting. Experts see it merely as a shadow of its charismatic president and have little difficulty in exposing its technical flaws.[1]

---

[1] It is difficult to define the constitution. Under normal conditions power resides in the cabinet and Parliament; but the president has the power of "arbitrage." Theoretically there is a dual source of power with the presi-

Yet, it has contributed to a period of political stability that made possible the liquidation of the Algerian war and the recognition by France of the new Algerian state. On the basis of the self-determination clause in the constitution, fifteen French-speaking countries in Africa and Madagascar have been granted independence. Six of these have elected to remain in a remodeled "French Community"; the rest, with other African states that have ties with France, have entered bilateral agreements on economic, technical, and financial aid, cultural cooperation, and diplomatic and military assistance. Certainly, the Fifth Republic has presided over the liquidation of the French Empire and has entered into constructive relations with the states which have emerged from its womb. The government has remained generous in its aid to these fledglings. Despite domestic criticism, the French taxpayer contributes a higher proportion of his income to foreign aid than the American. And in 1963, the Ministry for Cooperation initiated a version of the American Peace Corps known as the "French Association of the Volunteers for Progress."

The Fifth Republic was equally successful in dealing with the unpleasant by-products of colonial liquidation. The tension in Algeria at the close of the war drove 850,000 repatriates to metropolitan France, 700,000 during a three-month period in 1962. Public and private agencies cooperated to soften the consequences of this uprooting. The government provided generous loans for resettlement; jobs were located, training provided. Only 5,000 of the refugees remained on the list of the unemployed in December 1963. It is a tribute to the French people and government that the trauma caused by loss of home and possessions, often

---

dent defining the area of his competence. Professor Einaudi of Cornell argued, in a paper read before the New York State Association of European Historians in Oct. 1964, that the Fifth Republic died when De Gaulle set aside the constitutional method of revision in Article 89 and used Article 11 to bypass Parliament (October 1962).

achieved through the work of generations, could have been successfully assuaged.

Equally adroit was the defusing of the threat posed by the extremist organizations which developed in the agony of the French loss of North Africa. The O.A.S. and its satellites, led by ruthless men often with professional military training who were pledged to revenge, could have been a serious menace. They were met by the personal courage of General de Gaulle and by his confidence that they would be isolated and rendered harmless. They were. The activists were detached from their potential support in the army and among the repatriates, and the threat waned.

In the domestic field several developments lend validity to the Fifth Republic's appreciation of its own achievements. The vexing issue of aid to private, largely Catholic, schools was solved by compromise in the law of December 31, 1959. On the ground that educational freedom and diversity should be respected and that standards of education should be uniform, the law permitted the drafting of contracts between the state educational system and private schools that would allow the government to assume the latter's operating expenses and teachers' salaries. Special committees on the regional and national level facilitated the functioning of the law, and, by May 1963, more than 10,000 such contracts had been drawn with about 50,000 private-school-teachers' salaries absorbed by the state.

In 1958, the economic expansion that had marked France since Liberation seemed threatened. Inflation was undermining the gains made by workers and salaried persons.[2] The balance of payments deficit in 1957 was $1.28-billion. This outflow was temporarily halted by a 16.7% devalua-

---

[2] Wages increased by 11.6% in 1957, while consumer prices rose 10%. The first half of 1958 followed the same pattern. All statistics in this section supplied by Press and Information Division of the French Embassy, New York.

tion of the franc, but, by June 1958, the loss of foreign exchange had been resumed. France's reserves of gold and hard currencies were almost exhausted.[3] Earlier (June 18, 1957), France had been obliged to suspend trade liberalization, thus endangering her commitments to the Common Market before they became operative.

The financial stabilization of France under the Fifth Republic certainly owed a great deal to the cessation of the Algerian war. But bold governmental action aided. The currency was again devalued by 14.9% on December 28, 1958, and the appearance of the new or "heavy" franc in the next month restored confidence in the French monetary system. The result was the successful floating of the Pinay loan in 1958 which drew excess purchasing power from the economy and lessened the curve of inflation.

The drive of the De Gaulle government on the more stubborn problems of budgetary deficits, tax imbalances, agricultural production, and marketing problems made slower progress; but the government used its greater authority to press energetically for reform in all these fields. The result was that France resumed its impressive economic growth rate,[4] fulfilled its obligations under the Rome treaty,[5] and began to enjoy a surplus in international trade.[6] By every index, France had a healthy and expanding economy under the Fifth Republic.

The foreign policy of President de Gaulle wins fewer plaudits. He periodically reaffirmed the necessity of the At-

---

[3] There was only $19-million in the French Exchange Stabilization Fund, and by May 30, 1958, three-fourths of a $650-million international loan granted five months previously had been used up. Only $185-million of France's drawing rights on the International Monetary Fund and European Payments Union remained.

[4] There was a slight increase in rate of growth: in 1949–58, it was 4.9%; in 1958–63, it was 5.2%.

[5] France agreed to an even faster rate of tariff reductions with Common Market countries than the Treaty demanded.

[6] France had a substantial surplus in 1959, 1960 and 1961, substantial deficits in 1958 and 1963, and was about even in 1962.

lantic Alliance,[7] cites French loyalty during the Cuban crisis, and calls for the construction of a Western Europe. At least while Adenauer directed affairs at Bonn, the Franco–German treaty of January 22, 1963 was considered the great achievement of French foreign policy. But the emphasis on an independent French nuclear force, the veto on British entrance into the Common Market, the demand for revision of the NATO Pact, the recognition of Peking, the call for a neutralized Southeast Asia—these win only partial acceptance in France and very little in the United States. De Gaulle makes a case for each of these positions which contravene American policy. Only time will tell which is more nearly correct.

One might concede to the Fifth Republic that, on the whole, the balance sheet is favorable. But the present regime in France is not content with self-praise. General de Gaulle insisted on contrasting his success with the failures of the Fourth Republic. On this point, he gained wide assent, for the Fourth died without friends. In its later years, the nation had become indifferent to its functioning and unconcerned for its fate. The game of politics as played in the Palais Bourbon after the Second World War wearied public opinion. In the end, faith in existing political institutions was lost.[8] When its crisis came it found few defenders and it passed away unmourned and without benefit of decent burial. Its epitaph could be simply written: born 1945, died 1958.[9] This was a brief life span, even for France, justifying the advertisement in the Paris Métro during the summer of 1948: "The Republics pass; our paints remain."

The failure of the Fourth Republic was political in the

[7] Press Conference, May 15, 1962: "If the free world were attacked, on the old or the new continent, France would take part in the common defense at the side of her allies, with all the means that she has."

[8] Jean Lacouture, *Cinq hommes et la France* (Paris, 1961).

[9] Gordon Wright, *The Reshaping of French Democracy* (New York, 1948), 255–57, speculates on a Fifth Republic shortly after the birth of the Fourth.

broadest sense. Fundamentally, politics involves the art of making community decisions. This process requires an adjustment of conflicting aims and interests, difficult in any circumstance, increasingly so whenever the cement of common aspirations is weakened.

The Fourth Republic inherited a tradition of conflict that had been waged with sectarian bitterness for a century and a half.[10] It had spared no segment of the country's organized life. As a corollary, there was a record of governmental abuse of authority to maintain its position, facilitated by an immensely powerful administrative machine which provided a standing temptation to such abuse. The French response to their political past has been a general resistance to existing government with a willingness to surrender in crisis to an authoritarian savior.[11]

With this inheritance, Frenchmen had inaugurated the Fourth Republic with a high degree of agreement on one issue: the inadequacy of the Third.[12] The first referendum after Liberation rejected a return to the previous system, with only the radicals compaigning for a regime in which they had been the major beneficiaries. But the negative character of this consensus became apparent when only a fraction over one-third of the electorate voted in favor of a constitution which had been laboriously hammered out by the three political parties which shared the majority of popular support in the aftermath of Resistance.[13]

Inauspiciously launched, the Fourth Republic not merely

---

[10] Philip Williams, *Politics in Post-War France* (London, 1958), 2.

[11] Symbolized in the title of "Alain's" (Emile Chartier) classic, *Le Citoyen contre les pouvoirs* (Paris, 1926).

[12] Well summarized in David Thomson, *Democracy in France* (London, 1949), 170–210. But the Third Republic had satisfied the political elite and had given the major political groups, except for the working class and the Catholics, a permanent contact with their government through the political parties.

[13] In the elections for the Constituent Assembly of June 2, 1946 (which wrote the Constitution), the Communists and M.U.R.F. got 25.98%, the Socialists 21.14%, and the Mouvement Republicain Populaire 28.22% of the vote. Wright, 259.

carried France through the difficult period of reconstruction; it survived the abrupt withdrawal of De Gaulle from the premiership on January 20, 1946. It took the risk of admitting the Communists to office when it was necessary and expelled them in 1947 when they were still strongly rooted in large segments of the population. It was the expulsion of the Communists from government and their return to vigorous opposition which contributed to a return to the political behavior of the Third. After 1947, a heterogeneous complex of moderate parties faced extremists on the left and right with too narrow a terrain for maneuver in the serious problems threatening France and the world.

Although the Fourth Republic slipped back into the patterns of the Third, there was a diminution of the sharp ideological conflict which had marked French politics. This seems paradoxical, for never had republican institutions in France received so persistent a drum-fire as that provided by the Communists. Nor were they alone in opposition. The withdrawal of De Gaulle led to the formation of an intergroup of Gaullist deputies which soon crystallized into the RPF. Then came the Poujadists on the extreme right with their *Union de défense des commerçants et artisans* which may be described as an association against taxes which most of its members did not pay.[14]

This new right added to the difficulty of governing. But it remained an ill-defined opposition without strong ideological foundations. The classic right of the royalists had practically disappeared and the new brood claimed the republican title. Poujade found it convenient to invoke not only Joan of Arc but "our Robespierre" as well, and to propose a French Revolutionary institution as a solution for French problems. When, in 1957, a petition was circulated

[14] Stanley H. Hoffman, *Le Mouvement Poujade* (Paris, 1956); Jean Meynaud, "Un Essai d'interpretation du mouvement Poujade," *Revue de l'Institut de sociologie* (Paris, 1956), 3–38.

asking the government to participate officially in the second centennial of Robespierre's birth, it was signed not only by the leaders of the moderate groups including the Catholic Maurice Schumann, but by the representatives of the right!

The debates in the National Assembly of the Fourth Republic contain little reference to the great historic issues which had divided France.[15] The socialists did not renounce Marxism, but they mentioned it only occasionally and did not relate it to the problems at hand. Socialist deputies split on issues but no longer on the classic lines of revolutionaries *versus* reformists. As a group they retain a predisposition in favor of governmental activity for the wage earner, particularly for the civil servant; but the socialist parliamentarians made it clear that they had no desire for a radical modification of the existing system. Typical was the speech of one of their leaders in the National Assembly on July 5, 1956: "If we approve this measure [putting all nuclear fuels under Euratom ownership] as desirable, it is not, ladies and gentlemen, please believe me, because of any sectarian ideology hostile to private property." [16]

The other center parties were equally uncommitted. Edgar Faure defined radicalism as "a method of solving problems rather than a set of solutions." The effort of Mendès-France to give the Radical party a program during the Fourth Republic simply shattered it.[17] The MRP began with a set of principles, though it may be questioned if they were precisely defined. But when it appeared that they had little mass appeal, they were lost in the parliamentary

---

[15] Nathan Leites, *On the Game of Politics in France* (Stanford, 1959), 7–34; Maurice Duverger, *Les Partis politiques* (2d ed., Paris, 1954); Maurice Duverger, "Public Opinion and Political Parties in France," *American Political Science Review*, #46 (Dec. 1952), 1069–78; Jacques Fauvet, *Les Partis politiques dans la France actuelle* (Paris, 1947); Jacques Fauvet, *Les Forces politiques en France* (Paris, 1951); Georges Lavau, *Partis politiques et réalités sociales* (Paris, 1953); Maurice Duverger, ed., *Partis politiques et classes sociales en France* (Paris, 1955).

[16] Edward Spears, *Assignment to Catastrophe* (London, 1954), II, 304.

[17] Claude Nicolet, *Le Radicalisme* (Paris, 1957).

shuffle.[18] Gaullism had no other aim than to return their leader to power. When the prospect began to appear dim, the "Rally"—certainly a non-ideological term—declined.

Because the parties—the Communists always excepted—lacked a firm doctrinal base, their deputies divided on nearly every important issue during the course of the Fourth Republic. Sometimes the divergence was deep enough to cause the dissidents to leave their party;[19] more frequently the dissenters remained while siding with rival groups on specific issues.

A good index of the decline of ideological passion was the question of Catholic schools which would have flamed the fiercest passion before World War II. Though aid to these schools could still stir anti-clerical feeling in some segments of the electorate, the restraint of the deputies in these educational debates and the absence of provocative comments on either side prevented the serious cleavage so characteristic of Third-Republic days. Thus, on the crucial *Loi Barangé* which recognized the right of parents for some governmental assistance if their children attended non-public schools, 19 Radical deputies, including some with a left orientation, voted affirmatively.[20] Only in 1955 did the Radical party forbid its members to belong to the "Association for the Freedom of Education," probably because the vice-president of this Catholic pressure group was Bernard Lafay, a prominent radical, who made a pilgrimage to Santiago de Compostella. In the light of the history of the radicals, nothing could be more significant than this blurring of the clerical issue. No longer was it the basis for the classic division of right and left.

---

[18] Adrien Dansette, *Histoire réligieuse de la France contemporaine,* II, *Sous la Troisième République* (Paris, 1952); Adrien Dansette, *Destin du catholicisme français* (Paris, 1957): Réné Raymond, "Les Partis catholiques," *Vie intellectuelle* (Aug.–Sept. 1953), 173–89; Maurice Vaussard, *Histoire de la democratie chrétienne* (Paris, 1956).

[19] Mendès-France from the Radicals, Soustelle from RPF, Bidault from MRP.

[20] One of these was André Marie who had been Minister of Education in several cabinets.

This decline in doctrinal conflict might be viewed as a sign of political maturity. Under the Fourth Republic, French politics appears to the outsider as more reasonable and more moderate. The old fires undoubtedly burned beneath the surface, but the parliamentary idiom approached that of British and American practice.[21] Passionate debates on principles tended to be replaced by competition of interests, common to every representative body. Since the declining emphasis on doctrine was not accompanied by a growth in attachment to the common good, the role of economic pressure groups in Fourth-Republic parliaments was enlarged.

Special-interest groups are found in every modern society where there is any degree of free association. Within a larger community, men with some common bond will unite; in so doing they will seek means to achieve a common goal. While we are inclined to use the term "pressure group" pejoratively—particularly when we do not share its objectives—it is inevitable in a free society that groups of citizens will attempt to sway public opinion and governmental action. While a minimum of Rousseauist "general will" is essential as a cement, particular interests are a corollary of the democratic process.

What is significant in any political structure is the degree to which these particular interests have their way. Two correlations may be observed: a weak governmental authority with a diffusion of responsibility will encourage the activity of these groups. This is almost a definition of the political situation in the Fourth French Republic. An atmosphere of shifting coalitions and unstable majorities is ideal for pressure-group success.

A second factor is that a weak party structure deprives the politician of the protection afforded by party discipline. A British M.P. may resist the appeal of a special interest on the ground that the violation of the party program may

---

[21] The investiture debate on Laniel showed a reversion to the older form.

cost him his renomination. No such device could be available to his colleague of the Fourth Republic where the party structures were more fluid. As one who knew wrote: "Every deputy from Normandy voted for the apple; every deputy from Hérault voted for the grape." [22]

Though the conditions for the successful manipulation of the political machinery were somewhat less favorable in the Fourth than in the Third Republic because of changes in the electoral law and the appearance of a few larger and better-knit parties, they were infinitely greater than in a two-party system. In an American presidential election, voters are in effect presented with an "either–or" choice. But a deputy of the Fourth Republic could be pressured by voters who, if discontented, could slide but a single notch, say from MRP to RPF. Further, a British candidate of either party gravitates toward a common center to appeal to the undecided voters even at the risk of offending special interests. This would be impossible in France where a candidate would be at the mercy of any determined band of his supporters—and they all tend to be determined.

The advantageous position of the promoters of special interests in France should not obscure the greater stakes in the political game in all modern states. While we sometimes consider the state in the abstract as the defender of the common concern, in the concrete it is composed of human beings who have ties to many segments of the population. The realities of the modern state tend to accent the importance of these ties:

1. The great extension of the public intervention in the economy, made necessary by technology, enhances the value of governmental action and the efforts to obtain it;
2. The existence of a public sector and the use of public funds for investment have the same effect;

[22] J. Barthélemy, *Essai sur le Travail parlementaire et le système des commissions* (Paris, 1934), 86. They still did under the Fourth Republic.

3. Technological change threatens outmoded industries and stimulates their managers to seek protection by governmental action;

4. The demand for, and resistance to, efforts to redistribute national income by political means enlarges the area of pressure group activity.

All these factors were present during the Fourth Republic. Thus, the Radical Socialist deputies from Algeria participated in every metropolitan difficulty in order to build their power to preserve the privileges of the *colons*. Again, the modernization of the distribution system was a recognized need, but the organs of the small retailers were able to slow the process in the Fourth Republic. Although France, with Greece and Italy, has the heaviest proportion of taxation on consumers,[23] efforts at tax reform remained in the category of pious hope.

The demands of the particular interests tend to be contradictory: farmers and factory owners, workers and management, retailers and consumers. Their conflicting demands, in favorable circumstances, cancel each other out and may permit the formulation of a constructive policy. Then there are the unorganized interests which in a healthy political system will come to the surface with sufficient frequency to keep the particular interests within limits.[24] But

---

[23] The 1951 Report of the Ministry of Finance gives 70% of taxes from consumption, 25% from income, 5% from inheritance.

[24] Jean Meynaud, *Les Groupes de pression en France* (Cahiers de la fondation nationale des sciences politiques #95, Paris, 1958). Meynaud, the best French authority in this field, has also written: "Contribution à l'analyse des groupes d'intérêt dans la vie politique française," *Revue de l'Institut de Sociologie* (1956), 225–56; "L'intervention des groupes d'intérêt dans la politique économique," *Revue économique et sociale* (Oct. 1956), 256–77; "Essai d'analyse de l'influence des groupes d'intérêt," *Revue économique* (Mar. 1957), 177–220; "Les Groupes d'intérêt et l'administration en France," *Revue française de science politique* (July–Sept. 1957), 573–93; "Pouvoir politique et pouvoir économique," *Revue économique* (Nov. 1958), 923–57; with Alain Lancelot, "Groupes de pression et politique des logements: essai d'analyse monographique," *Revue française de science politique* (Dec. 1958), 821–60; with Jean Meyriat, "Les Groupes de pression en Europe occidentale," *Revue française de science politique* (Mar. 1959), 229–46. Also

these restraints worked poorly in France where the special interests readily found parliamentary spokesmen and where their determination contributed to *immobilisme* and economic retardation.[25] Thus, an industry in a region where its continued existence is irrational in the economic sense will use political pressure to escape the logic of its disappearance.

The sum total of these pressures inclines to relative economic stagnation; for while each seeks some growth, its primary concern is to defend the *status quo*. Thus, the pressure groups play an essentially conservative role. This made attacks upon entrenched positions difficult under the Fourth Republic, for a threat to one interest often inspired allies from other areas to join the defense. Mendès-France gave a pessimistic appraisal of the process: "Not wishing to oppose anyone, we end in total immobility." [26]

The difficulty of achieving social reform and economic progress under the Fourth Republic prompted Leo Hamon to pose the following questions:

1. In a multi-party system with sharp divisions among the electors, is it possible to reach any formulation at all of the general will?
2. Will not the parties in such a system hesitate to make unpopular but necessary decisions when they know that their action will be exploited by their rivals—particularly, as in the Fourth Republic—when the interests are so effectively organized?
3. If propaganda can effectively manipulate public opinion to the point where it can disguise specific purposes as the general interest, of what value is the eighteenth-century belief in the ultimate triumph of reason which is the foundation of universal suffrage? [27]

Francis Goguel contributed another factor in his discussion of the narrowing field in which Parliament can make deci-

---

Alfred Sauvy, "Lobbys et groupes de pression," 311–32, in *Politique et technique*, Gaston Berger, et al. (Paris, 1958), and "Lobbys et groupes de pression," 173–273 in *Le Pouvoir*, II (Paris, 1957).

[25] Leo Hamon, "Gouvernement et intérêts particuliers," *Esprit* (June 1953), 831–52.
[26] *Le Monde*, Apr. 10, 1952.
[27] *Op. cit.*

sions.[28] The relative decline of the legislature is characteristic of all twentieth-century democracies, but under the Fourth Republic it was impossible to define precisely where Parliament was exclusively competent short of an exact definition in the constitution. Goguel generalized that Parliament retained control of those areas of governmental action which had been characteristic of the nineteenth century, while the executive succeeded in preempting most of those which had become the concern of the twentieth. The practical consequence was that more and more economic, financial, and social matters were settled by governmental decree.

Parliament attempted to resist executive encroachment by an appeal to its historical position in the nation. Its refusal to surrender any of its *claims* vis-à-vis the executive brought the National Assembly impossible work-burdens, at the same time as it became increasingly difficult for it to accept measures which it knew were necessary yet which were certain to offend specific bodies of electors. Certain parliamentary customs strengthened this tendency,[29] as did the need to rely on technical experts who were functionaries of the administration. But behind these was the recognition of the power of organized interests to retaliate decisively in a situation in which the balance of force was so delicately poised.

The consequence was that in the course of the Fourth Republic the Parliament tended increasingly to abdicate to the executive in the face of specific pressures. On the negative side, this tendency prepared the electorate to look outside Parliament for decisive action, and so prepared the nation for the eclipse of the legislature in the Fifth. But on the positive side, it made possible a considerable measure

---

[28] "La Déficience du système parlementaire," *Esprit* (June 1953), 853–61.
[29] In specialized committees the government was put at a disadvantage in favor of the *rapporteur*.

of modernization. For the center of gravity of all political majorities in the Fourth Republic was not in the France of economic dynamism but in the relatively stagnant sections of the nation. Thus, were the details of an economic plan to be submitted to the National Assembly, the natural tendency of deputies to defend the existing situation would have destroyed its balance. To make more than token economic progress, a way had to be found around Parliament. The decisive fact is that such ways were discovered. Dramatic economic gains were made, but at the expense of the prestige of Parliament among the politically sophisticated.

One of these was provided by Article 25 of the Constitution. By establishing an Economic Council, the constitution makers provided the representatives of organized interests with an arena in which they could strive to influence public opinion. While the Economic Council ranked fourth in the hierarchy of representative bodies and while its responsibilities were purely consultative, its reports were circulated to all deputies, and its *rapporteurs* had access to relevant committees and could be invited to participate in their deliberations. Its recommendations were often ignored and it could be used as a forum for those who wished to preserve the *status quo*. But it also won increasing attention from the press and public, and its more serious proposals made an appeal to a growing body of enlightened opinion which sought economic modernization. Thus, the council had some influence in preparing the ground for such progressive measures as the 1949 demand of the trade unions for collective bargaining, the Schuman Plan, and the demand for an increase in family allowances. Not all of these necessarily promoted economic growth. But the proponents of such growth did find a public forum for their ideas.

This institution, and all others, would have been ineffective had there not been a fundamental reorientation in the thinking of an important segment of French society. Traditionally, the French managerial class has been slow to respond to technological change, cautious in its risk-taking, content with family-size enterprises that had low volume and high margin of profit. Before World War II, there were some signs of dissatisfaction with the slow rate of French economic developments. But a radical change appeared which was in part a reaction to the defeat and resistance. The Fourth Republic saw a new breed of managers who were receptive to technological change and who found support among governmental administrators. Jean Monnet was at once the leader of the new entrepreneurial type and a symbol of a new spirit in French economic life. He succeeded in gathering an enthusiastic group of progressive civil servants and in stimulating younger managers, economists, and even some labor leaders.[30]

The result might be called "the French miracle," an economic thrust that may be compared with developments in West Germany and in Italy. The Fourth Republic witnessed a remarkable experiment in voluntary planning, conceived and executed in a nation traditionally suspicious of governmental initiative. This planning required a substantial increase in the proportion of national income taken by government and its investment in power and other resources essential for the growth of the French economy. Its success assured France not only a recovery from the losses of the war but a healthy increase in industrial production. Even the most resistant segment of the French economy—agriculture—was stimulated by the appearance of new associations which encouraged mechanization and the introduction of new crops. Legislation made possible the consolidation of

---

[30] Some of the most competent of the new-type civil servant are in the French delegation to Euratom. It was in the parliamentary debates of July 1-11, 1956 that the Euratom Treaty was carried, thus assuring the continuance of French atomic research. It was the Fourth Republic by a curious combination of Europeans (MRP and some SFIO and Radicals) and nationalists that made possible De Gaulle's *Force de frappe*. The Socialist Prime Minister, Guy Mollet, promised France would not test before 1961. De Gaulle did not consider himself bound by this commitment.

parcels, and a near doubling in the use of fertilizers led to a steady increase in total yield.[31]

Thus, the Fourth Republic saw a truly dynamic France arise out of the relative stagnation of the pre-war period and the disaster of 1940. This new France owed much to American aid. But assistance from the Marshall Plan was used intelligently and for projects that had long-term promise rather than for immediate satisfactions.

The leaders of the Fourth Republic joined a policy of friendship for the United States, cemented in the Atlantic Alliance, with one of reconciliation with the traditional enemy beyond the Rhine. This rapprochement with Germany blossomed into the economic partnership of the coal-steel pact and was ultimately broadened into the Common Market. These achievements were made despite the handicap of an unstable executive and in the face of the determined opposition of the Communists and of assorted pressure groups. While the creative vision for the platform of internal reform and enlightened foreign policy often arose from associations outside government or from civil servants, the political system with all its limitations was obviously flexible enough to permit the implementation of these ambitious designs.

The spurt in French industrial production was accompanied by a tangible rise in national morale and by a growing birth rate. There was an increasing concern for the inadequacy of social services and for the condition of housing. But while the evidence of progress spurred the managers and administrators to expand their goals, their success made them impatient with the hesitations of government, particularly with the failure to handle the problems arising from the disintegration of the French Empire. It was this dynamic France which had achieved so much within the framework of the Fourth Republic that ultimately turned away from the system of parliamentary supremacy which

[31] Gordon Wright, *Rural Revolution in France* (Stanford, 1964).

was the cornerstone of French republicanism. In part, the drift toward a stronger executive was the work of those who looked not to an imaginary past but to a future that seemed within grasp.

Crisis and progress were both found in the Fourth French Republic. The former is more apparent, for the regime's failure to solve the Algerian problem brought it to an end. But the progress was real. We can dissect the flaws in the institutions and in the leaders of the Fourth Republic, but we cannot forget that they inherited a shattered country and left it an equal partner in a reconstituted Europe.

# A Select Bibliography of the Works of Ross J. S. Hoffman

*compiled by*

## PAUL R. ZIEGLER

BOOKS AND EDITED WORKS*

*American Political Thinking and the Vitorian Tradition* (Madrid: Institute Francisco de Vitoria del Consejo Superior de Investigaciones Cientificas, 1947), 18 pp.

*Burke's Politics: Selected Writings and Speeches on Reform, Revolution and War,* edited by Ross J. S. Hoffman and Paul Levack (New York: Alfred A. Knopf, 1948), 536 pp.

*The Common Good, Christian Democracy and American National Problems,* by Thomas P. Neill (CHRISTIAN DEMOCRACY SERIES; Editor-in-chief of the series: Ross J. S. Hoffman)–(Garden City, New York: Doubleday & Company, 1956), 640 pp.

*Conceived in Liberty: The History of the United States,* by Marshall Smelser and Harry W. Kirwin (CHRISTIAN DEMOCRACY SERIES; Editor-in-chief of the series: Ross J. S. Hoffman)–(Garden City, New York: Doubleday & Company, 1955 [revised edition, 1962]), 765 pp.

*Durable Peace: A Study in American National Policy* (New York: Oxford University Press, 1944), 120 pp.

*Edmund Burke, New York Agent, with His Letters to the New York Assembly and Intimate Correspondence with Charles O'Hara, 1761–1776* (MEMOIRS OF THE AMERICAN PHILOSOPHICAL SOCIETY, Volume XLI)–(Philadelphia: American Philosophical Society, 1956), 632 pp.

---

*For the purposes of this Bibliography "Edited Works" shall include those that Ross J. S. Hoffman has contributed to, edited, or generally edited.

*Great Britain and the German Trade Rivalry, 1875–1914* (Philadelphia: University of Pennsylvania Press, 1933 [reprinted, 1964]), 363 pp.
*The Great Republic: An Historical View of the International Community and the Organization of the Peace* (New York: Sheed and Ward, 1942), 167 pp.
*Man and his History: World History and Western Civilization,* by Ross J. S. Hoffman, Gaetano L. Vincitorio, and Morrison V. Swift (CHRISTIAN DEMOCRACY SERIES; Editor-in-chief of the series: Ross J. S. Hoffman)–(Garden City, New York: Doubleday & Company, 1958 [reprinted edition, 1960; revised edition, 1963]), 765 pp.
*Man the Citizen: The Foundations of Civil Society,* by Rev. Joseph N. Moody and Joseph F. X. McCarthy (CHRISTIAN DEMOCRACY SERIES; Editor-in-chief of the series: Ross J. S. Hoffman)–(Garden City, New York: Doubleday & Company, 1957), 512 pp.
*Medieval History,* revised by James J. Flynn (NEW STUDENTS OUTLINE SERIES)–(Ames, Iowa: Littlefield, Adams & Co., 1955), 175 pp.
*The Organic State: An Historical View of Contemporary Politics* (New York: Sheed and Ward, 1939), 116 pp.
*The Origins and Background of the Second World War,* by Ross J. S. Hoffman and Charles Groves Haines (New York: Oxford University Press, 1943 [revised edition, 1947]), 659 pp.
*The Relevance of Edmund Burke,* edited by Peter J. Stanlis and Ross J. S. Hoffman; based on contributions from Francis Canavan, S.J., Ross J. S. Hoffman, C. P. Ives, and Peter J. Stanlis (New York: P. J. Kenedy, 1964), 134 pp.
*Restoration* (New York: Sheed and Ward, 1934), 205 pp.
*The Spirit of Politics and the Future of Freedom* (Gabriel Richard Lecture, 1950)–(Milwaukee: Bruce Publishing Company), 98 pp.
*Symposium on Alexis de Tocqueville's Democracy in America,* edited by William J. Schlaerth; based on contributions from Ross J. S. Hoffman and others (FORDHAM UNIVERSITY STUDIES. BURKE SOCIETY SERIES, number 1)–(New York: Fordham University Press, 1945), 42 pp.
*Tradition and Progress, and other Historical Essays in Culture, Religion and Politics* (SCIENCE AND CULTURE SERIES)–(Milwaukee: Bruce Publishing Company, 1938), 165 pp.
*Visual Outline of Medieval History* (STUDENTS OUTLINE SERIES)– (New York: Longmans, Green & Co., 1933), 152 pp.

*The Will to Freedom* (New York: Sheed and Ward, 1935), 139 pp.

PERIODICAL ARTICLES AND SHORT PAPERS

"American Paradox; Reply," *The Tablet,* 199: 95 (February 2, 1952).
"The American Republic and Western Christendom," *Historical Records and Studies,* 35: 3–17 (1946).
"American Tradition and the Coming Peace," *Thought,* 18: 197–201 (June, 1943).
"Authority and Tyranny," *American Review,* 4: 385–409 (February, 1935).
"Bolshevism and National Socialism," *American Review,* 7: 322–326 (Summer, 1936).
"The Case for American Intervention," *Thought,* 15: 487–492 (September, 1940).
"Catholic Philosophy of History," THE MCAULEY LECTURES, 1957: *Some Aspects of History* (West Hartford, Connecticut: Saint Joseph College, 1957), 209–220.
"Catholic Women and Modern Problems," *The Catholic Mind,* 35: 289–292 (July 8, 1937).
"Catholicism and Historismus," *Catholic Historical Review,* 24: 401–412 (January, 1939).
"Catholic and the Modern State," *The Catholic World,* 142: 524–532 (February, 1936).
"Christendom and the Organization of Peace," *The Catholic World,* 151: 651–659 (September, 1940).
"Christian Democracy in Spain; Reply," *Commonweal,* 45: 93–94 (November 8, 1946).
"The Christian Republic," *The Tablet,* 180: 200–201, 213–215 (October 24–31, 1942); an excerpt from *The Great Republic* (New York: Sheed and Ward, 1942).
"Collectivism: A Problem for Christian Ethics; Comment," *Religion in Life,* 20: 4: 498–502 (1951).
"The Concert of Europe and the Balance of Power," *Thought,* 16: 681–696 (December, 1941).
"Conservatism," *Social Order,* 5: 448–452 (December, 1955).
"Dangerous Issues in Unknown Places," *Sign,* 23: 228–230 (November, 1943).
"Dodd's Diary; Abridged," *Catholic Digest,* 5: 62–63 (July, 1941).
"Edmund Burke as a Practical Politician," *The Burke Newsletter,*

2: 4–8: 266–276 (Winter, 1963–1964); reprinted from the Edmund Burke Symposium, Georgetown University (December 6–7, 1963).
"Education and the Attack on History," *American Review,* 6: 257–270 (January, 1936).
"Europe and the Atlantic Community," *Thought,* 20: 21–36 (March, 1945).
"The Exile's Triumph," *Sign,* 16: 89–90 (September, 1936).
"Faith and Liberty," *Sign,* 16: 529–530 (April, 1937).
"The Fascist State and the Exigencies of Modern Society," *The Spectator,* 1: 124–141 (Spring, 1938).
"Four Centuries of Political Idolatry," *Thought,* 17: 231–239 (June, 1942).
"General McArthur; Reply," *The Tablet,* 197: 443 (June 2, 1951).
"The Hayes Mission to Spain," *Thought,* 21: 5–12 (March, 1946).
"History: Basis of Prophecy," *The Catholic World,* 157: 348–354 (July, 1943).
"Holmes and Laski," *Thought,* 28: 446–453 (Autumn, 1953).
"Intellectual Confusion and Sophistry," *Sign,* 14: 631–633 (May, 1935).
"Introduction" to *The Catholic Philosophy of History* (PAPERS OF THE AMERICAN CATHOLIC HISTORICAL ASSOCIATION), Volume III (New York: P. J. Kenedy, 1936), pp. vii–x.
"Jacobin Heresy," *American Review,* 5: 349–360 (June, 1935).
"Lesson in Statesmanship," *The Catholic World,* 155: 721–724 (September, 1942).
"Liberty and Authority," *American Review,* 3: 562–590 (October, 1934).
"Marxian Philosophy of History," *American Review,* 7: 507–515 (October, 1936).
"Mr. Krutch and Europe," *American Review,* 4: 56–66 (November, 1934).
"The New History," *American Review,* 3: 516–520 (September, 1934).
"Nicholas Berdyaev's Philosophy of History," *American Review,* 8: 151–163 (December, 1936).
"The Origin and Development of Secularism," from *Man and Modern Secularism: Essays on the Conflict of the Two Cultures* (Chicago: National Catholic Alumni Federation, 1940), pp. 7–13.
"Paternalism in Government," IBO *Forum* (March, 1947).
"Peace to Come," *Sign,* 22: 464–466 (March, 1943).

"Peacemaking after Ideological Wars," *Thought*, 20: 404–426 (September, 1945).
"Planning and Freedom," *Thought*, 20: 5–9 (March, 1945).
"Postwar Europe," *Sign*, 23: 140–142 (October, 1943).
"Preface" to *Centenary Charter Lectures in Modern Political History* (FORDHAM UNIVERSITY STUDIES. BURKE SOCIETY SERIES, number 2)–(New York: Fordham University Press, 1946).
"Protest," *Christian Social Action*, 6: 13 (January, 1941).
"Religion of Faith and Works," *Sign*, 15: 9–11 (August, 1935).
"Reply to Mr. William Thomas Walsh," *The Catholic World*, 158: 256–263 (December, 1943).
"Return from Exile; The Position of the Church in the Modern World," *Sign*, 16: 9–11, 89–90 (August, 1936).
"Russia and the Versailles Order," *Historical Bulletin*, 21: 77–78 (May, 1943).
"The Schism of Henry VIII: In the Light of Authentic Scholarship," *The Catholic World*, 140: 524–531 (February, 1934).
"Should Germany have a Centralized Government?" *Sign*, 26: 31 (March, 1947).
"The Spanish Question in World Politics," *Thought*, 22: 19–30 (March, 1947).
"The Spanish Story," *Political Science Quarterly*, 63: 3: 424–429 (September, 1948).
"The Task of Restoring Christendom," *Thought*, 18: 12–24 (March, 1943).
"Theocratic Heresy in Politics," *Thought*, 21: 394–400 (September, 1949).
"Tocqueville and Burke," *The Burke Newsletter*, 2: 4–8: 44–47 (Spring-Summer, 1961); reprinted from an address delivered at the Tocqueville Centenary at Philadelphia (April 19, 1959).
"Totalitarian Regimes," *American Review*, 9: 321–338 (September, 1937).
"United States Foreign Policy," *Review of Politics*, 5: 404–414 (October, 1943).
"Vitoria and American Political Thinking," *Thought*, 21: 394–400 (September, 1946).
"The Verdict of History," from *The Road to Damascus*, edited by John A. O'Brien (New York: Doubleday & Company, 1949), pp. 72–98; reprinted from *Restoration* (New York: Sheed and Ward, 1934).
"The Watershed of the Nineteenth Century," *American Review*, 6: 502–506 (February, 1936).

"We are Native to Two Societies," *The Catholic World,* 148: 99–101 (October, 1938).

"Wentworth Papers of Burke, Rockingham, and Fitzwilliam," *Proceedings of the American Philosophical Society,* 94: 4: 352–356 (1950).

"The West and Russia," *Sign,* 23: 7–10 (August, 1943).

"The West and Soviet Eurasia," *Sign,* 25: 5–8 (August, 1945).

"What is Fascism?" *Sign,* 13: 749–752 (July, 1934).

"The Whigs and the Liberal Pope, 1848–1850," *Thought,* 24: 83–98 (March, 1949).

"Walter Lippmann Grows Wise with Age," *America,* 58: 150–151 (November 20, 1937).

REVIEW ARTICLES

Pauline Relyea Anderson, *The Background of Anti-English Feeling in Germany, 1890–1902* (Washington: American University Press, 1939), *American Historical Review,* 45: 3: 648–649 (April, 1940).

Herbert Butterfield, *Christianity and History* (New York: Charles Scribner's Sons, 1950), *Catholic Historical Review,* 36: 4: 450–453 (January, 1951).

Herbert Butterfield, *History and Human Relations* (New York: Macmillan Company, 1952), *Catholic Historical Review,* 38: 4: 438–439 (January, 1953).

Bernard Donoughue, *British Politics and the American Revolution* (London: Macmillan, 1964), *Catholic Historical Review,* 51: 3: 398–399.

Elio Gianturco, *Joseph de Maistre and Giambattista Vico: Italian Roots of de Maistre's Political Culture* (Washington: Murray and Heister, 1937), *American Historical Review,* 43: 3: 700–701 (April, 1938).

A. Goodwin, editor, *The American and French Revolutions, 1763–1783* (THE NEW CAMBRIDGE MODERN HISTORY, Volume VIII)- (New York: Cambridge University Press, 1965), *Catholic Historical Review,* 53: 3: 429–431 (October, 1967).

S. W. Halperin, *Germany Tried Democracy* (New York: Thomas Y. Crowell Company, 1946), *Political Science Quarterly* 62: 1: 128–130 (March, 1947).

E. J. Hughes, *The Church and the Liberal Society* (Princeton: Princeton University Press, 1944), *Journal of Modern History,* 16: 4: 306 (December, 1944).

Kenneth Ingram, *Years of Crisis* (New York: Macmillan Company, 1947), *Thought,* 23: 129–130 (March, 1948).
Sir Lewis Namier and John Brooke, *Charles Townshend* (London: Macmillan & Company, 1964), *The Burke Newsletter,* 6: 3–23: 446–448 (Spring, 1965).
Abel Plenn, *Wind in the Olive Trees* (New York: Boni & Gaer, 1946), *The Catholic World,* 163: 564–565 (September, 1946).
Gaetano Salvemini and George La Piana, *What to do with Italy* (New York: Duell, Sloan & Pearce, 1943), *Political Science Quarterly,* 59: 1: 131–133 (March, 1944).
Peter J. Stanlis, editor, *Edmund Burke: The Enlightenment and the Modern World* (Detroit: University of Detroit Press, 1967), *American Historical Review,* 74: 2: 604–605 (December, 1968).
J. W. Tyler, *Great Britain, United States and the Future* (London: Stevens & Sons, 1947), *Annals of the American Academy of Political Science,* 259: 169–170 (September, 1948).
Alan Valentine, *Lord North* (2 vols.; Norman, Oklahoma: Oklahoma University Press, 1967), *Studies in Burke and His Time,* 10: 1–33: 1070–1074 (Fall, 1968).
James Warburg, *Foreign Policy Begins at Home* (New York: Harcourt, Brace & Co., 1944), *Thought,* 20: 135 (March, 1945).
Sumner Welles, *Time for Decision* (New York: Harper & Brothers, 1944), *Political Quarterly,* 59: 4: 594–598 (December, 1944).

# INDEX NOMINUM

Abercromby, Sir Ralph, 174, 179
Acton, Lord, 87, 103, 283
Adenauer, Konrad, 295
d'Aiguillon, Duke of, 29, 30
Albareda, Anselmo, 260
Albert, King of the Belgians, 251
d'Alembert, Jean, 32
Amherst, Lord Jeffrey, 142
Asgill, Gen. Sir Charles, 177

Baker, William, 146
Balfour, Arthur, 247
Barral, 210
Barré, Col. Isaac, 114
Barrès, Maurice Auguste, 281
Barthélemy, Gen. Marie-Joseph, 233
Beauchamp, Lord, 140
Bedford, Duke of, 8, 10, 52, 53
Bellamont, Lord, 76
Benedek, General, 213
Benedetti, Count Vincent, 210
Beneš, Edward, 221, 222, 224, 225, 227–31; 235, 236, 240, 247–54
Bentham, Jeremy, 86, 101
Bentinck, Lord George, 199
Beresford, John, 162
Bessborough, Lord, 62, 64, 66, 67, 72, 75, 76, 78
Bingham, Sir Charles, 74–75, 76, 81
Bintinaye, Chevalier de la, 45
Bismarck, Prince Otto von, 203, 204–05, 207, 214, 217–19, 261
Blaquiere, Colonel, 57, 59, 60, 77–80
Blum, Léon, 264
Bompard, Admiral, 156
Bonomi, Ivanoe, 273, 275
Boyle, Robert, Earl of Cork, 67

Bridport, Admiral Lord, 156
Brickdale, Matthew, 113, 115, 117, 118
Bright, John, 84
Bristol, Lord, 55
Buckle, Henry, 85
Burgoyne, Gen. John, 139
Burke, Edmund, xvi–xviii, 2, 3, 7, 12, 14–45, 62, 64, 67, 72–75, 78, 79, 81, 83, 85–106, 115–18, 121, 124, 127, 143, 146–50, 153, 154
Burke, Richard, 44
Burke, William, 72, 148, 153, 154
Burzyinski, Count, 25
Bute, Lord, 142
Butterfield, Herbert, 1, 22, 132

Camden, Lord, 132, 154, 173, 174
Carhampton, Lord, 171, 174
Carlisle, Lord, 132
Carlow, Viscount, 76
Carysford, Lord, 76
Castlereagh, Lord, 166
Cathcart, Lord, 15, 24, 25, 26, 30, 31
Catherine the Great, 17, 18, 19, 23–25, 30–33, 38, 43, 44
Cavendish, Lord John, 153
Cavour, Count, 219
Chamberlain, Houston Stewart, 282
Champion, Richard, 113, 115, 118, 144, 148, 149, 150, 152, 154
Charlemont, Lord, 51, 57, 60, 77
Charles I, King, 35
Charles II, King, 49, 50, 52
Chatham, Lord, 2, 3, 10, 62, 66, 74, 132, 153
Chewton, Lord, 142

317

## 318  INDEX

Cheyney, Edward Potts, xv
Churchill, Sir Winston, 255
Cialdini, General, 213, 214, 215
Clare, Lord, 113, 115, 117
Clarendon, Lord, 204
Clemenceau, Georges, 229, 238, 240, 247
Clinton, George, 129
Cobden, Richard, 84
Cobham, Lord, 52
Cochrane, Alexander Baillie, 182–84, 186–87, 193, 195, 197
Codrington, Sir William, 114
Colpoys, Admiral, 156
Conway, Gen. Henry Seymour, 9, 17, 18, 24
Coolidge, Marcus A., 240, 241
Cooper, Sir Grey, 140
Coote, Gen. Eyre, 177
Copeland, Thomas W., 14
Cornwallis, Lord, 175, 177, 178, 179
Cranborne, Lord, 146
Croker, John Wilson, 184, 196
Cromwell, Oliver, 47, 49, 67
Crossfield, Major, 233
Cruger, Henry Sr., 108, 110, 111
Cruger, Henry Jr., 107–30
Cruger, John I, 107
Cruger, John II, 34, 35, 108, 110, 111
Cruger, John Harris, 111, 123, 24, 125–26
Cruger, Nicholas, 108, 123
Cruger, Telemon, 108
Cunningham, Sir Robert, 174
Curtis, E., 157
Cuza, Prince, 203
Czartoriski family, 15, 26

Damer, John, 75
Dartmouth, Lord, 11, 121
Daubeny, George, 124, 126
De Gasperi, Alcide, 256–75
De Gaulle, Charles, 288, 293, 294, 295, 297
Delugan, Don Giulio, 259, 274

Derby, Lord, 139
Devonshire, Duke of, 60, 66, 67, 69, 71, 72, 73, 75, 76
Dickens, Charles, 186
Diderot, Denis, 33
Disraeli, Benjamin, 181–99
Dmowski, Roman, 224, 238
Dollfuss, Engelbert, 262
Donoughmore, Earl of, 177
Dowdeswell, William, 1–13; 34
Drogheda, Marquess of, 171
Duer, William, 128
Duff, Gen. Sir James, 178
Dundas, Sir David, 168
Dunning, John, 11

Eden, William, 131, 132
Egerton, Sir Thomas, 142
Eliot, Lord, 195, 196, 198
Eugénie, Empress, 204
Eustace, Gen. Charles, 177, 178
Exelmans, General, 168

Faber, F. W., 185
Fawcett, Gen. William, 177, 178
Fernandez, Jiminez, 265
Fitzwilliam, Lord, 173
Flood, James, 51, 57, 60, 81
Fortescue, James, 60, 80, 81
Foster, Lt. R. C., 230, 232, 233, 234
Fownes, Sir William, 75
Fox, Charles, 44–45, 139
Foy, General, 168
Francis Joseph, Emperor, 202, 215, 217
Franco, Gen. Francisco, 265–66
Frederick the Great, 19–20, 24, 26, 31, 32, 33, 35, 36, 37, 39, 41, 222
Froude, J. A., 157

Gates, Horatio, 113, 114
George III, King, 1–4, 7, 8, 24, 27–31,

# INDEX 319

34, 35, 54–56, 58, 60, 79, 84, 117, 122, 132, 133, 134, 135, 151
Germaine, Lord George, 125, 132, 137
Gibbon, Edward, 40, 41
Gilson, Etienne, 263
Gobineau, Count, 282
Goguel, Francis, 303, 304
Gordon, Sir Robert, 189
Govone, Gen. William, 204
Gower, Lord, 11, 132, 134, 142
Grabski, Wladyslaw, 252, 253
Grafton, Duke of, 3, 4, 132, 134, 140, 142
Graham, Sir James, 197
de Gramont, Antoine, 209
Grant, Major, 121
Grantham, Lord, 29
Granville, Lord, 51
Grenville, George, 10, 13
Greville, Charles, 196
Gunning, Robert, 30, 31
Gutowski, Stanislaw, 231

Haines, Charles Groves, xv, 256
Halévy, Elie, 86
Halifax, Lord, 55
Hamilton, Alexander, 128, 129
Hamon, Leo, 303
Harcourt, Lord Simon, 56–61, 69, 70, 76, 78, 79, 80, 81, 82
Harding, Warren G., 284
Hardy, Admiral Sir Charles, 138, 152
Harford, Joseph, 113
Harris, Sir James, 27
Hastings, Warren, xvii, 103
Hayes, Carlton, J. H., 281
Hely-Hutchinson, General, 177, 178
Henlein, Konrad, 269
Henry VII, King, 50
Henry, Prince (Hohenzollern), 20
Herder, Johann Gottfried, 277
Hertford, Lord, 55, 60, 61, 62, 65, 66, 75, 78, 79, 83

Hickey, William, 72
Hitler, Adolf, 260, 261, 270, 278, 282, 285, 287
Hoche, Gen. Lazare, 156
Hoffman, Ross J. S., xiii–xix, 2, 256, 290, 309–15
Humbert, General, 176, 179
Horna, Dagmar, 229, 236
Hume, David, 86, 94
Hussy-Burgh, Walter, 51

James II, King, 50
Jay, John, 129
Jenkinson, Charles, 122, 123, 124, 125, 132, 134, 135, 147
Jerome Napoleon, 215
John XXIII, Pope, 283
Jones, John Paul, 151, 152
Johnson, Gen. Henry, 177, 178

Kaunitz, Prince, 20
Keene, Colonel, 61
Keppel, Admiral, 133, 138, 152
Kerner, Professor, 233–34
Kildare, Lord, 57
King, Rufus, 130
Kosciuszko, Count Thaddeus, 43
Kramar, Karel, 229, 231, 235, 240

Lafay, Bernard, 299
Lake, Gen. Gerard, 174–75, 177, 178
Langrishe, Hercules, 81
Lansing, Robert, 244
Laroche, Jules, 253
Latinik, Col. Franciszek, 232, 233, 234
Lecky, W. E. H., 47, 68, 85, 157
Leinster, Lord, 51
Leo XIII, Pope, 266
Lingelbach, William E., xv
Lippencott, Sir Henry, 124
Lloyd George, David, 237–38
Lodge, Sir Richard, 22
Longare, Bonin, 253

Lopez, Aaron, 111
Louis XIV, King, 33
Lucas, Charles, 51
Lyttleton, Lord George, 52

Macartney, Sir George, 17, 24
MacCunn, John, 86
MacLuhan, Marshall, 278
Malaguzzi, Count Alessandro, 202–03
Mallard, John, 114, 118
Manners, Lord John, 182, 184–87, 195, 197
Manteufel, General, 211
Maritain, Jacques, 263, 264
La Marmora, Gen. Alfonso, 202–06, 212, 219
Masaryk, Thomas, 224, 225, 228, 230–31, 234, 235, 236, 247, 248
Massey, Gen. Eyre, 177
Maurras, Charles, 281
Mayne, Sir William, 76, 78, 79, 82, 83
Mendès–France, Pierre, 298, 303
Meredith, Sir William, 119
Metternich, Prince Clemens, 189, 196
Metternich, Prince Richard, 202, 204, 206, 207, 208, 209, 210, 212
Mickiewicz, Adam, 43
Miller, Raymond C., xv
Milton, Baron, 66, 67, 72, 75, 76
Monnet, Jean, 306
Montini, Msgr. Giovanni Battista (Pope Paul VI), 272
Moore, Sir John, 166, 179
Morlet, John, 85, 86, 87, 103
Mountmorres, Lord, 76
Mussolini, Benito, 257, 258, 259, 266, 267, 270, 271, 273, 275

Napoleon I, 155, 157, 169, 180, 186
Napoleon III, 200–19
Nelson, Lord, 157
Newcastle, Duke of, 4, 143, 146

Newman, John Henry Cardinal, 185, 186
Niebuhr, Reinhold, 278
Nigra, Constantino, 204, 205
North, Lord, 3, 33, 36, 57, 59, 60, 61, 65, 66, 67–70, 74, 76–79, 82, 117, 119, 120, 131–42, 196
Northumberland, Lord, 55
Nugent, Maj. Gen. George, 179

O'Brien, William Smith, 193, 196, 199
O'Connell, Daniel, 188, 191, 192, 199
O'Hara, Charles, xvii, 3, 36
Oliver, Silver, 81, 82
Osborne, Sir William, 51
Ossicini, Adriano, 274

Paderewski, Ignacy, 225, 235–36, 237, 254
Paine, Thomas, 94
Pakenham, Thomas, 171
Palliser, Sir Hugh, 133
Panin, Count, 17, 24, 26, 30, 31, 32
Papen, Franz von, 261
Peach, Hannah, 109, 113
Peach, Samuel, 109, 126
Peach, Samuel (Cruger), 109
Peel, Sir Robert, 183–98
Pichon, Stephen, 229
Pilsudski, Marshal Jozef, 230, 231, 250
Pitt, William, the Elder (see also Chatham, Lord), 52
Pitt, William, the Younger, 175
Pius XI, Pope, 258, 260, 263, 265, 269, 275
Pius XII, Pope, 282–83
Polignac, Prince Jules de, 196
Ponsonby, Brabazon, 75
Ponsonby, John, 57, 75, 81
Portland, Duke of, 13, 145, 146, 148, 150
Poujade, Pierre, 297–98
Price, Francis, 75

# INDEX 321

Price, Richard, 94
Priestley, Joseph, 86
Prior, Thomas, 48

Randall, John Herman, Jr., 86
Rawlings, Lt. Col., 232, 233
Ricasoli, Bettino, 213, 214, 215, 216
Richmond, Duke of, 62, 63, 133, 136, 137, 140–41, 150
Righetti, Igino, 272
Robespierre, Maximilien, 298
Robinson, John, 132, 135
Robles, Gil, 265
Rochford, Lord, 25, 27, 28, 29, 30, 57, 58, 69
Rockingham, Marquess of, xviii, 2, 3, 4, 6–13, 33, 36, 60, 62–67, 70–76, 78, 79, 82, 83, 84, 118, 132–34, 137, 140, 143, 146, 147, 151, 152, 153
Rockingham, Lady, 5, 71, 151
Rodano, Franco, 274
Roosevelt, Franklin D., 267, 286
Rothschild, Baron, 209
Rousseau, Jean Jacques, 277, 278
Rutland, Duke of, 141

Salazar, Antonio, 266
Sandwich, Lord, 136, 137, 141
Savary, Admiral, 156
Savile, Sir George, 62, 63, 147
Sawbridge, Alderman, 139
Schumann, Maurice, 298
Seymour–Conway, Francis, 75
Seymour–Conway, Robert, 75
Shannon, Lord, 57, 76
Shelburne, Lord, 17, 60, 62, 65, 66, 74, 136, 137, 140, 152
Smith, Adam, 63–64
Smythe, George, 182–87, 194–98
Sorel, Albert, 22, 40
Spataro, Giuseppe, 273
Stalin, Joseph, 266, 287
Stanislaus, King (Poniatowski), 17, 18, 20, 28

Stephen, Sir Leslie, 85
Stewart, Gen. Sir James, 178
Stormont, Lord, 142
Stafford, Earl of, 67
Strauss, Leo, 104
Sturzo, Don Luigi, 257
Suffolk, Lord, 132
Sutton, Lord George, 145

Taine, Hippolyte, 281
Thorez, Maurice, 264
Thiers, Adolph, 210
Tighe, Edward, 81
Tisdall, Philip, 81, 83
Togliatti, Palmiro, 271, 287
Toniolo, Giuseppe, 264, 265
Townshend, Charles, 9, 10, 11, 55
Townshend, Lord Thomas, 55, 56, 57, 139
Toynbee, Arnold, 289
Truman, Harry S, 286
Tryon, Gov. William, 120
Tyler, John, 187
Tyler, Robert, 187
Tyrone, Lord, 51

Underdown, P. T., 117
Upper Ossory, Earl of, 60, 65, 66, 67, 71, 72, 73, 75

La Valette, 216
Vallency, Gen. Charles, 177
Van Schaack, Peter, 119, 120, 121
de Vattel, Emer, 39–40
Vaughan, Charles E., 86
Victor Emmanuel II, King, 211
Victor Emmanuel III, King, 257, 275
Victoria, Queen, 191
de Vischer, Charles, 268
Voltaire, 33, 39

Wade, Colonel, 233

Walpole, Horace, 61, 62, 66
Wandycz, Damian S., 231, 232
Weare, G. T. E., 117
Weaver, Richard M., 87
Wedderburn, Alexander, 11, 131, 132
Wellington, Duke of, 184, 191
Weymouth, Lord, 15, 55, 142
Whitney, Lois, 86
Wilde, Oscar, 1
Wilhelm II, Kaiser, 282

Wilkes, John, 112, 114
William III, King, 33, 37, 133
Wilson, Dr. Thomas, 115, 116
Wilson, Woodrow, 267, 286
Winchelsea, Lord, 142
Winter, Ernst Karl, 262

Yorke, Charles, 13
Young, Arthur, 48, 52, 53

D
6
C 65